THE TASTE OF FRANCE

*To my wife Jeannette and
my daughter Babette*

THE TASTE OF FRANCE

Photographs by
ROBERT FRESON

CONTRIBUTING AUTHORS
Adrian Bailey·Arabella Boxer·Caroline Conran
Alan Davidson·Nathalie Hambro·Douglas Johnson
Jill Norman·Richard Olney·Anne Willan

Recipes researched by Jacqueline Saulnier

Design by James Wageman

Webb&Bower
EXETER, ENGLAND

Based on **THE SUNDAY TIMES** Magazine Series

First published in Great Britain 1983 by
Webb & Bower (Publishers) Limited
9 Colleton Crescent, Exeter, Devon EX2 4BY

The text of this book originally appeared in
The Sunday Times Magazine as a series of articles by:
Adrian Bailey—Normandy, Brittany, and Bordelais
Arabella Boxer—Anjou and Touraine
Caroline Conran—Périgord
Alan Davidson—Languedoc and Pays Basque
Nathalie Hambro—Sologne
Douglas Johnson—Lyonnais and Burgundy
Jill Norman—Alsace
Richard Olney—Provence
Anne Willan—Ile de France

The recipes originally appeared
in Marie Claire magazine and
were researched and adapted
by Jacqueline Saulnier.

Frontispiece: Château de Nobles,
near Brancion in Burgundy

Right: Ingredients for brouillade
aux champignons (scrambled
eggs with mushrooms), in
Languedoc

Editorial supervision
by Leslie Stoker
Map by David Lindroth

British Library Cataloguing
in Publication Data

The Taste of France
    1. Cookery, French
    I. Freson, Robert
    641.5944   TX719

    ISBN 0 906671 82 5

Printed and bound in Italy

CONTENTS

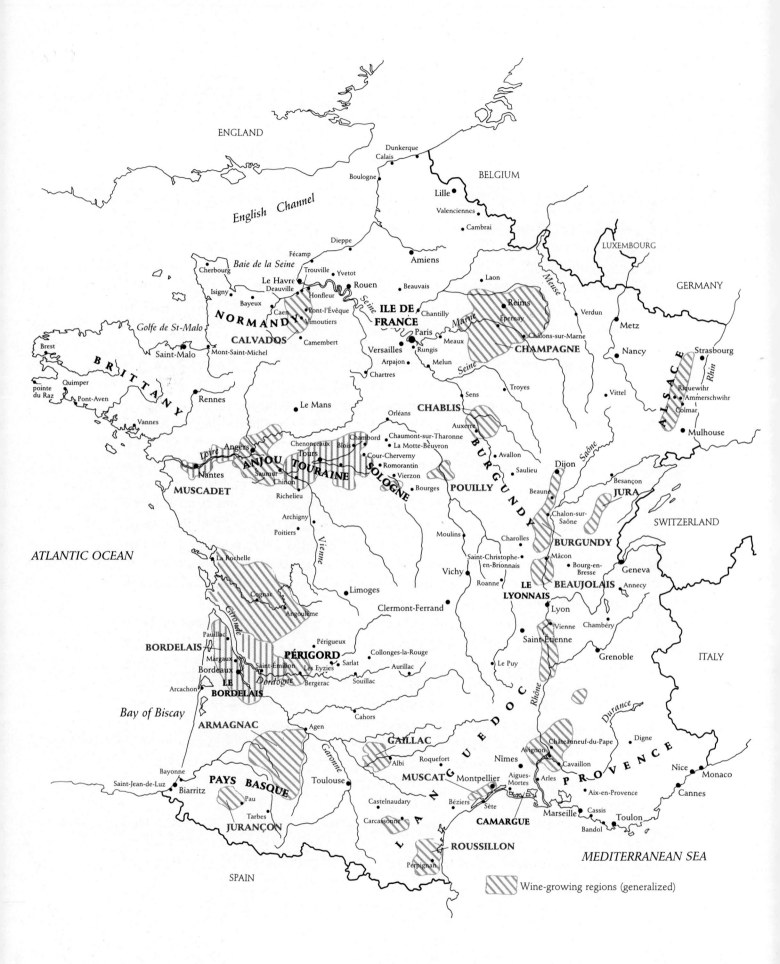

INTRODUCTION

I FIRST explored the gastronomic riches of the fourteen regions of France when I was commissioned to photograph the lovely French countryside and its delicious fare. In this effort, over several years, I sought to create pictures that would be evocative and sensuous, doing justice to the people who created this rich cuisine. As some of our favorite memories—especially travel memories—are associated with food, I wanted to evoke strong reminiscences through visual images that appeal to all of the senses.

In France, food is considered one of the foremost pleasures of life, and surely anyone who has spent time there is struck by the care and attention, the traditions and ceremony that surround the growing, marketing, and preparing of food.

Part of the special appeal of French cuisine is its tremendous regional variety. The peculiar personality of each region's cuisine has been determined to a great extent by climate, soil, foreign influences, and local tastes. A hearty *gigot à la bretonne* or coarse buckwheat *galettes*, for example, might be sampled near the rocky coast of Brittany. A refined *entrecôte, cèpes à la bordelaise*, and fine wines are the products of the rich Bordelais soil. In Normandy, *sole à la normande* and *tarte aux pommes* are created with local ingredients and served with cider. In Burgundy, where excellent—and abundant—*cuisine bourgeoise* reigns, wine is a frequent component in well-known dishes such as *bœuf à la bourguignonne* and *coq au vin*. Whether the cuisine is *paysanne, bourgeoise*, or *haute*, culinary resourcefulness is the cornerstone of the French kitchen.

This project has been a happy collaborative effort. I was fortunate to have worked with a most patient and determined culinary investigator, Jacqueline Saulnier. Mme. Saulnier coaxed many of the recipes—some of which had never been written down before—from local farmers' wives and proprietors of tiny village *auberges* and *café-restaurants*. She has compiled a rich collection of authentic recipes for the most characteristic dishes of regional French cuisine.

The text is the work of some of the most knowledgeable European food writers —Adrian Bailey, Arabella Boxer, Caroline Conran, Alan Davidson, Nathalie Hambro, Douglas Johnson, Jill Norman, Richard Olney, and Anne Willan—and serves as a culinary guide to the French provinces.

It is for their part in making me a gastronomically wiser photographer that I dedicate this book to all the anonymous French farmers, gardeners, and fishermen, as well as to the mothers of the sons and daughters who became the great chefs of France.

R. F.

NORMANDIE & BRETAGNE

NORMANDY

NORMANDY is one of the great gastronomic regions of France and one of the most prosperous. It is not only a land of milk and honey, but of cream, eggs, butter, cheese, and cider. These are the foundations of Norman cooking, and they are to be found on every small farm, with its apple trees and cider press, its white-and-liver–colored cows, its hens and vegetables. And a dish prepared *à la normande* may contain one or more of the typical ingredients that are the produce of Normandy's agriculture, not the least of which is the powerful apple brandy known as calvados.

At the Ferme de la Grande Cour, an unpretentious restaurant outside Honfleur, you can sit under the apple trees in the garden, amid the querulous hens, and enjoy *tripes à la mode* and chicken cooked with cream. Everywhere in Normandy, and in Brittany too, you are offered apple tart. At the hotel Domaine de Villequier, on the Seine, they serve their *tarte aux pommes* doused in calvados, and it arrives wreathed in dancing blue flames and is served with the slightly sourish, ivory-tinted Normandy cream. Norman appetites are legendary, and the French are pleased to observe that *normande* rhymes (almost) with

The tidal island of Mont-Saint-Michel in the English Channel, preceding overleaf, crowned with a Gothic Benedictine abbey, is at the border of the two regions. To the north and east stretch the rich pasturelands of Normandy; to the south and west the windswept peninsula of Brittany points into the Atlantic. Near the Norman village of Tancarville, a farmer, above, milks his Guernseys. The creamy milk of Normandy makes some of France's most distinguished cheeses, among them, right, Camembert, Pont-l'Évêque, and (unboxed, at bottom) the squared Neufchâtel and the rounded Livarot. Rich farmhouse butter and cream are essential to the classic dishes of Normandy.

The proprietors of Ferme du Lieu Marot, an auberge *and a working farm and orchard in the Norman town of Houlgate, are M. and Mme. Coisels, right. They share the cooking; he is bottler of their cider, and she prepares the pastries (she holds one of her strawberry tarts). Their* cuisine du pays *is prepared with their own dairy products, fresh vegetables, fruits—especially apples—and fish of the region. Opposite (clockwise from top left), some scenes and foods of Normandy: apple blossoms; a flambéed* crêpe Benedictine; *farm-made cheeses in the market of Pont-l'Évêque; a plate of typically Norman candies, including marzipan apples and calvados-filled chocolates; a basket of M. Coisels's hard cider; radishes and butter; a half-timbered house in the town of Pont-Audemer; a Camembert at its peak; and, center, a trio of First Communion girls who, when Mass is over, will celebrate* à la normande, *with a family feast.*

gourmande. A nineteenth-century visitor to Normandy, G. M. Musgrave, watched a young couple in Rouen eat fifteen dishes for lunch—or was it breakfast?—washed down by two bottles of Burgundy and one of Chablis.

So the French traveler, consulting his *guide*, in which he has penciled a selection of restaurants, approaches the land of cream and butter with reverence. And is not Normandy the place where men devour steaming bowls of tripe, cooked in the style of Caen, between ten and eleven in the morning, a prelude, as it were, to lunch? And is not lunch most likely to be a *sole à la normande*, or a *canard à la rouennaise*, and dishes smothered in rich, creamy sauces, flambéed in calvados, and flavored with cider apples?

In the Hôtel de la Poste in Domfront, a small town in the heart of the *bocage* region, an area of hedged meadows, pastures, and woods, you will discover that men do indeed find room for *tripes à la mode* between breakfast and lunch. This midmorning snack is taken very seriously and is available and more or less welcome at any time of the

day. The hotel specializes in traditional Norman cuisine, and the recipes were taught to the proprietor, Madame Le Prisé, by her mother, who probably learned them from *her* mother, which is why you will see on the menu, along with such specialties as *andouille* sausage and *poulet vallée d'Auge*, a pear and apple tart called *la portugaise de Grand-mère*, although the term *"Grand-mère"* on a menu generally implies old-fashioned, meaning "homemade."

Yet it is becoming increasingly difficult to maintain the authentic character of regional specialties, especially those that demand cream and butter; dairy produce has become too hygienic and mass-marketed. Madame Le Prisé, for example, has to go thirty miles to find farmhouse cream that isn't too thin and acid and holds its own in a sauce. No longer do you see in Normandy markets piles of farmhouse butter and cream, since farmers now send their produce directly to factories and wholesalers.

Traditional dishes are being maintained, says the proprietor of the Hôtel de la Poste, by the restaurants now that the French working wife cannot

spare the time or effort to prepare, for example, a regular quantity of *graisse normande*—beef and pork fat rendered, and simmered with herbs and vegetables. The fat is then drained off and used to sauté potatoes, to fry omelettes, and to give Norman cooking its distinctive flavor.

The promotion of regional cooking and its preservation was pioneered by the *Guide Michelin*, which, almost from its first edition in 1900, listed local specialties. The 1913 guide for Normandy tells motorists to go to Rouen for *canard à la rouennaise* and *pieds de mouton farcis*. In Brittany you were to go to Nantes for *alose à l'oseille* and to Concarneau for *sardines, thon,* and *petits pois*. The star ratings, which began in the 1920s, created fierce competition among restaurants and encouraged chefs to show their skills at *haute cuisine* rather than home cooking; nevertheless, many local recipes were probably saved from extinction, even though some may have been transformed into *haute cuisine* by the addition of fancy sauces.

A SURVEY of French eating habits recently revealed that sauces are on the decline, especially with the young, who prefer simpler dishes with fruit and vegetables, for which the *nouvelle cuisine* is in no small measure responsible. These trends are set temporarily aside during the vacation period, when French tourists rekindle their interest in *plats régionaux*, and it turns out that the favorites are the slow-cooking stews and *daubes*, such as *le bœuf bourguignon, tripes,* and *civet de lapin* or *lapin à la havraise*, dishes that appear infrequently in modern French homes. Most restaurants offer at least one regional choice on their menus, especially along the tourist routes, where you will find such classic examples as *sole à la normande*, one of the most famous—perhaps *the* most famous—recipe in the French culinary repertoire. The dish was named, according to Audot's *La Cuisinière de la Campagne* (1818), "on account of the excellence of Normany soles," and not because it originated in Normandy. Some say it was invented by the great chef Carême, who adapted an old Norman recipe, a *matelote* or stew of sole cooked in cider and cream. His recipe was later taken by Langlais (who cooked for Alexander Dumas), chef of the famous Paris restaurant Rocher de Cancale, who contributed oysters, mussels, truffles, and fried smelts. An English epicure of the Victorian era who called himself *"Fin Bec"* had a different theory. It was not Carême, nor Langlais, but the cook of a modest restaurant, Phillipe's, opposite the Rocher de Cancale, who really perfected the *sole à la normande*, adding crayfish, oysters, truffles, and *croutons* to the already top-heavy recipe. But whoever invented the dish, it had come a long way from its humble origins.

In theory, you can travel around the coast trying the local recipes for sole. Starting at Dieppe, you find *sole à la dieppoise*—sole in a white wine and cream sauce, garnished with mussels (for which Dieppe is famous), mushrooms, and crayfish. The mussels come from the sea, the crayfish from the local rivers—or in boxes from Paris. Fifty miles south along the coast road brings you to Fécamp, where Maupassant was born, where Benedictine liqueur is made, and where your journey may be rewarded with *sole à la fécampoise*, similar to the Dieppe variety but with shrimp butter in the sauce. In the port of Le Havre your *sole à la havraise* is garnished with shrimp instead of crayfish (there being no rivers to speak of), and they sometimes dispense with the mussels. At Trouville they omit the mushrooms and mussels, retain the shrimp, and serve a shrimp sauce; at Port-en-Bassin they throw in scallops.

Poulet vallée d'Auge—named after the valley of the little river Auge, where it was created—is a dish that calls for calvados and cream, quintessentially Norman ingredients, left. Cut up and cooked in butter, the chicken is flavored with fresh tarragon, salt, and pepper, and finished with a generous supply of mushrooms, right.

15

The fish markets in Trouville and Honfleur daily mount a display of seafood infinite in its variety, and glistening in its freshness, to tempt buyers who need no tempting. The fish are prepared for the tables of the little restaurants and cafés, faced and capped in gray slate, that cluster around the port. Here you may eat *plats de fruits de mer* straight from the sea—crabs, oysters, mussels, whelks, winkles, cockles, prawns, shrimp, and langoustines, and if you ask for a *plat impérial*, they add lobster.

This fashionable stretch of the Normandy coast, from Honfleur to Deauville and Houlgate, borders on the Pays d'Auge, perhaps the richest of all the regions in Normandy, a countryside of plump chickens, of cheeses—of Camembert, Pont-

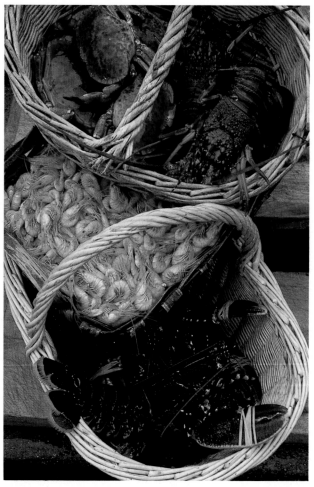

The shopping baskets of the chef from the restaurant Au Bon Accueil in Yport, right, hold fresh tourteaux *(crabs),* bouquets *(prawns), and* homards *(lobsters). The* crevettes au cidre *served at Ferme du Lieu Marot, below, are cooked in cider, water, and herbs; they are eaten with rye bread and butter and a glass of the same local cider.*

l'Évêque, and Livarot—and of the finest calvados and cider. Who would doubt that the most famous product ever to come out of Normandy is Camembert cheese? Even the Japanese make it, appreciating its mushroomy odor when fresh, its whiter-than-white rind flora and creamy texture. At Vimoutiers, near the village of Camembert, there's a statue of Marie Harel, the "inventor" of the cheese. Marie Harel did not really invent Camembert—it has been known in the district since the time of William the Conqueror—but she was the first to devise a rigid recipe and to standardize production. Camembert became an international delicacy instead of a local product when in the 1890s a Vimoutiers cheese factor, or *caviste*, a Monsieur Ridel, devised and patented the chipwood box that helped to preserve the cheese for export.

THE CITIES of Rouen and Caen compete for the title of gastronomic capital of Normandy, but honor is satisfied by designating Rouen the capital of Upper Normandy and Caen the capital of Lower Normandy. Both have given their names to a dish, regularly cooked throughout France. Caen bestowed *tripes à la mode de Caen*, perfected if not actually invented by a fourteenth-century chef named Benoit, a na-

At the foot of the narrow, medieval, cobbled street that rises sharply toward the spire of the Abbey of Mont-Saint-Michel—itself en route to heaven—is Mère Poulard's restaurant, which has been serving omelettes to tourists for well over a century. By popular request, they print and distribute the recipe in different languages, although the only thing special about *omelette de la Mère Poulard* is the ·oak-wood fire over which it is traditionally cooked. Here is the recipe: Use two eggs per person (have the eggs at room temperature); whip the eggs very well; melt plenty of salted butter in a tin-lined copper pan; cook very slowly, stirring with a fork all around the edges from time to time; remove from the fire often so that the omelette rises

Barbue à l'oseille, as prepared by the chef of Le Petit Coq aux Champs in Pont-Audemer, is presented with the fish —brill—napped with creamed sorrel, left. The ingredients, below, are simple—the brill, kept fresh on a bed of ice, the washed sorrel leaves, cream, salt, and pepper. White wine is a nearly inevitable accompaniment.

tive of the city. Today, he would have been given a Nobel prize. The tripe is cooked with beef fat and ox feet, plus root vegetables, garlic, herbs, allspice, cider, and calvados, enclosed in a special *tripière*, and left in the oven to simmer and philosophize for twelve hours. Tripe was originally a "take-out" dish, the product of a city already famous for its *charcuterie*, and prepared in the cookshops and bakeries in large quantities.

Rouen then responded with *canard à la rouennaise* —although the ducks are bred at Yvetot, some thirty miles away. The ducks are strangled so as to conserve the blood, which is an essential part of the sauce, and the dish became included in the repertoire of *haute cuisine* when it was adopted—in the late nineteenth century, as pressed duck or *canard au sang*—by Frederick, chef of the celebrated Tour d'Argent restaurant in Paris.

A local specialty will often find its main outlet in the nearest big town, so that Cherbourg, Avranches, and Mont-Saint-Michel are noted for their *pré-salés*, or salt-meadow mutton and lamb, which come in fact from sheep that graze on the coastal pastures of the Cotentin peninsula; you may see this featured on menus as *gigot des grèves du Mont-Saint-Michel*, and the meat acquires a delicate, slightly salty flavor of the sea.

like a soufflé; turn out of the pan and fold over; serve immediately. A version of this, called *omelette normande*, uses cream and suggests that you separate the eggs and fold the beaten egg whites into the yolks before cooking.

Vire, in the *bocage* country, is known for its black-skinned, prehistoric-looking chitterling sausages called *andouilles*. Built on top of a steep hill, the little town does a brisk trade in *charcuterie*—sausages and hams hang in windows in neat array. *Andouilles* and the smaller tripe sausages, *andouillettes*, are served in the town's restaurants; the *andouilles* with a purée of sorrel, the *andouillettes* grilled with puréed potatoes. Cut in slices, the *andouille de Vire* has a grayish marbled appearance; its flavor is rather bland and unremarkable. Why it has become a luxury article remains a mystery.

About half of the pastries turned out by Mme. Coisels of Ferme du Lieu Marot are made with apples grown on the farm. Both her tarte aux pommes *and* tarte aux fraises, *right, are usually served with her husband's cider. A carré feuilleté* aux pommes, *several kinds of small apple tarts, marzipan apples, and other delicacies, below, are all from her kitchen. Her unadorned chocolate cake, left, is fresh from the oven.*

BRITTANY

BRITTANY and Normandy are linked geographically but are poles apart in customs, in temperament, and in religion—the Bretons are Catholics, but somewhere, not too deep down in the Breton soul, are ties with the prehistoric people who erected the megaliths of Carnac. The two regions share, to some extent, similarities of produce and cooking, but in spite of disclaimers made in the *Larousse Gastronomique*, Brittany has no important culinary traditions, even though the raw materials are of excellent quality. The cider apple is such a vital crop that until recently you could not find a dessert apple from Pont-Audemer to Brest. The country lanes are lined with gnarled apple trees whose branches in the late summer bear small, golden, bittersweet fruit, later to be made into cider, and still later into *lambig (eau-de-vie)* in Brittany and calvados in Normandy.

Calvados from the region of the Pays d'Auge can develop into a fine, pale, and powerful apple brandy—given time. Elsewhere in Normandy, and throughout the Armorican peninsula, you can buy *eau-de-vie de cidre* made in ramshackle alembics by farmers' wives. It is rumored that Norman farmers keep small casks under the bed to refresh

Beaten by the sea into scores of jagged inlets and bays and rocky points of land, the ragged coastline of Brittany, some 750 miles long, juts farthest out into the Atlantic at the western headland of Finistère (roughly, the ends of the earth), top. The fish and shellfish Bretons take from the sea are the main

ingredients of some of the best of their cuisine. The cleaned mackerel, right, is marinating in oil, onion, carrots, lemon, bay leaf, thyme, and fennel. A highly seasoned wine sauce will be added, and then the dish will be marinated for two days more and eaten cold.

20

themselves on rising. Mrs. Robert Henry, in her recollections of life on *A Farm in Normandy* (1941), mentions that calvados was responsible for "stunted children and suicides in desolate farms."

IF THE Normans do not regard themselves as entirely French—they were originally of Viking stock—then by this standard of reference the Bretons might just as well be on an island in the mid-Atlantic. The Breton language, which has affinities with Welsh and Cornish, is still spoken in parts of Brittany. Breton produce such as vegetables and lobsters are "exported" to France

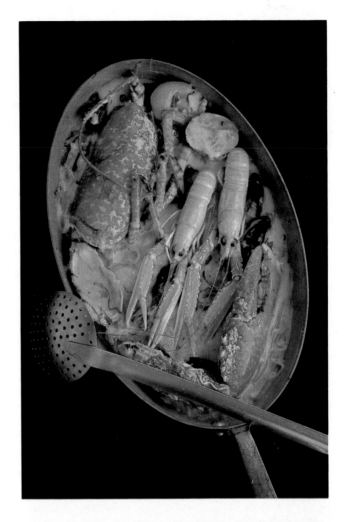

Pot-au-feu de homard Breton, *left, combines four kinds of shellfish—shrimp, scallops, oysters, and mussels—with the lobster in a* fumet. *The shellfish are simmered, right, in calvados and white wine, leeks, and shallots, and* crème fraîche *is added at the last minute. M. Corre of the Restaurant à la Pointe de Saint-Mathieu in the town of the same name is the chef. The main ingredients of the Breton fish stew called* cotriade, *below, are a large assortment of fish, shellfish, and, possibly, eel. They are cooked with garlic, onions, and potatoes in a fish and vegetable stock to which calvados and white wine are added. At the Relais la Coquille in the port of Concarneau, the* cotriade *is served traditionally—with a bowl of its own stock, fried bread, grated cheese, and a spicy sauce* rouille.

and other "foreign" countries, while French cheeses and wines are "imported" across the border.

Unlike their Norman neighbors, the Bretons do not attach fundamental importance to the fine art of cuisine. As late as the beginning of this century, meat—apart from salt pork and fishy-tasting goose—was rare on the table, although there was always plenty of butter: "Every Bretonne believes," wrote Edward Harrison Barker, who toured Brittany in the 1890s, "that human life cannot go on a single day unless it is copiously buttered."

These historical culinary facts remind us that a cuisine is a product of traditional cooking methods, of tastes, and of economics: When Barker toured Brittany, he found that the staples included rye bread, buckwheat pancakes, and black puddings. There was tripe, boiled bacon, sardines, and coffee. Today, Breton food is hardy, sustaining, and simple, and based on such dishes as *pré-salé* mutton with haricot beans, the celebrated *gigot aux haricots à la bretonne*. Buckwheat remains a staple. Buckwheat puddings, cooked in a muslin bag and known as *kik a'farz*, are boiled along with the family *pot-au-feu*, sliced and served with the meat. Throughout Brittany in towns and villages, *crêpe* vendors cook their *crêpes* on a thin metal griddle, skillfully spreading the thin batter with a wooden *rabot*. The *crêpes* are made of wholewheat flour, eggs, milk and water, sugar and vanilla, and spread with jam, chocolate, or apple purée.

It is noticeable in this part of France how habits and temperament reflect the landscape. Where Normandy is a tamed dairy countryside of pretty, half-timbered farmhouses, of wooded and gently undulating hills, Brittany is still wild and untamed. But the new and excellent motorways around the coast show Breton awareness of the importance of tourism and advanced industrial development. Some features may never change—the ubiquitous pig is still the mainstay of the average family, or, rather, it is the most popular meat in the Breton diet. Surprisingly, in view of the abundance of fish recipes and restaurants, the Bretons are indifferent to the "meat of Lent and Fridays." Fish is for tourists.

The three gâteaux Bretons *below are typically simple, unadorned sweets of the region. The sugared* gwen *(or* kuoing*)* amman *on the left is a yellow cake.* Le far, *in the middle, rich with eggs, tastes something like a flan. The* galette bretonne *has a cross-hatched crust. Opposite (clockwise from top left), glimpses of the marketplaces and towns of Brittany: a produce stall in Quimper; mussels in the Saint-Malo fishmarket; two* traditionally dressed women of Combrit, the place identified by the pattern of lace on their starched bigoudène hats; crabs in Saint-Malo; a fresh, live lobster awaiting the chef; two kinds of clams—palourdes (bottom) and amandes, in Quimper; there, too, a sign at a pâtisserie; shrimp of Quimper; and, center, in the harbor of le Conquet, a pair of lobsters plucked from a vivier, or holding pond.*

Brittany is divided fairly evenly between the farmland communities and the coastal communities. The farms start the day very early with coffee, and the men return home for breakfast at around 8 A.M. and sit down to a meal of buckwheat porridge, pork *pâté*, perhaps a slice of streaky pork eaten cold, with bread and wine. At lunchtime the family might have pork and potatoes, or a *galette*, washed down with *lait ribot* (buttermilk), beer, or cider. Only the townsfolk drink wine at lunchtime, although why the farmers deny themselves wine at lunch if they drink it for breakfast has never been clear. Lunch everywhere is terminated with a *mic*—coffee and a glass of *eau-de-vie*.

Brittany has culinary links with Wales. The Welsh, like the Bretons, drink buttermilk with their pancakes, although theirs are made with oatmeal instead of buckwheat. Breton farmers would appreciate the Welsh cawl, a stew of bacon, potatoes,

In Brittany, a galette *is a main-course* crêpe *into which eggs, meat, or fish can be folded. At the Crêperie des Artisans in Dinan, M. Moncet, the owner and chef, has assembled, left, the simple ingredients of* galettes—*buckwheat flour, water, and salt—along with mixing utensils and a griddle. The* galette *is cooked over a wood fire, below, with a fresh egg and, perhaps, ham or sausage, for filling. The dessert* crêpe, *right, is made with white flour, eggs, milk, butter, and sugar.*

cabbages, leeks, and beans thickened with oatmeal.

Although not a drop of wine is produced in Brittany, the Muscadet and Gros Plant vineyards being south of Nantes, it is said that a strong wine and an even stronger brandy are made on the Rhuys peninsula below Vannes. A Breton embarking on a bottle of Rhuys brandy needs, they say, four men to hold him up and a wall to prevent the five of them from falling backwards.

In all fairness to Breton cooking, the coasts and fishing ports have developed some fine dishes: *Cotriade*, the *bouillabaisse* of Brittany, is traditionally made from the portion of fish—the *godaille*—allocated to every fisherman once the bulk of the catch has been sold, which might include gurnard, gray mullet, John Dory, angler fish, conger eel, whiting, wrasse, mussels, or prawns. These are then cooked with potatoes, onions, carrots, garlic, herbs, Muscadet, and *eau-de-vie*. Seafood restaurants specialize in stuffed clams—*palourdes farcies*—skate with black butter sauce, mussels from Cancale, and, above all, the Breton lobster.

As you might expect, Brittany's finest restaurants are mainly along the coasts and tourist routes, and fish specialties are emphasized. At Pont-Aven, where Gauguin painted the peasant girls in their lace *coiffes* (which vary in design from area to area), there is the restaurant Moulin de Rosamadec, where the mill-

race tumbles past fuchsia blossoms and drooping willow fronds and in which, no doubt, brown trout repose. Inside the converted mill are pink flowers, pink candles, pink napkins, and matching table-cloths. You are offered plenty of fresh bread and, in keeping with Brittany's copiously buttered life style, a large slice of salted butter. The plump, moist turbot is an excellent choice because it is served with a *beurre blanc*, a specialty of Nantes and southern Brittany, and also of the Loire. Said to be tricky to make, *beurre blanc* is a pure, farmhouse butter sauce, emulsified by shallots, vinegar or white wine, and the cunning hand of the cook. Breton butter used to have a very pronounced and individual flavor before stringent laws of hygiene were introduced, and before the gorse on which cows were grazed gave way to fodder crops and corn. Perhaps this is why the *beurre blanc* of Nantes acquired a reputation superior to that of the *beurre blanc* of the Loire; bland, mass-produced butters are said not to be suitable for making *beurre blanc*—you need good old-fashioned farmhouse butter with all its faithful impurities, because these very impurities help in some way to emulsify the sauce.

Beurre blanc is made on the principle of mayonnaise, which requires the egg protein to "structure" the globules of oil and hold them together. The purée of shallots and the casein (milk protein), whey, and lactose in the butter all act as homogenizing agents. Although it is strictly against the rules (and is probably done in many restaurants), you can emulsify your butter with an egg yolk. You will need a teaspoonful of finely chopped shallots that you have cooked in cider vinegar or white wine until the liquid has evaporated and the shallots are soft, almost a purée consistency. Mix this with an egg yolk in a mixing bowl, and add four to six tablespoons of melted butter, drop by drop, while beating with an electric hand whisk or blender. This produces a passable *beurre blanc* to serve with poached or baked white fish.

Nantes, once the seat of the dukes of Brittany, has been the capital of the Pays de la Loire since the French Revolution, yet many Bretons still think of Nantes as a Breton town. Even the *Guide Michelin*, which should know, describes Nantes as "the biggest town in Brittany." The specialties of Nantes give a certain, perhaps unwanted, sophistication to Breton cooking: lampreys cooked with prunes, eel roe called *civelles*, ducklings cooked with young turnips and peas, mint-flavored *berlingots*, shad or *alose*—the herringlike fish of river estuaries—served with *beurre blanc*.

It is a fact, though, that there are more first-class restaurants in Brittany than in Normandy and the Loire together. The buckwheat, pork, sardines, and cider tradition has recently engendered an aware-ness of the importance of Breton produce. For the past century, Breton farmers along the coasts have been using marine fertilizers dredged from the sea, *sable coquiller*, which established the basis of fine crops of vegetables and fruits: early strawberries from Plougastel, and around Saint-Malo you will see fields of cauliflowers, artichokes, leeks, onions, garlic, carrots, cabbages, and beetroot, planted in neat rectangles of subtle purples, greens, and blues.

Given this bounty, Breton chefs have discovered latent skills, and are making impressive contributions to the repertoire. Tomorrow, the French traveler, clutching his *guide*, in which he has penciled a selection of restaurants, will pass through Normandy to sample the delights of *pot-au-feu de homard breton* in a progressive, modern country that has somehow managed to retain the essentials of a rustic Arcady.

Two kinds of cabbage ripen in the fall in a Breton farmer's field, opposite, near Cancale. The soil of Brittany, especially near the coast, is poor, due to salt spray and strong sea winds. Only sturdy crops that cling to the ground, such as cabbage, cauliflower, and artichokes, thrive. Below, a retired fisherman of Quiberon returns home from a day of harvesting cabbages with a load of discarded outer leaves to feed his rabbits.

CREVETTES AU CIDRE *Shrimps Cooked in Cider*

These are the delicate transparent shrimps sold live and
hopping like fleas in the markets of Normandy's coast.
In this recipe, instead of being cooked in water, they are
cooked in cider in the local way.

1 pound fresh shrimps or prawns (500 g)
2 cups hard cider (½ liter)
Salt, freshly ground pepper
1 bouquet garni—see Appendix

Bring the cider and 2 cups water to a boil, add plenty of
   salt, pepper, and the bouquet garni and boil for 10
   minutes. Add the shrimps, let the liquid return to a
   boil, and cook for 5 minutes.
Drain and serve steaming hot with bread and butter,
   and cider.

for 4 or 5 people / photograph on page 16

BARBUE À L'OSEILLE *Brill with Sorrel*

1 whole (4 pound) brill (or gray sole, flounder, or
   lemon sole), cleaned and gutted (2 kg)
2 pounds sorrel (1 kg)
1 cup heavy cream (250 ml)
Salt, freshly ground pepper

FOR THE COURT-BOUILLON
1 pound heads, bones, and trimmings of firm white fish
   (silver hake, haddock, sole, or flounder) (500 g)
1 onion, sliced
1 carrot, sliced
1 bouquet garni—see Appendix
1½ cups hard cider or white wine (395 ml)
Salt, freshly ground pepper

In a wide, shallow pan, prepare a *court-bouillon* made
   with the fish heads, bones, trimmings, onion, carrot,
   bouquet garni, cider, 1½ cups water, salt, and pepper,
   and let the mixture simmer 30 minutes. Skim off the
   impurities that rise to the surface, and gently poach
   fillets for 10 minutes or the whole brill for up to
   45 minutes.
Pick over and wash the sorrel. Put the leaves in a large
   saucepan full of boiling water for 30 seconds. Drain
   them and remove all the tough fibers and stems. Heat
   the sorrel in a frying pan with the cream, stirring
   constantly. Season with salt and pepper, and when it
   has reduced to a thick, green purée, serve it over the
   fish or on the side.

for 6 people / photograph on page 17

ESCALOPES CAUCHOISES
Veal Scallops with Cream and Mushroom Sauce

6 veal scallops
6 tablespoons butter (75 g)
1 onion, sliced
1 pound button mushrooms, sliced (500 g)
1 cup hard cider (250 ml)
½ cup calvados (125 ml)
½ cup *crème fraîche*—see Appendix—or
   heavy cream (125 ml)
Salt, freshly ground pepper

The scallops need not be pounded flat. Melt half the
   butter in a frying pan and cook the scallops for 3
   minutes on each side, until golden brown. Season
   lightly with salt and pepper; remove and keep warm.
Brown the sliced onion lightly in the same butter. Sauté
   the mushrooms in the remaining 3 tablespoons butter in a separate pan. When some of their juice has
   evaporated, set them aside.
Pour the cider into the pan with the onion and deglaze
   it by boiling rapidly until about half has evaporated.
   Add the calvados and reduce a little more, then put
   in the mushrooms and the *crème fraîche*. Return the
   scallops to the pan, with any juice that has run out,
   season, and heat gently for 5 minutes. Serve with
   snow peas cooked quickly in butter and sliced apples
   sautéed in butter.

for 6 people / photographs at left and opposite

FILETS DE SOLE NORMANDE   *Fillets of Sole, Normandy Style*

4 pounds Dover sole (or lemon sole), filleted (2 kg)

FOR THE FUMET
1 pound heads, bones, and trimmings of firm white fish
   (silver hake, haddock, cod, sole, or flounder) (500 g)
1 carrot, sliced
2 shallots, sliced
1½ cups hard cider or white wine (375 ml)
1 sprig of parsley
Salt, freshly ground pepper

FOR THE GARNISH
¾ pound raw, unpeeled shrimps or prawns (340 g)
   or 2 pounds mussels (1 kg) or 6 sea scallops

FOR THE SAUCE
1 pound button mushrooms (500 g)
Juice of 1 lemon
4 tablespoons butter (50 g)
1 egg yolk
1 cup *crème fraîche* (250 ml)—see Appendix
Salt, freshly ground pepper

To make the *fumet*, put the ingredients into a wide, shallow pan and simmer for 30 minutes. (If you are using mussels as a garnish, cook them and add their juices to the *fumet*.) Skim the surface, slip in the fish fillets, and cook them very gently for 10 minutes. Transfer them to a buttered gratin dish. Save the fish *fumet* and strain it, if desired.

Next prepare the garnish. If you have shrimps, cook them in 1 cup of cider and 1 cup of water for 5 minutes with a generous pinch of salt (see recipe for *crevettes au cidre*, page 30). Scallops should be poached for 1 to 2 minutes in the simmering fish *fumet*. Preheat the oven to 350°F.

Slice the mushrooms, sprinkle with lemon juice to prevent them from discoloring, and cook gently in 2 tablespoons of the butter. Add the sautéed mushrooms and the shrimps, mussels, or scallops to the fish fillets.

Beat the egg yolk with the cream and thin the sauce by whisking in 1 or 2 tablespoons of fish *fumet*. Season with salt and pepper, pour over the fish, dot with the remaining 2 tablespoons butter cut into small pieces, and heat through in the oven, for about 10 minutes.

for 6 people

TARTE AU SUCRE D'YPORT   *Apple Tart*

1 recipe *pâte brisée sucrée*—see Appendix
1½ pounds russet apples, peeled, cored, and sliced (800 g)
¼ cup calvados (60 ml)
5 heaping tablespoons sugar (60 g)
3 egg yolks
1 cup *crème fraîche*—see Appendix—or
   heavy cream (250 ml)
2 tablespoons finely slivered almonds

Soak the apple slices in calvados for 1 hour.
Preheat the oven to 425°F. Line a 9-inch tart pan with the *pâte brisée sucrée*, prick the crust with a fork, and bake blind for 15 minutes; reduce the heat to 350°F. Sprinkle 2 tablespoons of the sugar over the bottom of the crust. Drain the apple slices, reserving the calvados, and place the slices on top of the sugar. Bake in the moderate oven for 30 minutes; increase the heat to 425°F.
Beat together the egg yolks, cream, remaining sugar, and reserved calvados and pour the mixture over the apples. Scatter the almonds on top and bake for 15 minutes. Serve warm with a bowl of *crème fraîche* (or whipped, heavy cream) and a bottle of chilled cider.

for 6 people / photographs at right and opposite

COTRIADE   *Fish Stew*

3 to 3½ pounds whole fish—choose an assortment
    from angler fish, conger eel, silver hake, whiting,
    flounder, or monkfish—filleted, with heads and trim-
    mings reserved (1½ kg)
¾ pound mussels, cleaned (350 g)
½ pound langoustines or jumbo shrimp (225 g)
4 onions, chopped
4 carrots, chopped
4 tablespoons butter (50 g)
2 cloves garlic, crushed
¼ cup *eau-de-vie de cidre* or calvados (60 ml)
1 cup Muscadet or other dry white wine (250 ml)
1 bouquet garni—see Appendix
1 tablespoon tomato purée, diluted in a little water
Salt, freshly ground pepper, cayenne pepper
1½ pounds potatoes, thinly sliced (750 g)
Fresh herbs (thyme, bay leaf, savory, basil, parsley)
Pinch of saffron

Ask the fishmonger to fillet the fish and remove the
    gills, which can impart a bitter taste. Reserve the
    heads, bones, and trimmings.
Sauté the carrots and 2 of the onions in a large, heavy
saucepan with the butter and 1 clove of garlic. Sweat
    the vegetables by cooking them gently for 10 to 15
    minutes over a low heat, stirring occasionally, and
    then add the fish heads, bones, and trimmings. Stir,
    cover, and cook gently for 10 to 15 minutes more,
    then add the *eau-de-vie de cidre*, Muscadet, bouquet
    garni, and tomato purée.
Add enough water to cover the fish heads, bones, and
    trimmings and simmer for 1½ hours. Strain through a
    fine sieve, and season well with salt, pepper, and
    cayenne pepper.
Put the onions and garlic in the bottom of a large
    casserole, cover with the potatoes, season with salt,
    pepper, and cayenne and add the chopped herbs to
    taste and the saffron. Arrange the fish fillets on top
    and add enough strained stock to just cover the fish.
Preheat the oven to 400°F. Start cooking over a moder-
    ate heat on top of the stove for 10 minutes, then put
    the mussels and langoustines on top of the fish and
    bake for 20 minutes. Discard any mussels that don't
    open. Serve straight from the oven, with rounds of
    toasted French bread lightly rubbed with garlic.

for 6 to 8 people / photograph on page 23

POT-AU-FEU DE HOMARD BRETON   *Lobster Pot-au-Feu*

1 2-pound live lobster (900 g)
6 sea scallops
6 oysters
6 langoustines or jumbo shrimp, cleaned and deveined
1 pound mussels, well-scrubbed (500 g)
2 tablespoons butter (25 g)
1 tablespoon olive oil (15 ml)
¼ cup calvados or *eau-de-vie de cidre* (60 ml)
1 cup dry white wine (250 ml)
2 leeks, white parts only, finely sliced
3 shallots, finely chopped
1 bouquet garni of parsley, tarragon, and dill
Salt, freshly ground pepper
½ cup *crème fraîche* (125 ml)—see Appendix

FOR THE FUMET
¾ cup white wine (200 ml)
1 onion
1 carrot
1 shallot
1 bouquet garni—see Appendix
Salt
6 black peppercorns
1 pound fish bones, heads, and trimmings (500 g)

Combine the ingredients for the *fumet*, except the
    fish bones, and season lightly with salt. Cover with
    plenty of water and simmer for 40 minutes. Add the
fish bones and simmer for 20 minutes. Strain and
    boil rapidly until reduced to 3 cups.
Place the lobster on its back, cover the head and claws
    with a damp cloth to protect your hands, and, with a
    sharp knife, split it down the middle from head to
    tail. (For this recipe the lobster must be alive; if you
    can't bring yourself to split a live lobster, put it head
    first into a pan of boiling salted water for 2 minutes.)
    Remove the gravel (sand) sac from the head and pull
    off the claws. Crack them, and cut the lobster halves
    into two.
Heat the butter and olive oil in a large sauté pan, and
    sauté the lobster until it turns bright red. Remove it to
    a dish, and keep hot. Add the calvados or *eau-de-vie
    de cidre*, the white wine, and the 3 cups of *fumet* to the
    pan, and cook for 15 minutes over a high heat. When
    reduced, add the leeks, shallots, and bouquet garni.
    Season with salt and pepper and cook for 15 minutes
    more over medium heat, then add the scallops, oysters,
    langoustines, and mussels, and cook until just done,
    about 10 minutes. Discard any mussels that don't open.
Arrange the lobster on a hot serving dish surrounded
    with the mussels, scallops, oysters, and langoustines.
    Strain the pan juices, stir in the *crème fraîche*, taste for
    seasoning, and pour the sauce over the lobster. Serve
    with rice or steamed potatoes.

for 4 people / photograph on page 22

GIGOT À LA BRETONNE   *Leg of Lamb with Haricot Beans*

1 leg of lamb, weighing 5 to 6 pounds, boned but with
   shank on (2½ kg)
2 cloves garlic, slivered
4 tablespoons butter, softened (50 g)
Salt, freshly ground pepper
Thyme
6 shallots, sliced
2 carrots, sliced
½ cup white wine (125 ml)
1 cup lamb (or beef) stock or water (250 ml)

FOR THE BEANS

1 pound dried white beans, soaked overnight in water
   to cover (500 g)
About 3 tablespoons butter
1 carrot, diced
3 shallots, chopped
1 onion, stuck with a clove
1 bouquet garni, including celery tops—see Appendix
Salt, freshly ground pepper
2 tablespoons chopped parsley

Tie the leg of lamb into a neat roll with string. Make a
few incisions in the meat and push slivers of garlic
into them. Spread 2 tablespoons of the butter over
the lamb after seasoning it well with salt and pepper.

Preheat the oven to 450°F. Melt the remaining butter in
a roasting pan and put in a mixed layer of shallots
and carrots. Season with salt and pepper and sprinkle
with thyme. Place the leg of lamb on top of the
vegetables, sear for 10 minutes in the hot oven and
then reduce the heat to 400°F. Cook for 10 to 12
minutes per pound for rare meat, 15 minutes per
pound for medium, basting frequently. Let the lamb
stand in a warm place for 10 minutes before carving.

Meanwhile, cook the beans. Heat 2 tablespoons of the
butter in a cast-iron casserole and sauté the carrot
and shallots for 10 minutes, until softened. Add the
beans, the onion with a clove, bouquet garni, and
cover with water. Simmer for 1 hour, season with salt
and pepper and simmer until the beans are tender.
Remove the bouquet garni and discard it. Chop the
cooked onion and sieve it together with some of the
beans and enough of their liquid to make a thin,
velvety sauce. Drain the remaining beans and stir in
the creamy bean purée, the parsley, and the remaining tablespoon of butter. Taste for seasoning and heat
through.

Serve the lamb on a hot dish. Remove most of the fat
from the pan and deglaze the pan with the wine and
stock. Strain into a small pan. Skim any remaining
fat off the sauce, simmer 5 to 10 minutes, and taste
for seasoning. Serve the sliced lamb very hot with the
beans and sauce.

for 6 to 8 people / photograph below

ANJOU & TOURAINE

ANJOU & TOURAINE

ANJOU and Touraine together stretch from Angers in the west, to Blois, on the border of Sologne. This comparatively small area, no more than a hundred miles as the crow flies, lies along the banks of the Loire. The food of the region is based on two physical characteristics: the river itself, with its wealth of freshwater fish, and the extremely fertile soil. This, combined with the exceptionally mild climate, allows the cultivation of *primeurs* (early vegetables and fruit) some two weeks earlier than in the Ile de France, the area around Paris. The soft tufa stone of the river banks near Saumur houses countless caves, ideally suited to the cultivation of mushrooms. Thus it has become the main source of supply of *champignons de Paris* for the whole of France.

The local wines are justly famous—primarily the white wines, which are among the best in France. These, made for the most part from the Chenin Blanc grape, include Muscadet, Vouvray, Savennières, and Saumur. Sweet white wines are also a feature of the region; two of the best are Quart de Chaumes and Bonnezeaux. Anjou is well known for its rosés; these were formerly all slightly sweet, but a drier version

The pastoral peace of old France has not vanished from Anjou and Touraine; one glimpses it still in family farms, like the one near Langennerie, preceding overleaf, where the farmer has built a house-shaped meule, *or haystack. The Loire river and its tributaries water these fertile fields and also supply the freshwater fish that are part of many famous regional dishes. Above, a fisherman on La Creuze casts off of his flat-bottomed boat for perch, carp, and pike. The local* charcuterie, *right, includes* andouillettes *(rear), coils of blood sausage, pieds de porcs farcis (on tray), long, red* saucisses sèches au Vouvray, rillettes *and* rillons *(in bowls), and the triangular* jarrets de porc.

Family farms flourish in the exceedingly rich soil and mild climate of Anjou and Touraine, which escape the long winters of the north and the burning summers of the south. A farm in the Cher river valley, above, is built around a courtyard in traditional fashion. Centuries ago, a farmer's wealth (and the taxes he paid) were determined by the height of the manure pile in his courtyard; today, other measures are used. But the farmers of Archigny, below, still grow the abundant variety of fruits and vegetables for which these regions are renowned.

is now made to accommodate modern tastes. The local red wines are less well known internationally, since they are produced in relatively small quantities and do not travel well. They are unusual, light and flowery in character, almost like a white wine. Among the best are those of Chinon, Bourgeuil, Saint-Nicolas-de-Bourgeuil, and Saumur-Champigny. These are made from the Cabernet Franc grape, which is also used as the basis for most of the rosés.

Between Angers and Blois no fewer than thirteen tributaries run into the Loire, creating a strange, watery landscape that is almost unique. Some of these, like the Vienne, the Cher, the Indre, and the Loir, are almost as broad as the Loire itself. Others, like the Authion, are smaller but run parallel and very close to the Loire. Within the body of the Loire itself, strips of land emerge from the water, and winding channels form along the banks, making a curious interwoven pattern of earth and water. Trees grow on these narrow islets, and in the misty weather of late autumn, the whole area has a strange miragelike quality, for it is almost impossible to discern where the water ends and dry land begins.

Touraine, in the east, is densely wooded; there are the great forests of Blois, Russy, Amboise, Loches, and Chinon, as well as many smaller

*Honoré de Balzac lived and wrote in the village of Saché, in Touraine, where a woman tends her small herd of graceful goats, above. From their milk, she makes one of the glories of France—*fromage de chèvre. *At night she milks her goats, curdles the milk, and then pours it into perforated molds. A few days later, when the cheese has drained, she will sell it in a local market, like the one at Vernantes, below, as* chèvre frais. *What she can't sell, she will age. A variety of* chèvres, *from creamy, young cheeses to pungent, brown-skinned, aged ones, fill local market stalls.*

woods. It is to these forests that Touraine owes much of its past grandeur, for they were filled with wildlife. Many of the French kings shared with their nobles a passion for hunting, and this, combined with the beauty of the landscape, was the prime reason for the building of the innumerable castles along the banks of the Loire, both in medieval times and during the Renaissance. There is a peculiar lightness about these French forests; even in midsummer the foliage is delicate, mobile, and responsive to the slightest current of air. This is because most of the trees have small leaves, like the poplars and willows that are such a dominant feature of the Val de Loire.

The French still have a passion for *la chasse*; the hunting season starts on September 20, and by late October there is little wildlife left. If you wander in the Forest of Loches, or in the woods north of Langeais, in late autumn, you may not see a single animal, not even a bird. These French woods have an eerie stillness. Roe deer still live in the Forest of Loches, while fox hunting still takes place on private properties. The game birds include pheasants, partridges, and quail, together with thrushes and larks. (These little songbirds have always been considered fair game by the French, and are highly esteemed as food.) Along the banks of the rivers are wild ducks—teal and mallard. Pheasants are now raised commercially. If you drive through the pastureland near the ravishing Château d'Ussé, you'll pass a large field filled with pheasants in wire-netting cages. But live game birds are a rare sight. Most of the game birds that you will see will be hanging in butchers' shops. Partridges, however, cannot be bred. There are two sorts of partridge in France: The gray-legged variety is superior and usually roasted, while the red-legged variety has coarser flesh and is more often braised. Pheasants are treated in similar fashion; the young birds are roasted, and

the older ones are cooked in casseroles, braised *au chou*, or made into *terrines* and soups. A good example of the last is the *potage Saint-Hubert*, in which an elderly bird is combined with green lentils. Hares and rabbits are also popular; hares are made into *terrines* and *pâtés*, and rabbits, either wild or domestic, are cooked with herbs and white wine, sometimes with prunes.

One of the delicacies of the Val de Loire is the fish. Professional fishermen sell their catch directly to the best restaurants, as well as to the local markets. This includes salmon, salmon trout, perch, carp, pike, and shad. A particularly delicious fish is the *sandre*, a variety of large perch with very delicate flesh. Like the pike, it is usually served poached in *court-bouillon*, accompanied by a *beurre blanc*. Fashions change, even in country districts like these;

Matelote d'anguilles et de carpe, *left and below, a stew of eel and carp, gets its distinctive flavor and rich color from the fruity red* vin du pays *in which it is simmered with mushrooms and onions. At the Barrier, a two-star restaurant in Tours, it is a favorite of the chef, M. Barrier. Right, the ingredients for* sandre et perche de Loire beurre blanc *are assembled at Jeanne de Laval, a restaurant in les Rosiers. This braised dish is a specialty of Anjou. Culinary lore has it that* beurre blanc *was born in 1900 when an anonymous chef ruined a* béarnaise *sauce, in what turned out to be a happy accident.*

some years ago, almost every restaurant of repute had pike *quenelles* on its menu. (Although these are, strictly speaking, a dish from the Lyonnais, the preponderance of excellent Loire pike made them popular here also.) Today, they are much scarcer, though you may still find them in a charming small restaurant called Le Bon Laboureur et Château, in Chenonceaux. Their fat *quenelle*, shaped like a short chocolate éclair, is as light as the proverbial feather. The classic accompaniment to *quenelle de brochet* is *sauce Nantua*, a pale pink *velouté* made with fish *fumet*, cream, and pounded crayfish. Here it has little shreds of crayfish suspended within it. Restaurants commonly serve both pike and *sandre au nature* with *beurre blanc*.

Loire salmon are prized for their quality, and salmon trout are also caught. Salmon trout have been somewhat downgraded recently since they are now raised on fish farms, and few of them have actually seen the river. They resemble young salmon, and their flesh is solid enough to be cut and cooked in thick slices. Salmon are caught by netting, while shad are fished for from flat-bottomed boats. *Alose à l'oseille*—shad with sorrel—is a popular local dish. The river trout are excellent, found mostly in the smaller tributaries of the Loire and in large streams; they are often poached in a local white wine, usually a Vouvray, and served either hot, or, in summertime, *en gelée*. A good first course is a platter of tiny river fish lightly fried. Carp and perch are caught in the deep pools of the Loire and its larger tributaries; eels and crayfish are found in the canals. Eels are very popular; one of the best-known local specialties is the *matelote d'anguilles au vin de Bourgueil*, an eel stew made with local red wine, which gives it a unique character. Other examples of local dishes are *andouillettes grillées au vin de Vouvray*—coarse white sausages grilled and deglazed with white wine—*coq au vin de Chinon*, and *lapin poêlé au vin blanc d'Anjou*. The last is a semisweet white wine that transforms the rabbit casserole into an unusual dish.

Sorrel is widely grown and used in many local dishes; in addition to the shad already mentioned, there is a dish of roe deer with sorrel (*chevreuil à l'oseille*) that is renowned but unfortunately it is difficult, if not impossible, to find a restaurant that serves it.

The best known of all the local dishes, especially in and around Tours, are *rillons* and *rillettes*. These are found in all the local *traiteurs* and *charcuteries*, for nowadays they are more often bought than made at home. *Rillons* are strips of fat pork, quite large, which are eaten as an *hors d'œuvre*, hot, warm, or cold. *Rillettes*, as the name suggests, are a smaller version of *rillons*. Both are basically a form of potted pork made with either the breast or the belly cooked slowly for several hours in its own fat. *Rillettes* vary greatly from place to place: In Tours they are usually pounded into a smooth paste; in Angers and Saumur they have more texture, since the little strips of pork are left intact within the *paté*. Eaten with toast, as an *hors d'œuvre*, they go perfectly with the local red or white wines.

BOTH Anjou and Touraine are famous for their market gardens; they combine a particularly mild climate with an extremely fertile alluvial soil, the latter being the result of the many riverbeds that have shifted their course over the years, either naturally or because of canals. There is one especially fertile stretch of land between the Loire and the Authion, just east of Angers. The Château of Saint Mathurin, home of King René

Fishing in the placid waters of La Vienne, below, is thirsty work and often calls for a restorative nip of one of the local wines, like Bourgueil or Vouvray. Other sights and flavors of Anjou and Touraine include, opposite (clockwise from top left): the Grange de Meslay, a thirteenth-century tithing barn, seen through its fortified gate; tourangelle sweets at the Barrier in Tours; ripe Anjou pears; an outdoor food stall in Tours; a half-timbered village épicerie, or grocery store; Anjou apples, ready to be picked; grapes from a vineyard on the Loire; Williams-Duchesse pears; and, at center, a crème renversée, generously covered with caramel sauce.

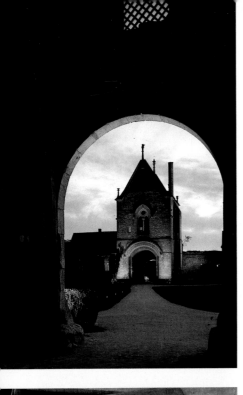

and Jeanne de Laval in the fifteenth century, is now owned by Vilmorin, the great market gardeners. Many of the *primeurs* are grown here for the Paris market.

On the banks of the Loire north of Saumur is a sandy area famed for its strawberries. Melons, peaches, apricots, and plums are also grown in abundance. Grapes are of the very best quality, and readers of Balzac's *Eugènie Grandet* will remember the tragic figure of Eugènie running upstairs to the attic to fetch some grapes to tempt her beloved cousin Charles. Grapes are stored throughout the winter in an ingenious way: Each bunch is cut at its peak and suspended from a rack, with the cut stalk inserted in a vial of water. This prevents them from shriveling up.

Tours is famous for its prunes, and a special variety of sweet damson is grown especially for drying. Prunes figure in many local dishes—not only in desserts, but also in casseroles of pork, veal, game, rabbit, and even eel. Dessert and greengage plums are also grown, as are many varieties of pear. Many of the local fruits have picturesque names that are directly linked with the ancient French nobility; one of the best plums is Reine Claude, named after the wife of François I, who lived at the Château d'Amboise. The Bon Chrétien pear came from the gardens of Louis XI near Tours, where it was grown from a cutting by Saint Francis of Paola, who was the King's spiritual adviser. Another local pear is the Jeanne d'Arc, named after Saint Joan, whose tragic campaign was enacted here.

A visit to a local market is one of the best ways of discovering local foods. Saumur, a pretty town built partly on an island and on both banks of the Loire, has a weekly market that is small but high in quality. Most of the stalls sell vegetables and fruit; there are also a few *charcuterie* stalls selling a variety of *andouilles* and *andouillettes*, including one made with horsemeat and another with eel. Some of the stalls sell only wild mushrooms; these are mostly kept by elderly women who have the time to search for them, and who know where to look. Some wild mushrooms, like the *girolle*, always grow in the same places, and these women guard their secrets fiercely.

In October, at the height of the mushroom season, you will find them cooked in many different ways. The very best, the *trompettes de la mort*, can be served simply sautéed as a garnish, with calf's liver or with a grilled lamb chop, for example. *Cèpes* can be fried and served with wild duck, or stuffed with chopped shallots, parsley, and ham to accompany a guinea fowl cooked in champagne. A small hotel in Richelieu serves an omelette stuffed to the bursting point with a mixture of *champignons sauvages*, while the ordinary *champignons de Paris* are served stuffed with *duxelles*.

You may want to spend some time looking for wild mushrooms in the forests. In this case, be sure to take them to a pharmacy to have them identified. This is a service that all the pharmacists perform during the mushroom season, which lasts for about a month. They display huge charts in their windows, and life-size models of each variety are laid out on trestle tables inside the shop. On a Saturday evening in the little town of Loches, a long line forms, all of men, carrying big baskets and boxes of mushrooms that they are prudently having verified before taking them home to their wives.

In Lencloître, on the borders of Touraine and Poitou, a big agricultural market is held monthly. Here you find a vast range of goods, from agricultural machinery to white Charolais bulls. Pink pigs are piled into crates, eight at a time, looking like fat *quenelles*. One stall sells six different varieties of strawberry plants, some still bearing fruit. Groups of farmers gather around little kiosklike bars, drinking

At the restaurant Les Cormorans, on the banks of the Loire, owner and chef Mme. Pitou makes her pâté de foie de volailles, *opposite, with liver from two kinds of poultry, fresh bacon, brandy, and herbs. Below,* champignons de Paris *grow in the caves of Anjou, where the temperature and humidity are stable.*

The ingredients for tournedos à la tourangelle, *left, with* artichokes and champignons de Paris, *are assembled by Mme. Yvette Marchand, who, with her husband, is gate-keeper at the Grange de Meslay near Tours. Anjou and Touraine supply mushrooms to all of France from the moist caves along the Loire river, which are ideally suited to their growth. Wild varieties, like* girolles, *right, are found in the woods; they are often browned and served with* crème fraîche.

the *vin du pays.* A couple in one stall sells *anguilles grillées au charbon,* a specialty of Poitou. This grilling of eels over charcoal makes a picturesque sight, curiously old-fashioned. The pair work together: The husband kills the eels by hitting their heads against a wall, and then lays them on a heavy iron rack, twenty-four at a time. The wife keeps the charcoal glowing fiercely, and the eels are grilled for about six minutes, weighed down with iron bars. They are then carefully turned, using a split stick like a primitive pair of tweezers, and grilled on the other side until crisp and slightly charred. The smell is delicious; although the eels are some-what expensive, there is no shortage of buyers.

One of the most interesting stalls sells goat cheeses. This region, especially the Plateau de Sainte-Maure, between Loches and Richelieu, is famous for *chèvres.* The goats are elegant creatures, dark brown, with a very dark stripe running down the center of their backs. They are seen everywhere, grazing quietly in the fields; often they have a wooden triangle around their necks to prevent them from squeezing through gaps in the fence. Goat cheeses vary both in shape and in condition. There are six different shapes, each denoting its origin: round and flattened, domed, square, heart-shaped, sausage-shaped, and pyramidal. They are bought at varying ages, according to personal taste. Some are sold *frais,* immediately after draining, still in their square white plastic cartons pierced with holes. Others have a firm, creamy white skin and are only a few days old. Still others have a greenish skin dotted with white mold; these are about a month old. The oldest are four months old and have grown a hard brown casing.

If you leave the market and drive back toward Loches, you pass through fields of golden asparagus plumes. Many of the fields are filled with livestock; you may even catch the charming sight

of cows and hens feeding together. A pretty tour-angelle bird is the *géline noire;* this little black hen with its scarlet comb scratches away in farmyards, along with speckled hens and white cockerels. It makes good eating, and is often stuffed and cooked in white wine or in a *pot-au-feu.*

Overlooking the river at the Château d'Amboise is the small Chapel of Saint Hubert, where Leonardo da Vinci lies buried. Over the door is a beautifully carved stone lintel depicting the vision of Saint Hubert, the patron saint of hunters. He is shown kneeling back in amazement before a stag, from whose head a crucifix is growing between the antlers. The different elements contained within this image—the woods, the animal, and the cross—seem to symbolize the whole region of Anjou-Touraine, with its hunting forests, its innumerable churches, abbeys, monasteries, and convents, and its strange atmosphere of the other world.

Fruits are the rule in the desserts of Anjou and Touraine. The ingredients of tarte aux poires Belle Angevine, *overleaf right, include Belle Angevine pears, a sweet-fleshed variety. In the finished product, overleaf left (top left), the poached pears are arranged over a* crème pâtissière. *Another regional specialty,* tarte aux prunes, *overleaf left (top right), is made*

with greengage plums. Small, golden mirabelle plums are often served with soupe dorée, *overleaf left (bottom left), a rough equivalent of French toast, but eaten in France as a dessert. The flavorings of* crêpe angevine, *overleaf left (bottom right), are the Angevine pears, vanilla, and orange zest.*

49

MATELOTE D'ANGUILLES ET DE CARPE *Stew of Eel and Carp*

2 pounds whole eel (1 kg)
2 pounds whole carp (1 kg)
½ cup white wine (125 ml)
2 bouquets garnis—see Appendix
1 onion, sliced
Salt, whole peppercorns
4 cups red wine, preferably Chinon (1 liter)
1 shallot, sliced
1 clove garlic
6 tablespoons butter (80 g)
Salt, freshly ground pepper
¼ cup cognac (60 ml)

FOR THE SAUCE
2 tablespoons butter (25 g)
1 tablespoon flour (10 g)
½ cup *crème fraîche*—see Appendix—or heavy cream (125 ml)

FOR THE GARNISH
Handful of finely chopped parsley
¼ pound button mushrooms, gently sautéed in butter (100 g)
¼ pound small onions, glazed (100 g)
6 heart-shaped pieces of bread, fried in butter

Have the eels cut in short lengths and the carp cleaned and scaled and cut into slices; reserve the heads and trimmings. Make a *fumet*: place the heads and trimmings in a pan with the white wine, a bouquet garni, the sliced onion, salt, and peppercorns and simmer for 30 minutes, adding a little water if necessary.

In a separate pan, bring the red wine to a boil with a sliced shallot, a clove of garlic, and a bouquet garni. Simmer for 30 minutes.

Heat the 6 tablespoons butter in a large sauté pan and turn the pieces of eel and fish in it to seal without browning. Season with salt and pepper, pour on the cognac, and flame. Strain the *fumet* and the reduced red wine and pour both over the fish. Bring slowly to a boil and remove from the heat—the fish will finish cooking in the hot liquid.

To make the sauce, heat the 2 tablespoons butter until it foams and then stir in the flour. Add enough of the fish cooking liquid to make a velvety sauce and stir in the *crème fraîche*.

Arrange the pieces of eel and carp in a heated dish and pour on a generous quantity of the sauce. Sprinkle with chopped parsley and serve with fried bread cut in heart shapes, small glazed onions, and gently fried mushrooms. Drink a good Chinon rouge with this excellent *matelote*.

for 6 people / photographs on pages 42 and 43

CUL DE VEAU À LA FAÇON DE GRAND-MÈRE *Veal Braised in the Old-Fashioned Way*

1 3-pound boned, rolled veal roast (1½ kg)
4 tablespoons butter (50 g)
2 onions, sliced
¼ pound smoked, streaky bacon, cut into lardons (100 g)
2 carrots, thinly sliced
2 celery ribs, thinly sliced
2 tomatoes, peeled and chopped
1 bouquet garni—see Appendix
2 generous pinches of fresh savory
Salt, freshly ground pepper
2 cups dry white wine, preferably Anjou (½ liter)
5 or 6 tablespoons heavy cream

Melt the butter in a casserole and sauté the onions, taking care not to let the butter brown. Add the bacon, and, when the fat starts to melt, add the veal and brown it on all sides.

Add the carrots, celery, and tomatoes to the casserole along with the bouquet garni and savory. Season with salt and pepper, stir the vegetables around to coat them with butter and bacon fat, and add the wine. Bring to a boil, reduce the heat to low until the liquid just simmers, and cover the pan.

Finish cooking the meat on top of the stove or in the oven. If you use the top of the stove, turn the meat occasionally. For oven-braising, set the temperature at 325°F. Allow the meat to cook for 1½ hours and test with a skewer to see if it is done. Serve at once, as it is, with the veal cut in thickish slices, and some of the fat skimmed off the pan juices. Or prepare this sauce: stir in the cream and reduce the liquid, by rapid boiling, until thick.

Green beans, fresh wild mushrooms when they are in season, or glazed carrots sprinkled with some of the sauce make good accompaniments.

for 6 people / photograph at right

CROÛTES AUX PRUNES OU SOUPE DORÉE   *Brioche Fritters with Prune Purée*

The method for making the *croûtes* is exactly the same as making French toast, but instead of bread, brioche is used, with a much more delicate result. These little golden tarts are extremely beautiful with their fluted edges, and taste delicious.

1 brioche loaf
3 eggs
3 tablespoons powdered sugar (25 g)
4 tablespoons butter (50 g)

FOR THE PRUNE PURÉE
½ pound prunes, soaked in cold water until plump (225 g)
½ cup sugar (100 g)
1 teaspoon *eau-de-vie de prunes*

Prepare the prune purée first. Cook the prunes in a little water until soft, about 20 minutes. Remove the pits, purée the prunes, and mix in the sugar and *eau-de-vie*. Allow to cool.

Cut the brioche, which should not be too fresh, into horizontal slices about ⅓ inch thick. Beat a whole egg and two egg yolks together with the powdered sugar. Melt the butter in a large frying pan. Dip the slices of brioche into the egg mixture and fry them gently until golden on both sides.

Transfer the prune purée to a dish and place the *croûtes* around the edges.

for 6 people / photograph on page 50

ARTICHAUTS FARCIS   *Stuffed Artichokes*

6 artichokes
½ lemon
6 thin slices lard or bacon
2 tablespoons butter (25 g)
2 tablespoons olive oil (30 ml)
½ bottle dry white Touraine wine

FOR THE STUFFING
⅓ pound lean pork, chopped (150 g)
⅓ pound veal, chopped (150 g)
½ pound mushrooms, chopped (250 g)
1 tablespoon heavy cream
2 tablespoons chopped parsley
Salt, freshly ground pepper

Prepare the artichokes. Cut off the tough outer leaves, and remove the entire upper part of the leaves with a sharp stainless-steel knife. Rub the cut edges with a lemon half to prevent discoloring. With a teaspoon, hollow out the middle and discard the hairy chokes. Blanch the artichokes for 10 minutes in a pot of salted boiling water before stuffing them to soften them; drain.

Prepare the stuffing. Combine the pork, veal, and mushrooms and season with salt and pepper. Bind the stuffing with the cream, and add the parsley.

Fill the inside of the artichokes with this stuffing. Seal each one by wrapping a slice of lard or bacon around it and tying it in place with a piece of string. In a flameproof casserole, melt the butter and oil; add the artichokes. Gently brown the artichokes and moisten them with the wine. Cover and cook for 1½ hours over low heat.

Remove the strings and lard or bacon from the artichokes, and serve, surrounded with cooked mushrooms.

for 6 people / photographs at left and opposite

SALADE TOURANGELLE   *Salad, Tourangelle Style*

This is a salad made with several different vegetables, raw and cooked, each kept separate, but served together in the same dish.

You can include:

Asparagus tips—cooked and sprinkled with a vinaigrette made with walnut oil and white wine vinegar to which you have added salt and pepper, some finely chopped shallots, and a little chopped parsley.

Cooked artichoke hearts—the vinaigrette for these is stronger and contains mustard, chopped fresh tarragon, chives, chervil, parsley, and salt and pepper.

Cooked green beans—seasoned with the same vinaigrette as for the asparagus.

Sticks of celery—remove all the strings and serve raw, sprinkled with lemon juice and salt.

Raw button mushrooms—slice finely and sprinkle with lemon juice. Dress with heavy cream flavored with mustard and seasoned with salt and pepper. Sprinkle with chopped fresh chervil.

Serve the salad with toast and fresh walnuts.

photograph opposite

TOURNEDOS À LA TOURANGELLE   *Tournedos, Tourangelle Style*

There is a choice of two versions for this recipe. In both cases, first be concerned with the sauce and the garnish.

Simple recipe:
4 *tournedos* (fillet steaks)
4 tablespoons butter (50 g)
4 shallots, chopped
4 thin slices of *pain de mie* (finely textured, firm white bread)
¾ cup white Loire wine (200 ml)
1 tablespoon oil
Salt, freshly ground pepper

Recipe for special occasions:
4 *tournedos* (fillet steaks)
4 artichoke hearts, cooked
2 tablespoons flour (20 g)
About 1 tablespoon lemon juice
8 tablespoons butter (100 g)
4 shallots, chopped
1 sprig of fresh tarragon
¾ cup white Loire wine (200 ml)
1 beef marrowbone, about 5 inches long
4 thin slices of *pain de mie* (finely textured, firm white bread)
3 tablespoons cognac
½ pound mushrooms (250 g)
1 tablespoon oil
Salt, freshly ground pepper
½ cup *crème fraîche*—see Appendix—or heavy cream (125 ml)

For the simple recipe, melt 1 tablespoon of butter and brown the shallots. Add the wine and reduce the sauce for 15 minutes over low heat.

Meanwhile, preheat the oven to 350°F. Toast the slices of bread. Fry the *tournedos* in 2 tablespoons butter and the oil for 3 to 4 minutes on each side (for medium rare). Put them on the slices of bread, season with salt and pepper, and keep warm. Deglaze the pan with the sauce and add the remaining tablespoon of butter. Taste for seasoning, pour over the *tournedos*, and serve immediately.

The recipe for special occasions is longer, but no more complicated. Prepare the garnish: wash the artichoke hearts. Put the flour in an enamel (stainless-steel or tin-lined copper) saucepan and mix in a bit of cold water to make a smooth paste. Add about 1 quart of cold water, the lemon juice, and salt. Bring to a boil, simmer for 5 minutes, and add the artichoke hearts. Return to a boil and simmer for 30 to 40 minutes, until the hearts are tender when pierced with a fork. Drain and transfer to a sauté pan with 2 tablespoons of melted, bubbling butter. Sauté until the hearts are heated through; set aside.

In another pan, brown the shallots and tarragon in 1 tablespoon of butter. Add the wine and reduce for 15 minutes over low heat.

Split the marrowbone in half lengthwise and remove the marrow. Cook the marrow for 2 minutes in boiling salted water. Take it out, cut into 4 pieces and season with salt and pepper. Set aside until later.

Sauté the mushrooms in 2 to 3 tablespoons of butter until lightly browned. Add lemon juice to taste and seasoning and keep them warm.

Toast the slices of bread as above, and reheat them just before serving. Cook the *tournedos* in 2 tablespoons of butter as above. When they are done, season with salt and pepper, and add the cognac. Let it get warm and flambé. Place the *tournedos* on the slices of bread and arrange the artichoke hearts on top. Top off with a circlet of marrow and surround with mushrooms.

Deglaze the frying pans you have used with the reduced sauce. Pour in the *crème fraîche*, taste the sauce, and correct the seasoning. Coat the *tournedos* with the sauce and serve immediately on very hot plates.

for 4 people / photograph on page 48

NOISETTE DE PORC AUX PRUNEAUX *Pork Chops with Prunes*

4 pork chops
½ pound prunes, soaked in cold water for a couple
   of hours if necessary (250 g)
5 tablespoons butter (60 g)
1 tablespoon vegetable oil (15 ml)
Chopped parsley

FOR THE SAUCE
1 carrot
1 onion
1 celery rib
2 tablespoons butter (25 g)
1 bouquet garni—see Appendix
1 clove
Salt, freshly ground pepper
2 tablespoons red wine vinegar (30 ml)
¾ cup red wine (200 ml)
1 tablespoon butter, softened (15 g)
1 tablespoon flour (10 g)

First make the sauce. Chop the vegetables and sauté
   them gently in the 2 tablespoons butter, together
with the bouquet garni, clove, and a little salt and
pepper. When they are golden, add the vinegar and
the red wine and simmer for 20 minutes. Strain the
sauce.

Meanwhile, poach the prunes in water just to cover for
20 minutes; drain.

Heat the butter and oil in a large frying pan and sauté the
pork chops on both sides, seasoning them with salt
and pepper. When they are cooked and golden brown,
remove and keep warm.

Work the butter and flour together with your fingers to
make a *beurre manié* and add it, broken into little
pieces, to the sauce. Let it cook gently for a few
minutes until the ingredients are well blended and
the sauce thickens. Add the hot prunes and taste
for seasoning.

To serve, arrange the chops on a dish, pour over the
sauce, placing the prunes around the edge, and sprinkle
with chopped parsley. Steamed potatoes are good with
these chops.

for 4 people / photograph at right

TARTE AUX POIRES BELLE ANGEVINE *Pear Tart*

The variety of pears called Belle Angevine are particularly good, but any sweet-fleshed, ripe pears can be
used.

FOR THE SWEET FLAN PASTRY
1 cup flour, sifted (125 g)
⅓ cup sugar (75 g)
Pinch of salt
5 tablespoons butter (60 g)

FOR THE PEARS AND SYRUP
1½ pounds pears (750 g)
½ cup sugar (100 g)

FOR THE CUSTARD
3 egg yolks
½ cup plus 2 tablespoons sugar (150 g)
3 tablespoons flour (25 g)
1 cup milk (250 ml)
1 vanilla bean

FOR THE GLAZE
3 or 4 tablespoons apricot or raspberry jam
A few drops *eau-de-vie de poire* (optional)

Prepare the pastry ahead of time. Mix the flour, sugar,
   and salt in a bowl, rub in the butter, and then add
   about 1 tablespoon water—the quantity may vary.
   Refrigerate for at least 1 hour.

Put the pears and sugar in a saucepan and add enough
   water to cover the pears; boil for 5 minutes. Peel,
   core, and halve the pears and place them in the syrup.
Bring to a boil, reduce the heat, and cook until just
tender, about 10 minutes. Remove the pears carefully
and reduce the syrup very gently, over a low heat,
until thickened.

Make the custard. Beat the egg yolks with the sugar,
and gradually add the flour, beating continuously until
blended. In another pan, bring the milk to a boil
together with the vanilla bean, remove from the heat,
and pour in a slow stream into the egg yolk mixture,
beating vigorously all the time. Return the mixture
to the milk saucepan and heat, stirring well until
smooth and thick. Set aside to cool, stirring occasionally to prevent a skin from forming.

Preheat the oven to 375°F. Roll out the pastry to about
⅛ inch thick and 2 inches larger all around than your
flan ring. Butter and flour an 8-inch flan ring and put
in the pastry, patting it into place with the palm of
your hand. Trim off the excess by rolling the pin over
the top of pan. Make the edges fairly deep, and prick
the bottom and sides with a fork, so that they don't
bubble.

Bake the pastry blind for 20 to 25 minutes. Cool slightly
and spread the custard evenly over the bottom. Arrange
the pears on top with their narrow ends toward the
middle. Make a glaze by mixing the reduced syrup
with the apricot jam. Cover the pears with this glaze
and sprinkle with a little *eau-de-vie de poire*. Serve at
room temperature.

for 6 people / photographs on pages 50 and 51

ILE DE FRANCE

ILE DE FRANCE

GASTRONOMICALLY, the Ile de France, with Paris as its center, must be the ideal island. It is bounded by the cathedral cities of Chartres, Beauvais, Soissons, and Sens, and its perimeter encloses the rich soil of the Paris basin, which for centuries has acted as market garden, bread basket, and dairy to the capital. Within an hour of Notre Dame Cathedral is the great cheese country of Brie; within half an hour, the wholesale markets of Rungis, nicknamed the "belly of France," such is the wealth of their produce; and within minutes, a unique concentration of fine restaurants.

The Ile de France is not an island at all, of course, though it is laced and girdled by rivers like the Seine and the Marne. The name is part history, part romance: This was "France proper" in the days when the original kingdom of the Franks was surrounded by the powerful, envious dynasties of Normandy, Burgundy, and Aquitaine. And the name has stuck, for Paris and its surroundings lie at the very heart of French civilization.

To many, the proximity of Paris to the open countryside comes as a surprise. Espaliered orchards bloom around Poissy, almost within sight

On the rue Mouffetard, in Paris, not far from the Sorbonne, restaurant chefs and housewives alike— not to mention students looking for bargains— shop for fresh produce, meat, fish, cheese, spices, and nearly every other ingredient of a French meal, including pastries and bread, preceding overleaf. Three indispensable and classic products of the French baker's art, opposite, are the slim loaves of bread called baguettes, the buttery breakfast croissants, and the wreath-shaped loaf called couronne d'épis. Wheat and other grains grow abundantly in the Ile de France, especially in the region called La Beauce, to the south of Paris. Chartres and its cathedral, top, is its center.

of the Eiffel Tower, and wild boar still inhabit the forest of Fontainebleau. Orly was once reputed for its floury potatoes rather than for its airport, and many other erstwhile villages, now mere suburbs of Paris, have given their names to cooking garnishes—Argenteuil was famous for its asparagus and Clamart for its peas, Montmorency for its cherries and Montreuil for its peaches. To this day, any dish *à la parisienne* almost always contains mushrooms, though only a single grower survives anywhere near Paris, the rest having moved to peaceful caves along the Loire. However, Arpajon, to the south of Paris, is still the proud home of what are reputed to be the finest green *flageolet* kidney beans. Developed a hundred years ago by selective planting, they were brought directly to market at Les Halles by a special railway running down the Boulevard Saint-Michel.

George Sala, an English journalist and gastronome who was in Paris in 1879, summed up the wholesale markets like Les Halles nicely: "The Halles Centrales form an Exposition Universelle of victuals. It is Grandgousier's larder. It is the Tom Tiddler's ground of things eatable. It is the grandest 'Grub Street' in Europe."

The bounty of Les Halles was reflected in the shops and street markets of a dozen Paris *quartiers*. You could live only minutes from butcher, poultry dealer, baker, and *charcutier*, not to mention countless vegetable stores, and even open-air markets. An 1828 list of Paris specialties includes "beef, peaches, melons, crayfish, eel, *goujons* [little fish], carp, *barbillons* [more fish], pastries, liqueurs, chocolate, galantines, jam and sweets. Everything for money," it concludes, "even fresh eggs from Lyon," a remark that is even more pertinent today. The shops around the Madeleine-Caviar Kaspia, La Maison de la Truffe, Hédiard (for exotic fruits and spices), Ferme Saint-Hubert (for cheese), and the Comptoir Gourmand of Michel Guérard (for prepared foods and *foie gras*) carry almost anything at a price.

In 1969, overcrowding finally forced the removal of Les Halles to Rungis, strategically placed near Orly airport. A visit to Rungis is a treat, for behind its slick modern façade is a romantic excitement that will catch you every time. Before you stretch the pavilions—1,500 acres of them—of what may well be the largest food market in the world. Inside extends what is undoubtedly the most varied collection of merchandise: poultry from fifteen French provinces, *foie gras* from Périgord and Israel, wild boar from Germany, potatoes from Picardy, mangoes from Peru. One pavilion is devoted entirely to sausages.

In one of the meat halls, a chef of La Varenne cooking school can be seen striding through a for-

Once a bistro serving the butchers and produce vendors of Les Halles at all hours of the night, the restaurant Au Pied de Cochon is now a large, gentrified establishment, still specializing, however, in a hearty onion soup, la gratinée, opposite. In a poultry shop in the rue Sainte-Dominique, above, birds of all sorts are offered. A first-class charcuterie in the rue Furstemberg, below, catches late shoppers on a winter evening.

A scoreboard proclaims that 431 tons of poultry have been delivered and that 83 tons are left from yesterday. The boxes of chickens are bedecked with red labels certifying their impeccable origin. Arriving at the fruits and vegetables, you watch as the chef takes a preliminary tour, poking here and there—it does not do to look only at the top of the basket. He collects trays of pears and plums, crates of half a dozen different vegetables, which are then trundled to his van by a minion. If you find yourself lingering wistfully by a basket of wild mushrooms, some knowing person may inform you that they're cultivated. For by no means is everything sold at Rungis top quality; on the contrary, a good deal of mediocre merchandise changes hands at (in theory) lower prices. But that is part of the charm—the search for a bargain.

T HE CHEF's last stop is at the *maraîchers* producers, who intensively cultivate tiny marsh gardens criss-crossed by drainage canals. Here grow the renowned *primeurs*—mini carrots and turnips, potatoes the size of a walnut, frail baby lettuces, and leeks no larger than a finger. Watercress is another specialty, tenderly cultivated in streams that are a chilly (but ideal) ten degrees Celsius—the *vert pré* or bouquet of watercress garnish for grilled meats and chicken is typically Parisian. For watercress, as for dozens of fruits and vegetables, there used to be a rhyming "cry of Paris" that itinerant vendors would intone as they walked the streets of the capital. Four centuries ago the artichoke man, for example, would commend his produce as "reheating body and soul, making your bottom more *chaud.*"

Thanks to these vegetables, Ile de France tables are distinguished by some splendid soups. A few, like onion soup, are *soupes* in the French sense of being bolstered with bread to form a complete supper. Others are rich, creamy *potages*—purées such as *Saint-Germain* (made with fresh green peas) and the carrot-based *potage Crécy* (a village to the east of Paris). Heartier is *potage soissonnaise*, laced with bacon and thickened with the white kidney beans of Soissons. *Potage aux primeurs*, a particularly tasty soup, comes from Marie-Antoine Carême, chef to Talleyrand, the Prince Regent, and Czar Alexander I.

Soup, in fact, was the theme of the first Paris restaurants, which were so named because they served *bouillons restauratifs*. Since 1467, the sale of cooked meat (*chair cuite*) inside the city walls had been the prerogative of the city *charcutiers*, but in 1765 a certain Boulanger is said to have circumvented the ordinance by serving sheep's feet in a soupy white sauce. Thirty years later, just after the Revolution, more than five hundred restaurants

An old saying has it that the markets of Paris are the belly of France, for in them all the foods of the country are sold. Above, game in a Left Bank shop. And opposite (clockwise from top left): chez Poilâne, fancy loaves; in the main market at Rungis, a farmer's chèvre from Loir et Cher; back in Paris, shellfish (including scallops with their roe, in foreground); circles of Coulommiers and Bries, known as le fromage des rois; so-called champignons de Paris, grown in caves mainly along the Loire; on a wall in the old wine market in Porte de Bercy, ghosts of old champagne bottles; baguettes and pains de deux for delivery in Paris; heart-shaped chèvres from Indre, southwest of Paris; and, from the Pont Alexandre III, an evening shopper's view of the spires of Paris.

est of carcasses, eyes alert. "Too dark, that," he says, "too much bone—it should be well-rounded, *dodu.*" He dodges out of the way of a passing truck, but if you are less nimble, you may get cursed, and catch the grin of the nearby *grossiste* out of the corner of your eye. Women are an unusual sight here, where hulking porters shift the carcasses (a major wholesaler can turn over $60,000 worth of meat in a day). Give the sausages a once-over—do you need casings for tomorrow's *boudin blanc?*—and follow the chef to the poultry pavilion.

were to be found in Paris. The Café Anglais, dating from 1802 during the short-lived Peace of Amiens, remains a legend of sumptuous good taste despite its disappearance in 1913. It was for many years presided over by Adolphe Duglére, the creator of *sole Duglére*. At one memorable dinner in 1867, he welcomed the Czar of Russia, the Czarevitch, the King of Prussia, and Otto von Bismarck to the table.

More typical is the mixed fortune of the Tour d'Argent, founded in 1582 outside the city walls (and therefore free to sell cooked meats). As a haunt of tax collectors in the eighteenth century, the Tour d'Argent was destroyed in the Revolution, but it was rebuilt in the 1860s and found fame with Frédéric, whose dignified figure preparing pressed duck is commemorated on tourist postcards. In 1912 André Terrail took over, moving the restaurant upstairs to its current site overlooking Notre Dame—at the time a bold step, inspired by a visit to the United States. Recently another Terrail, André's son Claude, installed a new young chef with his own brigade of almost a dozen—unheard of license considering that a chef normally inherits all but a couple of his predecessor's staff. The verdict on this change is yet to come: It depends on that very French institution, the gastronomic guide. *Michelin*, which gives its top, three-star, rating to the Tour d'Argent and to eighteen other restaurants in France, dominates the scene, but in the Ile de France it is Henri Gault and Christian Millau who have documented every gastronomic landmark —and there are many, for about a third of the hundred top-rated restaurants in France are in and around the capital.

Generally ignored by the guides, but far more vital to Paris life, are the cafés, bistros, and brasseries, with their "thousands of well-dressed people who sit all day, and during a great portion of the night, in and outside the boulevard cafés, smoking, drinking, playing at cards and dominoes, and otherwise enjoying themselves" (George Sala). Today's cafés range from the opulence of boulevard sites like the Café de la Paix, by the Opéra, to the most modest bar, but the best of them maintain the same clublike atmosphere that must have characterized the early generation of cafés in the Palais Royal. It was there, in front of the Café Foy, that Camille Desmoulins handed out chestnut-leaf cockades to the crowd who later stormed the Bastille.

If you stay in Paris long enough, you're likely to choose a local café as your own—perhaps one of the many cheerful, functional establishments with the traditional zinc countertop and iron-legged tables. Each morning you can greet the familiar faces and settle in to coffee and your newspaper while the proprietor delivers his orders on the phone.

"What was that junk you sent yesterday? Do you want to kill off my customers? You take me for an imbecile? *Hein?*" Or worse. Lunch on Thursday will be *petit salé* (a type of salt pork) with lentils; on Wednesday it was leg of lamb with *flageolets*; and Friday it may be skate with black butter or lemon sole *meunière*, or *brandade*, the Provençal purée of salt cod. Each day at the many local cafés customers are offered a *plat du jour* with a choice of two or three appetizers and, to finish, homemade chocolate mousse or *crème caramel*, or, if not, cheese or fruit. With coffee and a small carafe of wine, the bill comes to about $10 and the place is packed by 12:30.

More or less interchangeable with "café" is the term "bistro," a word of obscure origin possibly derived from *bistrouiller*, meaning to blend inferior wines. A brasserie, is different; bigger and less personal than a café, a brasserie originally did its own brewing on the spot. Many brasseries were kept by Alsatian cooks—hence the *coq au Riesling*, *choucroute garni*, and *saucisses frites*, which remain standard fare. Every railway station and many big

Soups are an Ile de France specialty, and potage aux primeurs, *left, is one of the best. It calls for the yolks of eggs, green spring vegetables, and* croûtons. *In* ris de veau, *below, as prepared at le Grand Veneur in Barbizon, sweetbreads simmer in a vegetable stock.*

street corners sport a brasserie, and some, like the Brasserie Lorraine in the Place Wagram, are expensive, with white linen tablecloths, champagne in ice buckets, and huge *cartes* offering plain, old-fashioned food—half a dozen different oysters, *langoustines mayonnaise*, grilled pig's trotters, huge steaks, scarcely smaller lamb chops, all served with superlative *frites*.

O N SUNDAYS many a Parisian repairs to the country for lunch at those *petites auberges* that encircle the city in an ever-expanding ring as transport improves. The seduction of their riverside settings was immortalized by the Impressionists, but already in the early 1800s, the gastronome Grimod de la Reynière was extolling the pure air of Saint-Germain-en-Laye, "whose vivacity excites the appetite and the digestion." Ambiance is all very well, but today the culinary interest of most Ile de France *auberges* is slight—many are glorified canteens for the quick service of tired *pâté*, tough lettuce, and overdone *coq au vin*.

Sunday tourists are in search of a vanishing species —the country cooking of the Ile de France. They are looking for the *gibelotte* of rabbit, simmered in white wine with a touch of bacon and onion, and chicken *à la ficelle*, basted in butter as it turns before the open fire. Once inns along the Oise made *matelote* stews of the day's catch of perch, pike, carp, and eel, sharpened with wine and enriched with cream. There must be some trace somewhere of the bream from the Loing, the *friture* of deep-fried little fish resembling whitebait, the *salmis* of Soissons goose, and the *navarin* lamb and vegetable stew of Montlhéry. But where?

First and last courses seem to have fared better.

Both Paris and the Ile de France are known for *pâtés* and *terrines*, the latter often based on game. Étampes, surrounded by cornfields, makes lark *pâté* (their little heads poking sadly out of the mold), and Barbizon, at the edge of the Fontainebleau forest, specializes in a *terrine* of wild boar with liver and truffles. The typical Parisian *pâté* comes in various shapes. A *friand*, for instance, is square, and a *pâté parisien*, round. More common are the rectangular *pâtés Pantin* (Pantin is one of the city gates), filled with strips of veal and ham, with a ground pork stuffing. A *pâté Pantin* can be large, in which case it is cut in wedges like a pie, but more often it is sold, like *friands* and *pâtés parisiens*, as an individual snack. Fillings are usually based on pork, but almost any meat can be used.

Dessert in the Ile de France is synonymous with pastry, and Paris could be called a city of *pâtissiers*. In one half-a-mile walk you can pass five or six *pâtisseries* of varying appearance and quality. One has harsh overhead lights and a minimum of decor and is filled with inexpensive, heavy cakes piled high with artificial cream. Another displays fancy and expensive *gâteaux* behind a tinted glass window. A third offers mostly chocolates. And a fourth fills his window with rows of enticing *hors d'œuvre* and *petits fours*. But how can they be fresh at 8:30 in the morning? You may scarcely notice the last, for all his window contains is breakfast croissants, brioches, and *pains au chocolat*.

Yet this is Millet, one of the finest *pâtisseries* in Paris. Here everything is baked that day, each cake a perfect replica of its fellow. Only the best ingredients are used—no need for a *guarantis pur beurre* sign. Decorations are simple—a crisp topping of caramel, a single giant chocolate rose, a border of perfect cream rosettes—for there is nothing to dress

Matelote de l'Oise is a fish stew usually made of pike, perch, carp, and eel and is a specialty of M. Murasan of the Auberge de la Rabette near Rambouillet. The cut-up fish are simmered, heads and all, below, with onions and scallions,

mushrooms, lemon, and parsley, so that the flavors, subtly blended, are caught in a sauce that is later thickened with cream and finally recombined with the fish.

up or hide. Specialties include *gâteau Saint-Honoré*, named after the patron saint of pastry cooks; vol-au-vents, which may be filled with a rich savory sauce or with *crème Chantilly*, the rich whipped cream that honors the Duc de Condé and his château at Chantilly; and brioches, which may have earned their name from the addition of Brie cheese.

Millet employs fifteen chefs and apprentices under master *pâtissier* Denis Ruffel. Only a small proportion of their confections reach the window, for most are made to order for restaurants and banquets. This reliance on outside caterers goes back a long way, for in 1557 the Venetian ambassador to France noted that within less than an hour "the *rôtisseurs* and *pâtissiers* can furnish a dinner for ten, twenty or even one hundred persons."

Entrecôte Bercy, below, is rib steak served with a wine and shallot sauce. It is named for the Quai de Bercy, once the location of the principal wine market in Paris. Wine, of course, is essential to the dish, and though most cooks claim that white is the correct color, chef François Medina at the Cochon d'Or in Paris, doesn't mind using red. He serves the entrecôte *with puff potatoes and garnishes it with watercress.*

The history of Parisian bread is less happy. Of all the cooking trades, the *boulangers* were most often in trouble for adulteration of flour with sand or sawdust, or for giving short weight. Now they're criticized for using preservatives and for replacing brick ovens with automated contraptions of steel. But recently the old artisan methods have been revived, notably by the Poilâne family. More and more shops are beginning to offer their own (or Poilâne's) country bread, wholewheat bread, rye bread, and interesting nut and raisin breads. Only the traditional crisp chewy *baguette* remains distressingly hard to find

Urban to the core and spending little time at home, Parisians have three answers to eating well—they eat out, they buy dishes to take home, and when they cook, they cook quickly.

"'A dash of vinegar,' 'swiftly sauté,' 'lightly browned,' 'quickly fried,' 'a taste of lemon juice, gherkins, and pepper'" was how cookbook writer Austin de Croze summed up the style in 1931. Typical of Paris cuisine are *châteaubriand*, a thick beef fillet that is grilled (rather than cooked in the oven); *entrecôte marchand de vin*, with its sauce of red wine and shallots; and the sister *entrecôte Bercy*, made with white wine. Another Parisian quick-fix is the medieval *sauce Robert*, a brown sauce designed to pep up plainly cooked meats, flavored with white wine, vinegar, and mustard.

Paris has been the home of chips (very thin French fries) since at least the sixteenth century, when they were sold at stalls on the Pont Neuf (in classic cookbooks a squat French fry is called *pomme Pont Neuf*). The superior *pommes soufflés* have a good story, which began at Saint-Germain-en-Laye, at the inauguration in 1837 of a little railway to carry vegetables into Paris. The train stuck on a steep gradient, and lunch was delayed until the whistle blew: The chef plunged his half-cooked potatoes into hot fat, where they puffed into beguiling little balls.

Quick Paris cooking is easy enough to find, but the opposite is also supposed to exist—*cuisine de concierge*. Elderly Frenchmen speak nostalgically of the little *plats* that simmered for hours on the stove, filling the apartment buildings with savory odors while the concierge scrubbed the stairs. *Pot-au-feu*, *hâchis parmentier* (shepherd's pie), and *boeuf miroton* (boiled beef simmered with onions and vinegar) are often cited, but rarely encountered in a *loge*.

A review of fast food in Paris is not complete without mention of the ubiquitous toasted cheese and ham *croque monsieur* sandwich. With full pomp, no less a body than the Académie Culinaire has debated whether *croque monsieur* should consist of one slice of bread or two, with the cheese a topping or a filling. Is *croque madame*, with a fried egg on top, a permissible variant? More insidious is the

Michel Petit, above, is the owner of Benoît, one of the best of
Paris's Right Bank bistros, on rue Saint-Martin. In the gracious
surroundings of turn-of-the-century polished brass and etched
glass one can have anything from a glass of wine to an entire

meal. Far more formal is the restaurant Grand Veneur, below,
at the edge of the forest of Fontainebleau. The fireplace in the
dining room has a broche, or rotisserie, where chicken and
game are roasted over a wood fire.

creeping menace of the hamburger, which, with
pizza, is fast taking over the teenage trade.

Cheese is an important part of the French meal,
and in the Ile de France this means Brie, above all.
(The Brie was part of the original Ile de France,
with its capital at Senlis.) To earn its *appellation
d'origine contrôlée* label, Brie must have a fat content
of 45 percent and a weight between 1.1 and 2.4
pounds, and have been aged for a month. In
addition, the milk must come from a specific area
that extends from Brie as far as the confines of
Lorraine. Here, however, standardization ends, as
you'll quickly appreciate when looking at the market stalls in Meaux, center of Brie production. The
familiar shallow wheels are classed as Brie de Meaux,
while Brie de Melun is smaller and thicker, with
Coulommiers, the third member of the Brie family,
resembling an overgrown Camembert. Each of them
also varies with age, from firm and almost chalky,
to creamy, then to butter-gold and oozing at the
seams. The conventional ideal of a perfumed,
creamy-soft Brie is only one stage at which locals
enjoy it. A crumbly, fresh variety is available (too
young under *appellation contrôlée* rules to be called
Brie) as well as crusty brown wedges that look to-
tally inedible. If the stall holder insists that you try
it, be brave—the sharp, nutty exterior is indeed
excellent, quite lacking the ammonia you'd expect.

B UT THERE is no escaping the ammonia smell as you follow Philippe Bobin, *maître affineur*, around the stacks of cheeses aging in his family's warehouse. He discusses the ideal conditions for ripening cheese—cool dampness is vital, as is the right combination of bacteria (the warehouse can never be disinfected). Among sixteen thousand cheeses there are a surprising number of varieties, and Monsieur Bobin explains that a dozen or more are made in Brie and nearby Champagne. High-fat types include Chaource, Brillat-Savarin, Fougéru, and Pierre-Robert; Butte de Brie is shaped like a brick, Vignelait is wrapped in vine leaves, and Fromage de Fontainebleau is fluffy and fresh, to be eaten with sugar and cream, or chopped garlic and herbs.

Wine can hardly be called native to the Ile de France, but vineyards prospered not so long ago at Pontoise and Suresnes, and in the Middle Ages the sunny slopes of Paris's Left Bank were covered with vines. Even today a token vintage is made in Montmartre and, to the south at Thoméry, Chasselas table grapes are grown on cuttings from François I's vine, still to be seen at Fontainebleau. But the vinous wealth of Paris is really in its wine cellars, stocked to last from here to eternity. During the siege of Paris in 1870, Restaurant Voisin was forced to serve up animals from the zoo but could still offer Château Palmer 1846 with its elephant consommé!

Cooks in the Ile de France have certainly tried everything. The province has been subject to so many diverse influences that it is impossible to decide what started here and what came from outside. In the past two hundred years alone, Paris has played host to governments that included the *ancien régime*, the first and second empires, the first through fifth republics, not to mention occupying forces. Foreigners have introduced such anomalies as the 1820s craze for roast beef and Yorkshire pudding, and the current taste for couscous and spring rolls. A case can even be made that the best French provincial cooking is to be found not on the spot, but in Paris, where hundreds of country cooks have made good in the restaurant trade. In fact, the lover of French cuisine could do worse than to simply stay in Paris. For when all is said and done, France leads the Western world in cooking, and Paris, with the Ile de France, lies at its heart.

The beautiful boulangerie *of M. Poujaran on the rue Jean Nicot, in Paris, above left, is notable for its nineteenth-century atmosphere. Below stairs at Poilâne, in the rue du Cherche-Midi,* boulanger *Michel Lory slides a batch of bread into the oven as dough behind him rises. Fromage de Fontainebleau à la crème, above, is a mixture of* fromage blanc *and* crème fraîche, *sprinkled with sugar. A Paris-Brest cake, opposite, baked by M. Ruffel of Pâtisserie Millet in Paris, is a puff pastry filled with a* crème pâtissière pralinée. *The first Paris-Brest was the creation of a turn-of-the-century chef who wished to honor the famous bicycle race of the same name and made the cake circular—and inflated—like a bike wheel.*

ENTRECÔTE BERCY   *Entrecôte Steak with Sauce Bercy*

A garnish or sauce "Bercy" always includes white wine, for the Quai de Bercy, on the Right Bank of the Seine, used to be the landing point for barges carrying wine to the capital. Today most wine is delivered directly to retail outlets by truck, but rows of giant casks are still to be seen in the half-deserted warehouses lining the Quai. For this *entrecôte*, soufflé potatoes or, more mundanely, French fries are the standard accompaniment.

4 *entrecôte* or rib steaks, each about ¾ inch thick (2 cm)
2 shallots, finely chopped
½ cup white wine (125 ml)
2 cups brown stock (½ liter)
2½ teaspoons arrowroot or potato starch, mixed with 2½ tablespoons cold water
2 teaspoons oil
Salt, freshly ground pepper
1 tablespoon chopped parsley

For the Bercy sauce: in a heavy-bottomed pan boil the shallots with the wine until the liquid is reduced to about 1 tablespoon. Add the stock, reserving ½ cup, and bring to a boil. Whisk the arrowroot paste into the boiling sauce, a little at a time; it will thicken at once. Add only enough paste to give the sauce the consistency of very thin cream. Taste for seasoning and adjust if necessary. The sauce can be made up to 2 hours ahead.

To finish: heat the oil in a heavy frying pan or griddle. Add the steaks and fry them over fairly high heat, allowing 3 to 5 minutes on each side for rare steak. Sprinkle them with salt and pepper after turning. Transfer to a serving plate and keep warm. Reheat the sauce. Add the reserved ½ cup stock to the frying pan and boil, stirring well to dissolve the pan juices. Add to the sauce and strain. Bring just back to the boil, stir in the parsley, and taste. Spoon a little sauce over the steaks and serve the rest separately.

for 4 people / photograph on page 72

TERRINE DE GIBIER   *Game Terrine*

¾ pound bacon, sliced (350 g)
1 pound game meat (hare, rabbit, venison, or wild boar) (500 g)
¼ pound uncooked ham, diced (125 g)
¼ pound pork fat, sliced (125 g)
¼ cup brandy (60 ml)
¼ cup Madeira (60 ml)
½ teaspoon ground allspice
Pinch of ground cloves
Pinch of ground nutmeg
Salt, freshly ground pepper
1 pound minced pork (half fat and half lean) (500 g)
1 egg

FOR THE LUTING PASTE
¼ cup plus 2 tablespoons flour (90 g)
2 to 3 tablespoons water

You need a 1½-quart terrine mold with a lid and a steam hole. Line the terrine with the bacon, reserving 2 or 3 slices. Cut half the game meat into finger-sized strips. In a bowl, mix the strips of meat, ham, and pork fat with the brandy, Madeira, allspice, cloves, nutmeg, salt, and pepper. Cover and marinate for 1 to 2 hours.

To assemble the terrine: preheat the oven to 350°F. Grind the remaining game meat through the fine blade of a meat grinder, with the minced pork and 1 slice of reserved bacon. Drain any marinade from the game strips into the ground meat mixture, beat in the egg, and season well with salt and pepper. Stir until the stuffing holds together. Fry a ball of this stuffing and taste—it should be quite spicy. Adjust the seasoning in the remaining mixture if necessary. Spread a quarter of the stuffing in the terrine, add a layer of one-third of the strips of game with a few cubes of ham and pork fat, and cover with another layer of stuffing. Continue adding meat and stuffing until all are used, ending with a layer of stuffing. Cover with the remaining slices of bacon and put on the lid.

For the luting paste: put the flour into a bowl and lightly stir in the water to make a stiff paste. Form the dough into a long strand by rolling it back and forth on a board with your hands. Set the dough around the lid of the terrine to fill the gap and press down lightly to seal.

Set the terrine mold in a roasting pan filled with water and bring to a boil on top of the stove. Then cook the terrine in the hot oven for 1¼ to 1½ hours, or until a skewer inserted in the center of the mixture (through the steam hole) is hot to the touch when withdrawn after 30 seconds. Cool the terrine to tepid and then remove the luting paste and lid. Set a flat plate with a 2-pound weight on top to press down the terrine. Refrigerate overnight. When cold, remove the weight and replace the terrine lid. The terrine is best kept at least 3 days (up to a week in the refrigerator) so the flavor mellows.

To serve, turn out the terrine onto a plate and slice it, or leave it for slicing in the terrine mold. Serve it with crusty wholewheat or country bread.

for 12 people / photograph opposite

GÂTEAU PARIS-BREST

The pastry cream may be flavored with coffee, as it is here, or with praline.

FOR THE CHOUX PASTRY RING
1 cup flour (150 g)
7 tablespoons butter (90 g)
1 teaspoon salt
6 eggs
1 tablespoon plus 2 teaspoons sliced, blanched
    almonds
Powdered sugar (for sprinkling)

FOR THE CREAM FILLING
5 egg yolks
¼ cup plus 3 tablespoons sugar (90 g)
¼ cup plus 2 tablespoons flour (45 g)
1½ cups milk (375 ml)
Pinch of salt
2½ teaspoons instant coffee
Butter

Preheat the oven to 400°F and butter a baking sheet.

For the *choux* pastry: sift the flour onto a piece of wax paper. In a saucepan heat a scant cup of water, butter, and salt until the butter is melted. Bring to a boil and remove from the heat. Add all the flour at once and beat vigorously with a wooden spoon until the mixture comes away from the sides of the pan in a ball. The heat of the water will cook the flour to make a dough. Put back on the heat for 30 seconds to 1 minute, stirring, to dry the dough. Transfer the dough to a bowl.

With a wooden spoon, or using an electric mixer, beat 4 eggs, one by one, into the dough, beating well after each addition. Break another egg into a bowl and whisk until mixed. Beat enough of this egg into the dough to make a mixture that is very shiny and just falls from the spoon; it should still hold its shape. All the egg may not be needed, and if too much is added, the dough will be too soft to shape.

Scoop the dough into a pastry bag fitted with a ¾-inch plain tip, and pipe a 10- to 12-inch ring on the prepared baking sheet. Pipe a smaller ring just inside it. With the remaining dough, pipe a third ring on top of the other two. Beat the remaining egg with a pinch of salt and brush the dough with it; sprinkle with the sliced almonds. Bake for 30 to 35 minutes, or until the pastry is very firm. It will brown on top before it is cooked, so be sure the cracks on the sides of the ring are brown before removing it from the oven. Transfer the ring to a rack. While still warm, slice the ring horizontally into layers so steam can escape.

For the cream filling: beat the egg yolks with the sugar until thick and light. Stir in the flour. Bring the milk to a boil with the salt and coffee, stirring until the coffee dissolves. Whisk the milk into the egg mixture, return it to the pan, and whisk over gentle heat until boiling. If lumps form as the cream thickens, take it from the heat and whisk hard until smooth. After thickening, cook the cream gently 1 to 2 minutes, whisking constantly. Pour into a bowl and rub the surface with butter to prevent the formation of a skin. Leave until cold. The *choux* pastry ring and the coffee cream filling can be made up to 8 hours ahead. Keep the pastry in an airtight container and the cream in the refrigerator.

To finish: scoop the cream into a pastry bag fitted with a star tip. Put the lower half of the pastry ring on a serving plate. Pipe the cream in rosettes onto the ring and set the upper ring on top. The cream should show at the sides. Sprinkle with powdered sugar. The *gâteau* can be filled up to 2 hours before serving. Keep it in the refrigerator.

for 10 people / photograph on page 75

POTAGE AUX PRIMEURS   *Spring Vegetable Soup*

3 leeks, white part only, cut in julienne strips
Leaves of 2 bunches of celery, cut in julienne strips
½ head of romaine lettuce, cut in julienne strips
2 quarts beef or chicken consommé (or stock or broth)
    (2 liters)
⅔ cup green peas (150 g)
Salt, freshly ground pepper
6 egg yolks
Croûtons—see Appendix

Wash and drain the leek, celery, and lettuce strips. Bring the consommé to a boil and add the vegetables, including the peas. Taste for seasoning and adjust if necessary. Simmer 10 to 15 minutes, or until the vegetables are tender.

Prepare the *croûtons*.

To serve: bring the soup to boil. Mix the egg yolks in a bowl with a whisk. Slowly stir in 3 or 4 spoonfuls of hot soup. Off the heat, whisk this mixture into the remaining soup. Taste for seasoning. Spoon the soup into bowls and serve at once. Pass the *croûtons* separately.

for 8 people / photograph on page 68

GIBELOTTE DE LAPIN *Fricassée of Rabbit*

A *gibelotte* is simply a fricassée—it can also be made with chicken.

2 rabbits, weighing about 2 pounds each, each cut into
    6 pieces (1 kg each)
½ pound bacon, diced (250 g)
4 tablespoons butter (50 g)
30 baby onions, peeled
1 tablespoon flour (15 g)
1 cup white wine (250 ml)
About 1½ cups veal or chicken stock (300 to 400 ml)
1 clove garlic, crushed
1 bouquet garni—see Appendix
Salt, freshly ground pepper
½ pound mushrooms (250 g)
2½ teaspoons Dijon mustard
1 tablespoon chopped parsley

Blanch the bacon by putting it in cold water, simmering 5 minutes, and then draining. In a flameproof casserole, melt the butter and fry the bacon until transparent. Add the onions and cook, shaking the pan occasionally, until the onions and bacon are lightly browned. Remove them from the pan and reserve.

Preheat the oven to 350°F, unless you choose to prepare the fricassée on top of the stove.

Fry the rabbit in the pan, a few pieces at a time, until brown all over. Return all the rabbit to the pan, sprinkle with flour, and cook until straw colored. Add the white wine, stock, and garlic and bring to a boil. Add the bouquet garni, salt, and pepper and cover with the lid. Simmer very gently on top of the stove or cook in the oven for 15 minutes. Add the onions, bacon, and up to ½ cup additional stock if the sauce is too thick; cook for 15 minutes longer.

Clean the mushrooms and, if they are large, cut them in half or quarters, otherwise leave them whole. Add them to the casserole and continue cooking 10 to 15 minutes, or until the rabbit is tender and the mushrooms are cooked. Discard the bouquet garni and taste for seasoning. The rabbit can be cooked up to 3 days ahead and refrigerated or frozen.

To serve, reheat the rabbit, if necessary, on top of the stove. Remove from the heat and stir in the mustard. Transfer the rabbit to a deep dish or serve it in the casserole, sprinkled with parsley. Potatoes sautéed in butter are a good accompaniment.

for 6 to 8 people / photographs below

SOLOGNE

SOLOGNE

IF YOU travel about seventy-five miles south from Paris, you can enter the province of Sologne by crossing the Loire at Orléans. There the highway runs out. A further forty-five miles or so along smaller roads takes you to Romorantin, Sologne's "capital," close to the southern border and boasting a modest 19,000 inhabitants. From east to west, Sologne lies between the Loire and the Cher, stretching about fifty-five miles. It is no longer an administrative entity; in 1941 the department boundaries were redrawn, and Sologne now forms a part of three departments, Le Loiret, Le Cher, and Loire-et-Cher, but it does not contain any of their administrative capitals. As a result of being consigned to this bureaucratic oblivion, Sologne might have lost its identity in people's minds, but this has not happened, because it is physically so different from its neighbors, and its name, in French, still has a romantic ring.

The cooking in Sologne is dominated by game, for shooting and hunting parties are still vital today to the economy of the area. Some of the finest "shoots" in France are to be found here.

The heyday of the great "shoots" was between the wars. Then

An old farmhouse near the village of Yvoy-le-Marron, preceding overleaf, has an air of peaceful rusticity that is characteristic of Sologne. Much of the region is heavily forested, and, in season, solognot farmers spend as much time hunting game as tilling the soil. A couple who live in Vernon-en-Sologne, *top, return from their daily round with sacks of potatoes and firewood they have gathered from fields and woods. The game that teems in the countryside and makes hunting the region's main resource includes, opposite (left to right), rabbit, hare, red partridge, and pheasant.*

aristocrats would gather at a hunting lodge for a day of felling game that had been carefully raised for the occasion. Released by a gamekeeper, a fattened pheasant or deer would be brought down by the hunter's bullet. Today such shooting parties are organized by successful businessmen from Paris, and occasionally attended by wealthy visiting Middle Eastern sportsmen.

There are many hotels and restaurants in Sologne where farmers and gamekeepers meet for lunch (they are usually closed in the evenings) that serve traditional game dishes such as simple rabbit *pot-au-feu*, and *civet de lièvre* (rather like jugged hare). Pheasant is frequently served in a more elaborate way—such as in a *ballotine*—boned, stuffed, and rolled up like a bundle, sometimes served hot—or with juniper berries, roasted on a bed of cabbage, accompanied by a *galette* of potatoes. Partridges are served from the end of the summer to mid-autumn, sometimes wrapped in vine leaves and cooked in *verjus*—sour grape juice. As a side dish, a *croûte aux champignons* may be presented—a whole-grain–flour pastry filled with sautéed mushrooms.

In addition to the more familiar pheasant and partridge, there are large numbers of roe deer, wild boar, and a wide variety of wild fowl on the lakes and mires in this lichen-carpeted marshy land.

The cooking of Solonge is not *grande cuisine*, and

it is by no means *nouvelle*; instead, it represents an imaginative use of the ingredients at hand. An example of this is the use of *nèfles* (medlar fruits), which when puréed and sweetened make an unusual and fragrant filling for a tart. They are sold at the wine cooperative in the town of Olivet, where their woody smell pervades the room.

Olivet, right at the north of Sologne, is celebrated for its pears, which are of many varieties, with evocative names like *beurre hardi*, with its blushing skin and its pinkish flesh, and *comice*, Jeanne d'Arc, *conférence*, Canada, and William. The Bon Chrétien variety, so appreciated by Marcel Proust, disappeared altogether after the last war. The *eau-de-vie de poire William*, sold with a whole pear mysteriously grown to full size inside the bottle, has a fragrance and a delicacy that puts Swiss *Williamine* to shame.

Sunday morning near Nouans-les-Fontaines, opposite (top), the generations mix as a party of local hunters—farmers, tradesmen, craftsmen—heads for the woods. Alexandre Marchand, opposite (bottom), is a visitor from Tours. A hunter, below, disdains the orange vests and scarlet shirts many American hunters favor, in order to blend in with the landscape. Above: perdreaux au verjus, *in which the partridges are wrapped in vine leaves, sautéed, and then cooked in a casserole with tiny onions and the juice of white grapes.*

It would hardly be an exaggeration to say that Sologne is the land of lakes; a survey of 1518 estimated there to be 4,000 of them. They are caused not only by damp climate but also by the accumulation on a clay soil of waters from the Massif Central, to the south. Several attempts were made to drain the country, in particular under the initiative of Napoleon III in the mid-nineteenth century. The Canal de la Sauldre was dug, as were many drainage channels, but as the land is not rich loam, the efforts were largely a waste of time.

Perhaps it was the mists, which the abundant stagnant water generates, and the brooding melancholy of the landscape, particularly in autumn, that led to the strong belief in the supernatural among the inhabitants of Sologne. Local spirits, which may

Partridge eggs, below, appear in many local markets. A marcassin, or young boar, right, although farm-raised to replenish game, is still a dangerous beast. Its rich meat is marinated for a day or more to make marinade de civet de marcassin, *opposite. The marinade calls for white wine, onions, shallots, garlic, carrots, celery, and a bouquet garni. It is a specialty of Mme. Crouzier, the proprietor of the Croix Blanche auberge, in Chaumont-sur-Tharonne.*

have had their origin in the pre-Christian days, became transformed into local saints and were closely associated with sacred springs and fountains. The patron saint of Sologne is Sainte Montaine, a farm girl of great devotion, who was one day sent to collect water from a nearby spring, with a jug in each hand. On her way back she dropped and broke the jugs. When she returned to the farm, her mistress was angry and to mock the poor girl's clumsiness ordered her to return to the spring for more water, but this time handed her two wicker baskets in which she was to fetch it. Montaine prayed and a miracle happened; she was able to bring back the baskets full of water.

Today the lakes are the haunts only of fishermen. The fishing season begins on September 29, Saint Michael's Day, and the common catch in the lakes consists of carp, rainbow perch, tench, pike (*brochet*), and eels. Many of the *quenelles de brochet* served in the grand restaurants of France come from the humble ponds of Sologne. The eels are often cooked *à la poulette* (in a cream and egg-yolk sauce with mushrooms). Given the marshy nature of the land, you might expect to find fresh frogs for sale in the market, but although the forests no doubt abound with them, those that you can buy are actually reared in captivity like most of the trout and carp that are offered.

The market, partly in a covered hall, is the mainspring of Romorantin, which has been prosperous to a greater or lesser extent since the sixteenth century. Several of the buildings of that date remain, such as the Chancellerie and the Hôtel Saint-Pol. Joan of Arc stayed in the town on her way to Orléans, they say, and Claude de France, the wife of François I, was born in the château. The Sauldre gently meanders through the center of the town, where it briefly divides to form the island of La Motte (which, together with the land to one side of it, now forms a pretty public garden). It is there that Leonardo da Vinci is supposed to have had the idea for a château to rival Chambord. King François had commissioned him to produce such a building, and though work on it was never even begun, plans for it exist in libraries in England and Italy. Had it been built, the history of Sologne would have been different.

The château de Chambord itself lies on the edge of Sologne, close to the Loire, although its large hunting forest extends well into the territory of Sologne. The château was patronized by generations of French kings but then fell into disrepair after revolutions and wars. The only other major château in Sologne is Cheverny, which lies right on the western border. There is still much deer hunting there in the grand manner.

THE PEOPLE of Romorantin take their gastronomy rather seriously, and every year on the last weekend of October, the marketplace is devoted to a kind of Patangruelic festival, in which all, from the professional chef to the interested amateur, are invited to display their own homemade produce. The result of this abundance, of course, is that if you try to sample everything, you will reach your limit before you have gotten very far; you can make a tour of the marketplace, perhaps sampling only those items that appear to be more or less regional.

One year there were some interesting kinds of *charcuterie*, involving *rillettes* made from wild duck and *lapin de Garenne* (a species of hare). There was a blood sausage, a specialty from the village of Pruniers a few miles away, that included mushrooms and walnuts in the stuffing. There were game pies and *pâtés* of various textures, from the coarse rabbit *terrine* to the smoother pheasant *pâté*.

Another treat was the *tartouillat*, a savory pumpkin pie, which should be eaten just warm and is a specialty of the village of Millançay. The best of

In lièvre à la solognote, *below, the stuffed hare is cooked with vegetables, wine, and herbs and will be served cold with prunes. The hare, opposite, is stuffed with bacon, bread, lard,* and herbs. Red wine is the likely accompaniment, preferably a Chinon from nearby Touraine. This dish is another specialty of Mme. Crouzier.

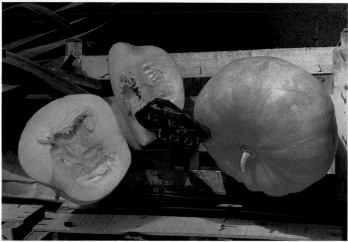

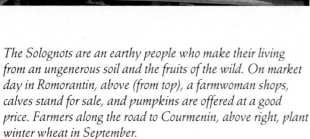

The Solognots are an earthy people who make their living from an ungenerous soil and the fruits of the wild. On market day in Romorantin, above (from top), a farmwoman shops, calves stand for sale, and pumpkins are offered at a good price. Farmers along the road to Courmenin, above right, plant winter wheat in September.

the *confiserie* were made by professionals, like Monsieur Benoist's truffles, which have a *prâline* center covered with *nougâtine* and rolled in cocoa. He had also made some marvelous *croquets aux amandes*, which are a little like brittle brandysnaps and are excellent on top of ice cream; a specialty of Neung-sur-Beuvron, they are called *aristocrates*, apparently because they were first made at the time of the 1789 Revolution.

Close to Romorantin is the village of Lantheney, where pilgrims used to visit the statue of Sainte

Claire. Apparently people used to meet outside the church on Easter Monday to eat hard-boiled eggs dyed green in spinach juice, a curious custom, but perhaps not much odder than drinking green beer on Saint Patrick's Day.

North again from Romorantin, you come to the little town of Lamotte-Beuvron. This is a purely agricultural town, but it has become famous because it is the place where the Demoiselles Tatin created the tart of the same name.

The story, which is wonderfully related by Jane Grigson in her book *Food for the Famous*, is that the Tatin sisters ran a hotel, which is still standing, close to the station on the newly constructed line from Paris. The wealthy, arriving for their shooting weekends, would often dine at the then new, but today rather ugly, Hôtel Tatin et Terminus. The stove in the kitchen was of an old design, with no oven, as most pastries would have been brought in from the local *pâtisserie*, and game would have been roasted before the fire. The only way to cook an apple tart on such a range (apples being the most

*Fall lingers long in Sologne and brings out its best. Even a
shuttered old house in Courmenin, above left, has a late-
flowering garden at the front door. In the market of Romorantin,
an extravagant wild mushroom, left, is a special find. Mme.
Crouzier's preserves, above, include homemade tomato paste,
two kinds of cherries, two kinds of beans, pears, mushrooms,
and even game—venison and pheasant. Pommes de terre
sautées, opposite, is an all-season dish, prepared with potatoes and plenty of butter, garlic, and chopped parsley.*

plentiful and excellent fruit in Sologne, especially
the Reinette d'Orléans) was to cover one of the
hotplates with a metal dome, with the tart inside.
Obviously the problem would be that the pastry,
being a poor conductor of heat, would burn before
the apples were cooked. So the tart was inverted,
the apple and sugar and butter being allowed to
caramelize while the pastry cooked. The result was
the marvelous upside-down confection known
today throughout France as the *tarte Tatin*, its fame,
no doubt, partly due to copies made of it in Paris
by the chefs of the returning sportsmen.

BACK in the twelfth and thirteenth centuries,
the wine from the part of Sologne nearest
to Orléans was more appreciated than it
is today. It was exported by the merchants
of Saint-Omer to the Plantagenet kings of England

and was considered of a quality to match the wines of Bordeaux. Today, the vines in the region are mostly the Gris Meunier and the Gamay Rouge, which both give a light refreshing wine, not at all heady, and go well with Sologne's *charcuterie*, and with white meat and poultry. The Cabernet, which grows in the sandy soil, makes a red wine deep in color, with a high tannin content, as well as a fragrant rosé, which is particularly good with the local goat cheeses, such as the *cendré* from Olivet and the one from Pannes, which is ripened under the ashes of the vine shoots and then wrapped in walnut leaves. Further northeast you'll find a Menetou-Salon, a delicious, light, and fruity red wine with an aftertaste of raspberries.

Another alcoholic drink, perhaps less pleasant, is the *hydromel*, a kind of mead from the local honey. Sologne has extensive pine forests and heather-carpeted moors of a purplish pink, which provide the food supply for endless beehives. The honey is used in many ways—to make a base for *pain d'épices* (gingerbread) and to make *nonnettes* (little ginger-

bread cakes with an apricot glaze) and *sablés de Nançay*. Little biscuits of this name are now made industrially and are rather disappointing, but you can still find the real thing in the village of Neuvy-sur-Barangeon, in a rather decrepit *café-boulangerie* where you're likely to see farmers and gamekeepers nibbling at them over what appear to be some rather robust spirits.

Honey is used in cooking other dishes too. At a restaurant at Brinon-sur-Sauldre, one of the main courses is breast of duck, thinly sliced, and coated with a sauce made with a thin gravy blended with the local honey. As a side dish, you can have *cèpes*, sautéed, with a hint of garlic and parsley—it makes a perfect combination.

If some of the many traditional dishes of Sologne have been forgotten, it is possibly because they were not particularly palatable—such as *la miausée*, a gruel made from rye bread in milk and honey, and *la trempée*, made by frying bread soaked in red wine. But many robust regional dishes have stood the test of time admirably.

The ingredients of escargots aux champignons, *opposite, here include four kinds of mushrooms:* girolles *(on the plate, with sliced almonds),* button-sized champignons de Paris, *and the much bigger* cèpes, *and* bolets. Tartouillat, *below, is a strudel-like dessert filled with pumpkin and apples.*

Honey is the basis of many regional sweets, below, and even goes into a sweet wine called Hydromel. The little round cakes are nonnettes, *and the loaf cake is a* pain d'épices. *A French version of honey butter is made by whipping together the honey and the honeycomb.*

CÈPES FORESTIÈRE   *Cèpes in Cream and Garlic Sauce*

2 pounds fresh *cèpes* (1 kg)
8 tablespoons butter (100 g)
3 shallots, chopped
1 clove garlic, chopped
2 tablespoons parsley, chopped
Salt, freshly ground pepper
About ¼ cup meat juice or good meat stock
2 to 3 tablespoons heavy cream (optional)

Trim the *cèpes* and wipe them clean; they should not be washed. (If you are using dried *cèpes*, reconstitute them by pouring boiling water over and leaving them for 1 hour.)

Melt the butter in a casserole and add the *cèpes*, shallots, garlic, and parsley. Season lightly with salt and pepper and allow to cook briskly at first, then more slowly with the lid half covering the pan. They will take about 40 minutes to cook.

Before serving, add the meat juice to the cooking liquid and, if you like, a few tablespoons of cream. Sprinkle with additional parsley, taste for seasoning, and serve.

for 6 people

TERRINE DE LIÈVRE À LA SOLOGNOTE   *Hare or Rabbit Terrine*

1 hare or large rabbit, skinned and cleaned
2 or 3 thin slices pork fat back

FOR THE MARINADE
2 cups good white wine (½ liter)
1 teaspoon olive oil
2 large onions
1 clove garlic
1 clove
1 carrot
1 celery rib
1 bouquet garni—see Appendix

FOR THE JELLY
Reserved bones from the hare or rabbit
Half a calf's foot
¾ cup white wine (200 ml)
1 bouquet garni—see Appendix
Salt
A few peppercorns

FOR THE FARCE
½ pound streaky bacon (250 g)
¼ pound lean breast or shoulder of veal (125 g)
1 truffle
Salt, freshly ground pepper
1 egg, beaten

You can make this terrine by removing the fillets from the back and beneath the ribs of the hare and cutting them into strips, which are alternated with the *farce* in the terrine. All the remaining meat is taken off the bone, chopped, and mixed with the *farce*.

Alternatively, as shown in the picture on p. 88, the hare can be boned and stuffed whole, which looks very impressive. In either case, simmer the marinade ingre-dients for 30 minutes, allow to cool, and then marinate the boned whole hare or meat of the hare overnight in the refrigerator. Turn and baste the meat occasionally.

Reserve the bones for the jelly. In a pan combine the bones, the half calf's foot, white wine, bouquet garni, salt, and peppercorns with 2 cups of water. Bring to a boil, skim, and simmer, reducing slowly to about 1 cup. Set the jelly aside.

Prepare the *farce*: chop the bacon and veal (and the remaining meat of the hare if you have taken it off the bone) in a food processor, or use a knife with a large, sharp blade. Slice the truffle thinly and add to the chopped meat. Season the mixture well with salt and pepper and bind it with a beaten egg. Cook 1 teaspoon of the mixture in a frying pan to see if it is correctly seasoned—if not, add more, as a terrine should be highly seasoned.

Preheat the oven to 350°F. Line a large terrine with about half the pork fat back; flatten with a rolling pin. Drain the marinated hare, reserving the marinade.

If you have boned the whole hare, spread it out in the terrine. Fill it with the *farce*. Close the belly of the hare over the top and cover with the remaining pork fat.

If you have cut the fillets into strips, lay them lengthwise in the terrine alternating with layers of the *farce*. Cover with the remaining fat.

Cover the terrine, set it in a *bain-marie*, and bake for 1 hour. Add the reserved jelly and, if necessary, add a little of the marinade. Cook for 1½ hours.

Allow to cool, and wait 48 hours before you eat the *pâté*.

for 12 people / photographs on pages 88 and 89

BALLOTINE DE FAISAN AU GENÉVRIÈRE   *Ballotine of Pheasant with Juniper*

1 pheasant, plucked and cleaned, with its giblets
About 2 cups dry white wine, preferably Sancerre (½ liter)
1 bouquet garni—see Appendix
2 tablespoons butter (25 g)

FOR THE FARCE
3 or 4 chestnuts
1 thick slice smoked ham
½ cup plain yogurt (125 ml)
A few juniper berries
Salt, freshly ground pepper
2 eggs, beaten
Dash of old *marc* or juniper liqueur
Small can of *foie gras*, chopped (optional)

FOR THE GARNISH
Cooked, shelled chestnuts and, if possible, *chanterelles*
   (small, golden, trumpet-shaped wild mushrooms)

Bone the pheasant so that the flesh remains intact and
   the bird can be put back together into its original
   shape—see Appendix. Season it inside and out and
   put in a cool place.
Make the stock: place the bones in a saucepan with
   about 1 cup of the wine and the bouquet garni. Season
with salt and pepper and simmer gently for 30 minutes, adding more wine if the liquid becomes too
   reduced. Strain and set aside until later.
Cover the chestnuts with boiling water and simmer for
   15 to 20 minutes, until tender. Drain, remove the
   shells and skin, and crush them.
Make the *farce*: chop the ham and the liver and heart
   of the pheasant. Add the crushed chestnuts, the yogurt,
   and the juniper berries. Season with salt and pepper
   and bind with the eggs. Sprinkle the mixture with
   the *marc* and, if you like, the *foie gras*, which will
   give an even better flavor.
Spread out the boned pheasant and spread it with the
   stuffing. Roll it up and tie it carefully with string.
   Heat the butter in a casserole and brown the pheasant on all sides. Add the remaining wine and the
   reserved stock, cover the pan, and simmer gently for
   45 minutes, until tender.
Serve hot, surrounded by cooked chestnuts and, if you
   can get them, *chanterelles*. Leftover *ballotine* is delicious served cold with a salad.

for 4 people / photograph below

BALLOTINE DE FAISAN AU GENÉVRIÈRE   *Ballotine of Pheasant with Juniper*

PERDREAUX AU VERJUS   *Partridges with Verjus*

4 partridges, plucked and cleaned
2 tablespoons butter (25 g)
Salt, freshly ground pepper
4 tender vine leaves
20 button or pickling onions, peeled
1 carrot, sliced
1 bouquet garni—see Appendix
About ¼ cup chicken stock
½ pound slightly unripe white grapes (250 g)

Truss the partridges and season with salt and pepper.
   Wrap each bird in a vine leaf and tie thread around it.
Heat the butter in a small casserole and sauté the
   partridges for 2 minutes over a brisk heat. Add the
   onions, carrot, and the bouquet garni to the casserole.

Moisten with the chicken stock, season, and cover
   the pan, letting it simmer gently for 20 to 25 minutes.
Remove the partridges, unwrap the vine leaves, and
   return the birds to the casserole to cook for 10 to 15
   minutes, or until tender. Crush the grapes, which
   should be picked about a week before they are ripe.
   Strain the grape juice and add it to the casserole about
   5 minutes before the end of the cooking time. Remove the partridges to a hot dish and bring the sauce
   to the boil for 1 minute. Taste for seasoning and add
   a little pepper—it should be quite sharp and strongly
   flavored. Serve very hot.

for 4 people / photograph on page 85

PAIN D'ÉPICES AU MIEL DE SOLOGNE   *Honey Spice Bread*

⅓ cup shelled almonds and hazelnuts, coarsely
   chopped (50 g)
1 cup flour (150 g)
½ cup thin honey (150 g)
1 egg yolk
Pinch of ground cinnamon
Pinch of ground cloves
Pinch of *quatre épices* (a mixture of white pepper or
   allspice and nutmeg, cloves, and ginger or cinnamon)
1 teaspoon baking powder

Preheat the oven to 325°F. Mix all the ingredients
   together thoroughly in a bowl. If the honey is thick,
   first heat it gently until it liquifies, then add it.
Butter a small loaf pan and spoon in the mixture. Bake
   until set, up to 45 minutes.

for 6 to 8 people / photograph on page 95

PÂTE DE COINGS OU COTIGNAC   *Quince Paste*

6 pounds ripe quinces (3 kg)
4½ cups sugar (1 kg)
Granulated sugar (for sprinkling)

Peel the quinces and cut them in quarters, removing the
   cores. Tie the peels and cores in a piece of cheesecloth
   and combine in a large saucepan with the quinces,
   sugar, and 1 tablespoon of water.
Cook until the quinces are tender and have turned into

a soft purée. Remove the peels and cores and transfer
   the purée to a flat baking pan or other large flat dish.
Turn the oven to its lowest setting, put in the quince
   paste, and leave the oven door ajar. It takes about 10
   hours for the paste to set. When it is firm, cut it into
   squares and sprinkle generously with granulated
   sugar.
The paste keeps quite well in an airtight container.

CROQUETS   *Almond Cookies*

2 egg whites
1 cup sugar (250 g)
A few spoonfuls of flour
¾ cup almonds, chopped (125 g)
Grated lemon peel or ½ teaspoon vanilla (for flavoring)

Preheat the oven to 325°F. Beat the egg whites until
   they stand in peaks. Slowly add the sugar and then—
   a little at a time—add flour, until fairly firm. (The
   exact quantity of flour required for these cookies

depends on how much the egg whites can absorb,
   which can vary by as much as a tablespoon.) Add the
   almonds. Roll out the dough and cut into long
   rectangles, about 1 inch wide. Place on a buttered and
   floured baking sheet and bake for 30 minutes; then
   turn up the heat to 350°F and bake for 15 minutes,
   while continuing to keep an eye on them. The
   cookies turn a rather dark brown.
Open the oven door, turn off the oven, and leave the
   cookies to dry a little more as they cool. They should
   be very dry and fairly brittle.

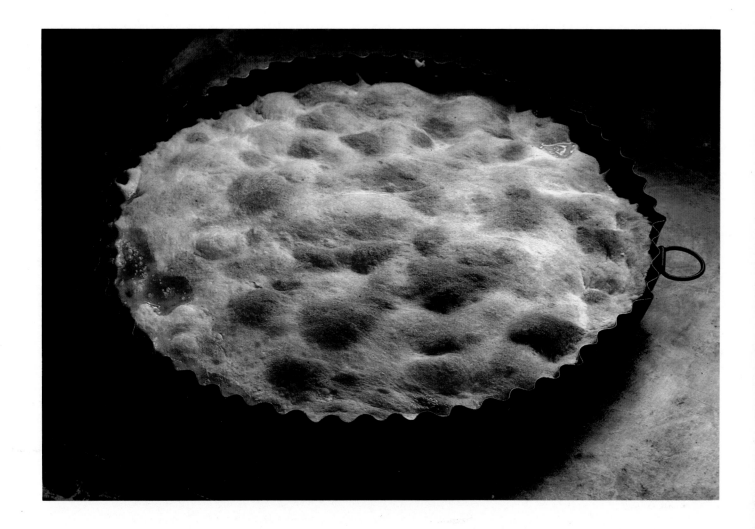

TARTE DE DEMOISELLES TATIN OU TARTE À L'ENVERS *Upside-Down Apple Tart*

This tart is an extraordinary culinary invention. The pastry, cooked on top of the apples, stays light and crisp, and the tart is then turned upside down. You can apply the same principle to other fruit tarts, such as pear or plum.

1 recipe *pâte brisée sucrée*—see Appendix
3 pounds russet apples (1½ kg)
½ cup powdered sugar (50 g)
4 tablespoons butter, melted (50 g)
Vanilla sugar or cinnamon
Crème fraîche—see Appendix—or heavy cream
   (optional)

Make the *pâte brisée sucrée*, and refrigerate, wrapped in plastic wrap, for 30 minutes before use.
Peel, core, and quarter the apples. Sprinkle the bottom of a heavy, round, seamless cake pan or deep flan pan 7 inches across, with the powdered sugar, put in some of the apples, and cover them with melted butter and generous quantities of sugar. Repeat the layers, drizzling the top with butter, sugar, and vanilla sugar or cinnamon.
Preheat the oven to 425°F. Before baking, cover the pan and place on the stove over a very low heat and let the apples cook gently, until the sugar in the bottom has started to caramelize. If the apples are watery, this can take a fairly long time. You will be able

to smell it, so don't allow it to burn. Roll out the pastry into a round about ⅛ inch thick, slightly larger than the pan. Cover the apple mixture with a layer of the pastry and bake for 15 to 20 minutes, covering the pastry with foil if it starts to get too brown.
Take the tart out of the oven and turn it upside down onto a plate. Eat hot or lukewarm with cream, and drink a Vouvray or Côteau du Layon with it.

for 6 to 8 people / photographs above and below

99

ALSACE

ALSACE

ALSACE is the easternmost province of France, extending from the eastern slopes of the Vosges mountains across the fertile plain of the Rhine, which forms its border with Germany. High in the Vosges are the mountain pastures where cows graze in summer and skiing enthusiasts gather in winter. The steep inclines to the plain are densely forested with pine, beech, and fir, which give way to the vineyards in the foothills. In his *Journal de Voyage* of 1580, Montaigne described Alsace as "a large and beautiful plain, flanked on the left by hillsides covered with most beautiful and carefully tended vines." Through these hillsides meanders the famous Route du Vin, just over a hundred miles long, connecting the picturesque villages of the wine growers.

Small town and prosperous-looking villages dominate the Alsatian scene. Houses with high-steepled roofs cluster around a church in a haphazardly harmonious pattern of little streets and alleys. Many of the fortified villages of the wine road retain gates or parts of their walls, and the more prominent hills are usually dominated by the ruins of a castle, symbol of the many wars and marches across this

Not far from the Rhine, a field of poppies blooming in June are a treat for the tourist, but a weed to the farmer, preceding overleaf. In the Alsatian town of Eguisheim, top, the indigenous architecture is a reminder of Alsace's historical links with Germany.

Delicacies from the Glasser shop in Colmar, opposite, include: various sausages and a loaf of peasant bread in the picnic basket; a bottle of local Riesling (top); and more bread, meat pastries, and Munster cheese (bottom).

much-disputed bit of Europe.

The alluvial plain is intensively cultivated with corn, hops, tobacco, wheat, rye, barley, potatoes, sugar beet. Winter vegetables are limited to cabbage and a great variety of roots, but in summer there is excellent asparagus, and every kind of fruit tree grows in the many orchards, as do chestnut, almond, and walnut trees. The fruits are an essential part of Alsatian cuisine: Soft fruits and apples are used for tarts; apples, *quetsches*, and pears are dried in slices (*schnitzen*) for winter keeping; and all manner of fruits are used to make the *alcools blancs*, or *eaux-de-vie*, for which the region is renowned.

The food we think of as typically Alsatian, and which may indeed have been eaten in the region for centuries, did not necessarily originate there. *Choucroute* may well be Tartar in origin, *foie gras* is special also to Périgord, *bäckeoffe* resembles many peasant dishes throughout Middle Europe, the *kugelhopf* mold is found all over northern Germany —but nowhere else did a gastronomic culture take shape that effortlessly combines all these disparate elements into one great tradition of good food and good living. Montaigne's *Journal* acknowledges that the Alsatians were excellent cooks, particularly of fish, that they never served water with their wine, and that they mixed different meats in one dish.

Basically, Alsatian cuisine is of peasant origin, but the competitive spirit of the free villages extended quite early to a pride in local specialties and variants. In the more prosperous towns, the original economy of ingredients and methods was deliberately ignored in ostentatious (and wasteful) attempts to be seen to be richer and grander, and a new tradition was born of garantuan feasts demanding legendary appetites.

The diet of the peasants and artisans of the region was far more austere than popular tradition would have us believe. In the Middle Ages bread was the staple food, with a few green vegetables in summer, and dried peas, beans, and lentils in winter. During the wine harvest, vineyard work-

The quintessential Alsatian dish choucroute, *opposite, features sauerkraut, flavored with bacon, onions, and juniper berries, which is then combined with sausages, smoked pork, and dumplings. Riesling, of course, is the wine of choice, here in the Maison des Tanneurs restaurant in Strasbourg. Along the roads and in the towns of Alsace, left from top, signs of the region: a stork's nest, obligingly perched on a roof in Illhaeusern; a farmer's wife selling her vegetables in Colmar; corn for pigs drying on a wall near Strasbourg; and freshly picked wild strawberries from a field near Roschwirr.*

ers were given wholewheat bread with cabbage and turnips, blood sausages, and tripe. Monastery records show that at Murbach Abbey the monks received every day, rye bread, two goblets of wine, two dishes of vegetables (one seasoned with salt, the other with lard or oil, according to the season), and cheese. Pork or chicken was eaten on feast days; a bit of fat bacon was much prized in winter: Meat was rare and continued to be so until the eighteenth century, when it began to be a regular part of the Sunday meal.

Special dishes and special menus were created for religious and secular feasts. Different breads, cakes, and *petits fours* came to be associated with the great religious festivals, but in Alsace everything can be made into a celebration: New Year, Twelfth Night, carnival, Saint Joseph, Saint Martin, Saint Hubert (the patron of hunters), Saint Urbain (the patron of vineyards), the patron saints of the different villages, and every family occasion from birth through marriage to death. In our own more touristy times, many towns have a wine festival, Ribeauvillé has a *kugelhopf* festival, Colmar has *choucroute* days, Munster has a *tourte* festival, others celebrate beer, hops, or onion tarts—and all are occasions for good eating and inspired drinking. Even washdays had their special food, *bäckeoffe* (baker's oven), a meat and potato stew that apparently dates back to the mid-nineteenth century. The meat could be marinated the night before, and early in the morning the layers of pork, beef, lamb, onions, and potatoes were assembled in an earthenware casserole that was taken to the baker to cook while the women went off to the washplace.

Choucroute is often the first thing we think of when Alsatian food is mentioned, but the Alsatians seem to eat little of it now (one wryly said it was fed to foreign visitors and that homesick Alsatians would eat it in Paris). It is sold in the *charcuteries*, and older people in the countryside still make their own. Fifteenth-century records speak of two types: *Gumbostkrut* (cabbage "*en compôte*"), which is the whole cabbage, well blanched, kept in a mixture of water, vinegar, salt, and mustard, often together with similarly blanched turnips; and *surkrut*, made of cabbage shredded by the *surkrutschnieder* (a profession that survived until the early twentieth century), then salted and packed in barrels with cumin and elderberry leaves. Other traditional seasonings were dill, horseradish, and parsley; nowadays cloves, bay leaves, and juniper are more usual.

Peasants ate boiled root vegetables and *lard fumé* with their *choucroute*, and on special occasions sausages or better cuts of salted pork were added. *Choucroute* with sausages was served on feast days in the seminary attended by Julien Sorel (in Stendhal's *Le Rouge et le Noir*), to the delight of his fellow students, mostly poor peasant boys for whom a square meal had always been an event. The Jews of Alsace ate their *choucroute* with preserved goose. Like some other great peasant dishes (green pea soup, for example), *choucroute* improves with reheating. Today, if you order it in a restaurant, the portions are decidedly daunting: A mound of *choucroute* will be surrounded by boiled potatoes and topped with the traditional *lard fumé* plus at least two different sausages and one other smoked and boiled meat—the whole quite sufficient for a small family. Brillat-Savarin ranked *choucroute* among his nineteen greatest dishes; *nouvelle cuisine* chefs in Alsace prefer simple salads of *choucroute*, pickles, and *crudités*.

Noodles have been popular in Alsace for several centuries, and they are still frequently made at home. They are the traditional accompaniment to many local specialties such as jugged hare, *matelote*, and chicken fricassée. *Spaetzle*, similar to noodles but more chewy, are small curls of dough boiled and then served with melted butter or fried golden in butter. Like noodles, they are always served as an accompaniment to another dish: Alsatians do not eat pasta as a dish on its own. They are also fond of small dumplings, *knepfle*, made with flour or semolina (rather like *gnocchi*). Until the beginning of this century, they were a traditional Friday main course, served with dried fruit. They are still served today, either in the traditional way or with a salad.

PORK is the favorite meat of Alsace. It is presented in many guises: as roast loin, chops, or leg; salted or smoked hams, hocks, knuckles, trotters, belly, and shoulder; bacon; and local specialties such as Strasbourg sausages and *tourte de la vallée de Munster*. Until early in this century, every rural family kept pigs. The annual pig killing, and the attendant feast to eat the parts that will not keep, are vividly remembered by the older inhabitants. In some villages butchers still go from house to house to kill the pig and make sausages and *charcuterie*.

The range of *charcuterie* in Alsace is enormous, and the fame of local manufacturers is such that they can still hold their own against the industrialized suppliers to supermarkets. When you walk

Tarte à l'oignon *is served hot, with cold white wine to wash it down. It's an uncomplicated dish, opposite, in which the flavors of onion and bacon are blended in an egg and cream filling and baked in a plain crust. This country dish is a long-time favorite at Le Caveau restaurant in Eguisheim.*

down the main street in any Alsatian town or village, your eye will be drawn to the *charcutier*'s window. The display is always appetizing and seldom less than sumptuous. There is every variety of *terrine* and *pâté*, together with sausages with cumin or with garlic, *saucisses de Strasbourg* (pork and beef, a plump variant of the frankfurter), highly spiced *cervelas* (originally containing pig's brain—hence the name), *burelewerwurscht* and *waedele* (both calf's-liver sausages), dried and smoked sausages and salamis, blood sausages, bacon, hams, and all kinds of meat *en brioche*.

The choice of game is very wide too: hare, rabbit, partridge, pheasant, quail, woodcock, wild duck, deer, buck, and wild boar all find their way to the table, often served with the fruits of the region, including grapes, and with noodles or *spaetzle*. Pheasant replaces smoked pork in a grand *choucroute*. All appear in different forms in *charcuterie*.

Flocks of geese were kept in both country and town well into the twentieth century. Geese are altogether useful creatures. Omnivorous as are pigs (and therefore cheap to rear), they provide a great deal of meat and cooking fat, with feathers and quills as byproducts. Roast goose stuffed with chestnuts or apples is served at Christmas and New Year, and there are regional specialties, such as stuffed neck of goose or goose leg with *choucroute*. Most famous is the incomparable *foie gras*, served as a *terrine* or a *pâté en croûte*, or sautéed in butter and garnished with apple slices. As a garnish, *foie gras* turns up in salads, with noodles, or in stuffed goose neck, and it is also used as a mousse or in aspic. Said to mature with age like a great wine, it is the most esteemed dish of Alsatian cuisine, always served on special occasions.

The inventor of the *pâté de foie gras en croûte* is said to have been Jean-Pierre Clause, chef to Marshal de Contades, military governor of Alsace. Clause surrounded the liver with chopped veal and bacon and then wrapped the whole in a pie crust. An immediate success when tried out in 1780, this

Each region of France prepares snails in its own way. In Alsace, one method is escargots en brioche, left, in which the snails are cooked, taken from the shell, and baked briefly on slices of brioche covered with garlic butter. The brioche absorbs all the butter so that none is lost. They are served as a first

course at Le Caveau in Eguisheim. Ecrevisses au Pinot Rouge, below, before and after cooking, are made with river crayfish and wine. The crayfish, which take on a rosy hue after cooking, are sprinkled with fresh parsley.

ture, but where at least they found a climate of religious tolerance. The Jewish element in Alsatian cooking has partly economic, partly religious, aspects. Where the Gentile Alsatians had a predeliction for pigs and pork, the Jewish Alsatians used geese and goose fat, and the region's famous *carpe à la juive* was a sabbath dish because it could be made a day ahead and served cold.

THE RHINE and its tributary the Ill used to yield salmon, eel, lamprey, pike, carp, and perch in abundance, and although supplies are much more limited now, the Alsatians still enjoy a wide range of freshwater fish dishes. The two most famous fish dishes are *matelote à l'alsacienne* and *carpe à la juive*. The *matelote* is made of pike, tench, perch, trout, and eel cut into pieces and simmered in a *fumet* and Riesling. When the fish is cooked, the cooking liquid is thickened with

In râble de lièvre aux nouilles fraîches, *left (here at Brasserie Flo in Paris), the hare is marinated before it is roasted and served over noodles.* Truffes sous la cendre, *below, is* foie gras *rolled in chopped truffles shaped into balls the size of small potatoes, and served with a softening of meat jelly.*

dish made its creator's fortune: In 1784 Clause married the widow of a *pâtissier* and devoted the remaining forty-odd years of his life to the manufacture and sale of his *pâté*, adding others based on venison, wild boar, hare, quail, partridge, duck, turkey, and freshwater fish—an amazing forty-two varieties in all.

But he was hardly the first to think of serving *pâtés en croûte*. These appear at least 120 years before his time in the paintings of Sebastian Stosskopf. The Musée des Beaux Arts in Strasbourg has a fine collection of his still-lifes. A particularly lovely one is a blue and white bowl lined with strawberry leaves and piled high with ripe and unripe strawberries, but another fine one shows a marble table on which are a basket containing wine glasses and a *pâté en croûte* sliced through to show the inside clearly.

Alsace has long had a substantial Jewish strain in its population, and the Jewish influence on Alsatian cuisine has been considerable. The first Jewish settlements were recorded in Strasbourg in the thirteenth century, the period when Alsace turned into an autonomous society with rapidly expanding trade links. The Thirty Years' War uprooted large numbers of the poorer Jews, whose economic situation did not improve much in Alsace, where they were not allowed to engage in agricul-

beurre manié, and the sauce finished with cream and egg yolk. The *matelote* is traditionally served with noodles. An interesting *salade de matelote* was devised by François Stéphan, the enterprising young chef at the Hohlandsbourg Restaurant in Trois Epis.

Frogs have been eaten in Alsace at least since the thirteenth century, and Strasbourg used to have a frog market next to the fish market. There were three traditional ways of cooking and serving frogs: in a soup (a true regional dish), boiled with onion and herbs and served with a light stock and flour sauce, or fried in batter with grated lemon and egg white. These days frog soup is still widely found on restaurant menus, but otherwise the ubiquitous Provençal sauce of garlic and tomato has taken over. New ways have appeared as well, however: *grenouilles au Riesling* (started in butter with shallots) and a delicate *mousseline de grenouille*, which is a specialty of the Auberge de l'Ill at Illhaeusern.

Terrine d'anguilles, right, is featured at the Auberge de l'Ill in the beautiful village of Illhaeusern. The eels are fresh from the Ill river. Another dish of the Auberge is the coarsely textured but finely flavored terrine de canard au foie gras en brioche, *below.*

If any shop windows rival those of the *charcutiers*, it is the bakers'. The range of breads is amazing. There are all shapes and sizes and flavors—cinnamon, cumin, sweet spices, almonds; breads made from every type of flour—rye, wheat, barley, bran; large peasant loaves with heavily scored crusts, small brown loaves with walnuts, delicate white ones in the form of a crown; bread with pork fat; wholegrain bread, milk bread, and a profusion of rolls.

Certain breads are associated with different festivals. On New Year's Day the children used to take a brioche, called a *neujohrweka*, to their uncles, aunts, and godparents. February 5, Saint Agatha's Day, is the festival of the bakers: On that day, in the Sundgau, people still buy a big loaf early in the morning, carry it to Mass to be blessed, and make sure that every member of the family eats some of it during the day. For Saint Nicholas, December 6, the baker makes small brioche figures called *bonshommes*, and these together with dried fruit and nuts are put out for the children on the night before. The history of other breads often goes back several centuries to a village festival, probably that of the patron saint. As their fame spread through the region, others started to imitate them.

Berawecka is a rich bread made from dried pears with dried *quetsch*, prunes, figs, raisins, and walnuts, spiced with cinnamon, cloves, and lemon zest, and

111

flavored with kirsch or *eau-de-vie de poire*. The fruit is soaked, then chopped and mixed into a bread dough made with milk. It was traditionally eaten on Christmas Eve, before midnight mass; nowadays it appears for Christmas breakfast or on New Year's Day.

The universally known *kugelhopf* is a light yeast cake with raisins and almonds that is baked in a special fluted and twisted mold. It is very good for breakfast, and is also served in the afternoon with a glass of Muscat or Traminer. It was the custom until the 1940s for people to bring their own milk, eggs, butter, and *eau-de-vie* to the baker, with their own *kugelhopf* mold. The baker would provide flour, sugar, raisins, almonds, and yeast. This practice is still found in a few villages, mainly in the farm areas.

In addition to breads, Alsace is noted for its fine *pâtisserie*. *Bredle*, a sort of *petit four*, are traditionally associated with Christmas. Made in sculpted wooden molds in a great variety of shapes, they replaced the wafer Hosts as Christmas decorations very early on, just as colored balls replaced the original red apples. Alsatian tradition has it that the decorated Christmas tree originated in Selestat around the year 1500, and certainly there was great competition between various villages as to the most beautiful decoration of the village tree. Nowadays *bredle* can be bought all year round. *Anisbredle* are the simplest ones (egg, sugar, flour, and aniseed), *butterbredle* are richer (more butter and sugar), and *schwowebredle* are made with ground almonds.

Alsace has almost as many fruit tarts as *pâtés*. All the colors and flavors of the orchard appear in tarts: plums, *quetsches*, cherries, blueberries, pears, apples. A custard of egg yolk and cream is often added to the fruit filling, or the fruit may simply be sprinkled with sugar and cinnamon. Savory tarts are as popular as are sweet ones, especially onion tart or *zewelwai*, for which thinly sliced onions are softened in goose fat or butter before being spread in the pie shell and covered with the egg and cream filling.

The only cheese special to Alsace is Munster— and that really belongs more to the mountain ranges of the Vosges, where the milk of the mountain herds was always preserved as cheese, whey, and buttermilk. Some butter was made there, but pork fat was the main spread. Munster is a semi-soft cheese with a red or orange crust and a very strong and distinctive smell. It is usually served in fairly small portions with a little dish of caraway seeds.

ALSACE is as renowned for its drink as for its food. Excellent white wines, *eaux-de-vie*, and beers are made here. Wines have been made along the left bank of the Rhine for centuries, and although wine production had been hampered or halted at regular intervals by wars, revolutions, and epidemics, it has always recovered, increased its reputation, and widened its market. Until the French Revolution the vineyards were owned by abbeys, secular rulers, and individual wine growers of many nationalities. When the vineyards were split up, the many new owners concentrated on quantity rather than quality, and for the next hundred years, Alsatian wines did not fare well: Beer became a serious competitor at home, and abroad Switzerland and Germany imposed taxes on imported wines. Annexation by Germany led to the mass production of indifferent wines, and at the same time mildew, phylloxera, and other diseases ravaged the vines. Only after 1918 were serious efforts made to restore quality.

These efforts bore miraculous fruit, and the wines of Alsace now have a distinct character all their own. Recognition has been slow, however: Not until 1962 was the region granted one single *appellation contrôlée* for all its many different wines. Alsace or Vin d'Alsace may be followed by the varietal (grape) names that distinguish the wines of Alsace. Outside the region, its wines are still listed on menus as "Riesling d'Alsace" and the like—never a year, never a grower, never the name of a place or a vineyard. Yet in Alsace itself the many great restaurants will carefully detail fifteen different Rieslings, ten Gewürztraminers, several Pinot Gris (or Tokay d'Alsace, as they are more commonly known), and the odd Muscat or Pinot Noir. The detail will always include the name of the grower, however small his input may be.

The slopes of the Vosges face in many different directions, for they are all river gorges coming down from the mountains toward the plain. Variations in soil and exposure to sun and wind create an infinity of microclimates, each with its own wine. Proud indeed are the few names of vineyards such as Schoenberg or Sporen that have been in the fam-

Alsatian pastries come in all shapes and sizes, from rich cakes to fruit-filled tarts. They are the essential accompaniment to afternoon coffee and the favorite way to end a meal. A selection, opposite, in the little medieval town of Kaysersberg, includes a cross-hatched tarte aux quetsches *(top), made with quetsch plums;* kugelhopf, *an exceptionally light tube cake and one of the most popular Alsatian desserts; a* tresse en brioche *(next to it); a buttery, almond-flavored pastry (front left); a loaf called* chinois; *and a round brioche cake, sticky with sugar and nuts.*

ily for generations, constantly producing the best Reisling wine.

Alsace produces a greater variety of *eaux-de-vie* and fruit liqueurs than any other part of France, or probably of the world. Every fruit from the orchards and every wild fruit and berry from the Vosges is distilled. The liqueurs have some faint color and are sweetish, the *eaux-de-vie* are colorless, dry, and intensely perfumed with the fruit. They are made in small distilleries and by some of the large wine producers. In Riquewihr, the wine capital of Alsace, even the smallest wine stores offer kirsch, William pear, *quetsch*, plum, raspberry and wild raspberry, quince, strawberry and wild strawberry, sloe, mirabelle, elder, blackcurrant, sorb, pine bud, blueberry, gentiane, holly berry, and wild rose (intriguingly called *gratte-cul*).

Strasbourg rivals Munich in claiming to be the beer capital of the world. Certainly Mutzig, Meteor, and Kronenbourg are internationally known beers. Nine-tenths of Alsatian beer is exported, and the quantity produced is a quarter of France's total output. This is not to say that Alsatian beer is not appreciated at home. Alsatians enjoy their beer as much as their wine and still prefer to drink it from an earthenware mug rather than a glass. The museums of Strasbourg and Colmar preserve many handsome old beer mugs with the coats of arms of religious communities, bishops, and noblemen.

In the eighteenth and nineteenth centuries every village or town had its potter, making domestic and agricultural crocks. Now there are just two centers left, both in northern Alsace, that specialize in earthenware. Soufflenheim potters, whose shops are all along the main street of the village, make lead-glazed pottery often in bright colors and decorated with flowers, animals, and inscriptions. In Oberbetschdorf they make gray salt-glazed stoneware with blue ornaments. The museums of the region have handsome examples of early work in both styles.

The Musée des Beaux Arts in Strasbourg has a splendid collection of dishes and terrines in the form of cabbages, cauliflower, turkeys, ducks, and geese, made by three generations of the Hannong family in the eighteenth century. The Musée Alsacien in Strasbourg and the Unterlinden Museum in Colmar both have excellent collections of wooden gingerbread molds, glazed earthenware and copper molds for *kugelhopfs* and other cakes, and iron molds for waffles and wafers. The molds are in a variety of forms: Fish were used for New Year's cakes, crayfish as a symbol of fertility for wedding cakes, stars for Christmas, and the lamb for Easter.

The purple quetsch *plum, nearly tasteless when raw, is ideal for baking, however, because once cooked it develops a rich plum flavor. At the Maison des Tanneurs in Strasbourg, another version of the* tarte aux quetsches, *opposite, is cooked in a flan ring. The plums, boiled with sugar and water, are arranged over a plum-flavored* crème pâtissière, *baked, sprinkled with sugar, and served warm. Situated on the Ill river, the Auberge d'Ill has a garden for warm-weather dining. Two of its dessert specialties, right, are the* gâteau du chef, *a butter-cream layer cake, and a fresh strawberry tart, both to be eaten with a glass of cold Sylvaner.*

RÂBLE DE LIÈVRE AUX NOUILLES FRAÎCHES *Saddle of Hare with Freshly Made Noodles*

If you eat fresh noodles frequently, it might be worth investing in a pasta machine, which helps to knead the dough and roll it out. However, it can also be done by hand in the traditional way, as below.

1 large saddle of hare
8 tablespoons butter, melted (100 g)
½ cup *crème fraîche*—see Appendix—or heavy cream (125 ml)
Salt, freshly ground pepper

FOR THE MARINADE
1 bottle Riesling
1 sprig each of fresh thyme and parsley
1 bay leaf
1 carrot, cut into rounds
1 onion, finely sliced
Pinch of ground coriander
Pinch of grated nutmeg

FOR THE NOODLES
3 cups flour (400 g)
3 eggs
1 tablespoon oil (15 ml)
¼ teaspoon salt
Flour (for dusting)

Prepare the marinade by putting all of the ingredients in a saucepan and bringing them to a boil. Pour the hot mixture over the hare and set aside for 24 hours.

To prepare the noodles: arrange the flour in a mound on a board and make a well in the center. Put in the eggs, oil, and salt and start to draw in the flour, mixing it to a paste with the fingertips of one hand. If the dough seems too dry, add a little water. Break the dough into little pieces and crush and smear them across the working top with the palm of your hand, then scrape them up and put them all together to form a mass. Do this 2 or 3 times and then leave the dough to rest, covered with a damp cloth for 1 hour; do not refrigerate. Cut the dough into 4 pieces. On a floured cloth, roll out each piece into a large rectangle, making it as thin as possible. Then sprinkle lightly with flour, and cut into ¼-inch strips. Separate the noodles and spread them out loosely on a dish towel; let them dry for 30 minutes. They can now be kept for up to 3 days in an airtight tin or a plastic container.

To cook the hare: first marinate it in the white wine marinade for 24 hours. Preheat the oven to 375°F. Remove the hare from the marinade and pat it dry; reserve the marinade. Roast for 40 minutes, basting with the melted butter. Pierce the meat with a skewer; it is perfectly cooked when the juices run clear.

Remove the saddle to a heated dish and deglaze the roasting pan with some of the marinade. Add the *crème fraîche*, simmer for a moment, taste, and season if necessary.

Just before you serve the hare, cook the noodles. Bring a large pot of salted water to a boil and cook them for 2 to 3 minutes; then drain. If you like them tender, as the French prefer them, take the pan off the heat and leave the noodles to poach in their cooking water for a further 5 minutes.

Put the saddle on top of the noodles, pour some of the sauce over the top, and serve the rest separately. Some cooks add *morels* (wild mushrooms) to the sauce.

for 6 people / photograph on page 110

CUISSES DE GRENOUILLES AU RIESLING *Frogs' Legs Cooked in Riesling*

24 frogs' legs
Dry white wine
A little flour
8 tablespoons butter (100 g)
Salt, freshly ground pepper

FOR THE SAUCE
2 shallots, chopped
1 clove garlic, chopped
1 tablespoon chopped parsley
¼ bottle dry white wine, preferably Riesling
½ cup *crème fraîche*—see Appendix—or heavy cream (125 ml)
1 egg yolk
Salt, freshly ground pepper
Pinch of grated nutmeg (optional)
A little chopped parsley or other herbs

Buy ready-prepared frogs' legs and marinate them for 2 hours in dry white wine to cover.

Wipe them dry and dust with flour to make sure that they are very dry, shaking off the excess. Melt the butter in a skillet and sauté the frogs' legs gently without letting them brown. When they are tender and pale golden, season with salt and pepper and transfer them to a dish to keep hot.

Prepare the sauce: in the same butter, sauté the shallots and garlic. When golden, add the parsley and white wine and reduce for 20 minutes over a moderate heat.

Beat the egg yolk with the *crème fraîche* and, away from the heat, bind the sauce with this mixture. Stir over low heat until it thickens. Season with salt and pepper, and add a pinch of nutmeg if you like. Pour this velvety, deliciously scented sauce over the frogs' legs, sprinkle with a little chopped parsley or other herbs, and serve.

for 4 people / photograph opposite

FAISAN À LA CHOUCROUTE   *Pheasant with Sauerkraut*

A *choucroute* can be accompanied by an infinite variety of things—from all sorts of sausages, *boudins* and *quenelles*, various kinds of salt pork, bacon, and ham (smoked or unsmoked), to *confits* of goose or duck. It can also be cooked with game, as in this recipe, where it is partnered by a pheasant.

1 pheasant, cleaned and plucked
2 pounds sauerkraut (1 kg)
4 tablespoons lard (125 g)
½ pound streaky bacon, cut into thick slices (250 g)
1 onion, stuck with a clove
2 bouquets garnis—see Appendix
3 cloves garlic
8 juniper berries
About ¾ cup white wine (200 ml)
About ¾ cup homemade chicken stock (200 ml)
1 *cervelas* boiling sausage
Pork fat (for covering the pheasant)
1 onion, sliced
1 carrot, sliced
Salt, freshly ground pepper

Wash the sauerkraut thoroughly, loosening the strands carefully. Press it lightly in a colander to strain off all the liquid. Grease a flameproof casserole with 2 tablespoons of the lard, put in a layer of half the sauerkraut, and add the bacon, the onion stuck with a clove, 1 bouquet garni, the garlic, and juniper berries. Cover with the remaining sauerkraut. Season with pepper but add very little salt, as the bacon is salty. Moisten with the white wine and stock and cover the pan. Cook very gently over low heat for 3 hours, making sure that the sauerkraut does not stick, and adding more wine or stock if necessary. Add the sausage to the sauerkraut after 3 hours.

Now start the pheasant. Truss it and tie slices of pork fat around the bird with a string. Melt the remaining 2 tablespoons of lard in a skillet and brown the pheasant on all sides. Add the sliced onion and carrot and the second bouquet garni and season with salt and pepper. Cover the pan and cook gently for 40 minutes, basting the pheasant frequently with its cooking juices. If it seems too dry, add a few tablespoons of chicken stock.

When ready to serve, carve the pheasant into pieces. Pile the sauerkraut on a dish with the pheasant pieces, the sausage cut in thick slices, and the pieces of bacon.

Deglaze the cooking juices from the pheasant with a little chicken stock and serve separately in a sauceboat.

for 4 people / photograph above

118

SALADE DE MATELOTE *Freshwater Fish in a Salad*

2 whole trout, weighing about ½ pound each, cleaned
  and gutted (200 g)
½ pound eel, skinned (250 g)
½ pound pike fillets (250 g)
2 medium carrots
¼ pound very thin green beans (100 g)
¾ cup white wine (200 ml)
1 head of lettuce
¼ pound watercress (100 g)
4 mushrooms, thinly sliced
1 small onion, chopped
1 lemon, quartered
Freshly ground pepper

FOR THE COURT-BOUILLON
A few slices carrot and onion
1 lemon slice
Salt, freshly ground pepper
1 bay leaf
1 clove
¾ cup white wine (200 ml)

FOR THE DRESSING
4 tablespoons sunflower oil (60 ml)
1 tablespoon wine vinegar (15 ml)
1 tablespoon sherry vinegar (15 ml)
¼ cup *crème fraîche*—see Appendix—or heavy cream
  (60 ml)
Juice of 1 lemon
Salt, freshly ground pepper

Combine all of the ingredients for the *court-bouillon*,
  except the wine, in a saucepan, along with 2 cups of
  water, bring to a boil, and simmer for 15 minutes.
Peel the carrots, cut into rounds, and cook in boiling
  salted water for 10 minutes. Cook the green beans in
  boiling salted water for 5 minutes. Drain the vegetables and set aside at room temperature.
To poach the fish: add the wine to the prepared *court-
  bouillon*. Cut the eels into 8 pieces, and simmer in the
  liquid for 10 minutes. Add the trout to the pan, and
  simmer for a further 3 minutes. Cut the pike fillets
  into 8 pieces, put them in, and cook for 2 minutes.
  Remove all of the fish from the cooking liquid and let
  cool slightly.
To serve, put the lettuce leaves on individual plates and
  arrange some watercress and mushrooms over them.
  Mix the ingredients for the dressing together and
  sprinkle over the salad. Fillet the trout, place a fillet in
  the center of each plate, and surround with pieces of
  eel and pike. Sprinkle on chopped onion. Garnish
  with rounds of carrot and small bundles of beans. Put
  a quarter of lemon on each fillet of trout and sprinkle
  with freshly ground pepper just before serving. The
  dish should be served lukewarm.

for 4 people

TARTE AUX QUETSCHES *Quetsch Plum Tart*

The *quetsch* is a long, oval black plum, which is tasteless when raw, but develops an unmistakable, rich
flavor when cooked.

1 recipe *pâte brisée*—see Appendix
2 pounds *quetsch* plums (1 kg)
1½ cups sugar (300 g)
4 eggs
1 cup flour (150 g)
⅔ cup milk or cream (150 ml)
¼ cup *eau-de-vie de prune* or mirabelle (60 ml)
Powdered sugar (for sprinkling)

Pit the plums and combine with 1 cup sugar. Cook
  them for 15 minutes, until tender; allow them to
  cool. (A few cracked plumstones, tied in a piece of

muslin and cooked with the plums, give a subtle
  flavor to the dish.)
Preheat the oven to 425°F. Line a large (10-inch) flan
  ring or a false-bottom cake pan with the pastry. Bake
  it blind in the usual way and allow to cool.
Meanwhile, prepare the filling. Beat the eggs, adding
  the flour, then the milk, and the remaining ½ cup
  sugar to make a smooth batter. Beat in the *eau-de-vie*.
  Fill the pastry crust with the cooked plums and the
  filling mixture.
Bake for 25 minutes, until set, protecting the top of
  the crust (by covering it with aluminum foil) if
  necessary. Serve lukewarm or cold, with powdered
  sugar sprinkled on top.

for 8 people / photographs on pages 113 and 114

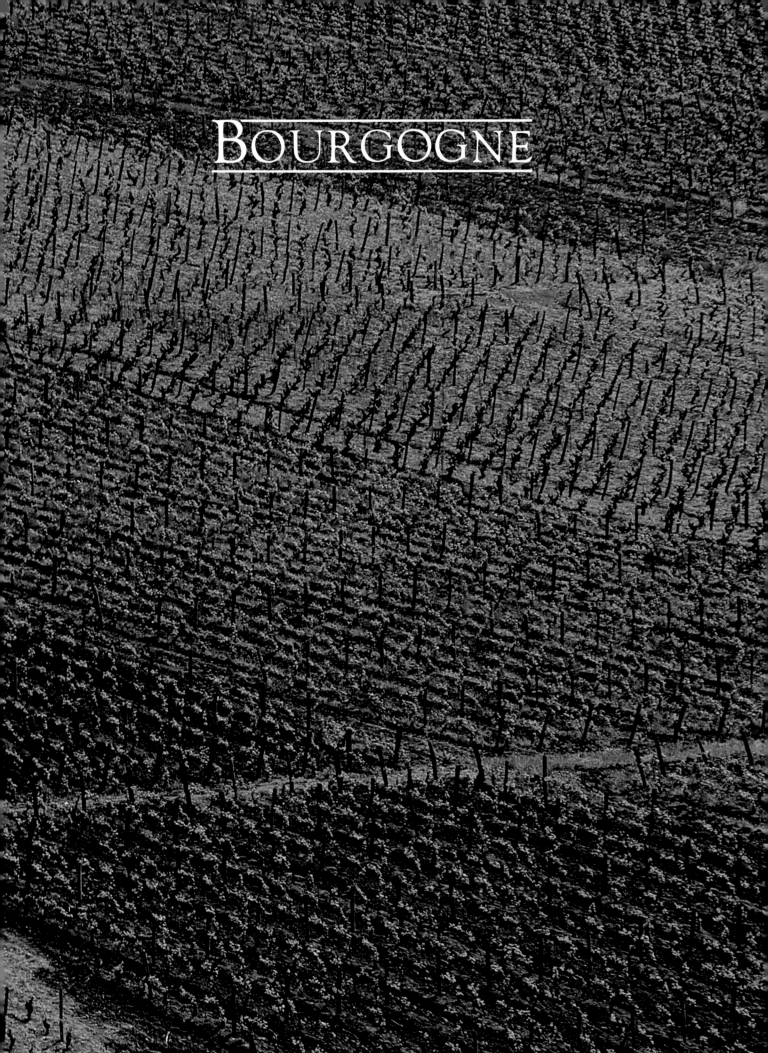

BOURGOGNE

BURGUNDY

URGUNDY is a rich and fruitful plain, confined on the east by the Jura mountains and on the west by the granite mass of the Morvan. In contemporary terms, it is usually defined as consisting of four departments, the Côte d'Or, the Nièvre, Saône-et-Loire, and the Yonne, but there is good reason to include the regions of Bugey and Bresse, which are within the departments of the Ain.

Bugey is famous in the annals of gastronomy because its chief town is Belley, the birthplace of Brillat-Savarin (1775–1826), a lawyer whose most famous book, *The Physiology of Taste,* is regarded as the bible of gourmets. One of these gourmets felt that considering the book a bible was not sufficient, and that the Christian religion could not honor Brillat-Savarin enough, so he wanted a mosque to be erected at Bugey, where at regular intervals a muezzin would summon the faithful with the cry, "There is one God, Brillat, and Savarin is his prophet."

Bresse, with its capital at Bourg-en-Bresse, belonged (like Bugey) to the House of Savoy, and as far as records go back, its farmers have raised the most famous poultry in France. The market, with its *volaille,*

In a corner of the vineyards of Mercurey, near Aubigny, plots belonging to different farmers are separated by narrow paths, preceding overleaf. In the village of Eguilly, top, the simple elegance of burgundian architecture complements the graceful landscape. Opposite: Citeaux, Brillat-Savarin (poised on the Citeaux), and various chèvres *are favorites among the cheeses. Pommard and Savigny-les-Beaunes are red Burgundies; Meursault is a white wine. Blackcurrants are used to make cassis, a gentle fermentation of the fruit with a dash of marc. The loaf is* pain d'épices; *the oval cakes are a smaller version topped with a* glacé; *and the little cakes in foil are* nonnettes.

which are soaked in milk to give a gleaming whiteness to the skin, is a tourist attraction in itself.

The addition of Bugey and Bresse to Burgundy further enriches the gastronomic variety of an already rich area. Indeed, some would say it is wrong to talk about Burgundian cooking. Just as the world-famous wines around the Hautes-Côtes of Beaune are very different from the many local wines to be found in Bugey, for example, or around Tannay, in the Nièvre department, so it is said that the term *cuisine bourguignonne* is too vast to be meaningful.

One should talk, rather, of a whole series of different *pays*. That of the Morvan, for example, with its many rivers, which have the reputation of producing the finest of fish, with its forests, which are the home of remarkable game, its valleys, which produce delicate mushrooms. The inhabitants of this area, which even today remains somewhat isolated, are not far removed from the times in the nineteenth century when the northern women were reputed to be the best midwives and were heavily in demand in Paris, and the southern women were famous laundresses, and *la cuisine de Morvan* is similarly specialized and idiosyncratic. That famous gourmet and mayor of Lyons, Edouard Herriot, appreciated it. When he was the leader of the Radical Party and the President of the National Assembly, he would return to Paris at times of crisis, but when the newspaper headlines said, "The Republic is in danger: M. Herriot is on his way back," those who knew him knew that part of his hasty return involved his sitting in a restaurant in Saulieu, or Rouvray, or Avallon, napkin tucked under chin, and appetite aroused.

In contrast, there is *la cuisine de Dijon*, which is associated with the dukes of Burgundy. It is said that whereas other men had ovens in their kitchens, the dukes had kitchens in their ovens. Their receptions were famous for the quality of the fare.

Farther south, near the Charolais beef area, the Mâconnais forms yet another region. To the east the quantities of food eaten seem to grow, and are dominated by large chickens and by crayfish, *sauce Nantua*, truffles, and morels.

However, if one must generalize about Burgundian cooking, it is often said that it is based on four principles: wine, cream, pork fat, and pastry. There is controversy about cooking in wine, since many claim that the best results can be obtained only by using the best wines—and even that the wine drunk with a dish should be the same as that in which it is cooked. Thus a *soupe d'escargots au Meursault* (a specialty of the Beaune region) should be accompanied by this great white Burgundy. On the other hand, some prefer the cooking to be based on more ordinary, rougher wines, especially when a recipe entails a fairly long cooking time and the addition of herbs. At all events, wine is used in a *marinade*,

A Poulet de Bresse, *opposite, with the ingredients to make a* Poulet de Bresse en civet, *was fed on corn, buckwheat, and milk, and then bathed in milk; it must have an official stamp to be marketed under the name. In the market of Bourg-en-Bresse, below left, an area is reserved for small farmers to sell their produce—eggs, vegetables, cornichons, cheese, even flowers, and, of course, chickens. A supplier brings in his chickens live and by the crateful, center. An experienced shopper, right, gauges the quality of a chicken by the color of the skin of its legs.*

as a *meurette* or red wine sauce, and in a *matelote* or fish stew made with wine (sometimes called *pochouse* or *pauchouse*). *Marc* (a powerful spirit distilled from the skins and seeds of pressed grapes after the wine has been made), vinegar, or *verjus* (a wine that has soured, sometimes called *vin vert*) can also be used. The phrase *à la bourguignonne* invariably means cooked in wine.

The cream should not be the ordinary storebought type. With typical attention to detail, the Burgundians prefer cream scooped with a wooden spoon from milk that has been standing for some time. It has a nutty taste and, as most vegetables in Burgundy can be served *à la crème* (cabbage, turnips, spinach, asparagus, summer squash, beet), as can

Pochouse bourguignonne, *below, is a fish stew cooked in wine—here, in Chambertin—as prepared by M. Hure, chef of the Hostellerie de la Poste in Avallon. It is best savored with a glass of the same red Burgundy. An assortment of freshwater fish, opposite, and, if possible, crayfish are the basis of* pochouse. *They are browned with bacon and onions, then cooked with herbs, cloves, and the wine, flamed with* marc, *then served with mushrooms, garlic* croûtons, *and, perhaps, a bit of cream.*

many special dishes (mushrooms and sweetbreads especially), the cream is regarded as important.

The pork fat is no longer so often made by the housewife and kept for months in earthenware dishes, but it is bought from the butcher, rather than in packets from the supermarket. In Burgundy this is the basis for cooking, as is butter in Normandy or oil in the south, although these can also be used.

As for the pastry, the expert on traditions recommends the preparation of a whole ball of dough on Wednesday so it will be ready on Sunday when it is most likely to be in demand. In Burgundy traditional pastry dishes are used at all times: The *gougère*, for example, which is made with grated cheese, usually a Gruyère these days but traditionally an expensive cheese from Franche-Comté, should be served as an appetizer. Some good restaurants will serve small *gougères*, hot or cold, with *apéritifs*. There is also *chorlatte*, diced pumpkin enclosed in pastry and baked in a cabbage leaf, which is a vegetable course, *galette au fromage* (made with short pastry), which is a savory dish, and, of course, many desserts.

THERE are other remarkable ingredients in the region, like the snails around which a great deal of local knowledge is proudly displayed. But, while it is agreed that they are best when collected when they leave their winter hibernation and before the warm days of April, there is disagreement as to whether snails should be kept without nourishment for some ten days, or should be fed for a week or so on lettuce, fresh water, and thyme.

Mustard is a specialty of Dijon, and no less a person than Bossuet, who was born there and who became Bishop of Meaux ("L'Aigle de Meaux"), explained to the Duke of Burgundy at the end of the seventeenth century how to mix the right quantities of mustard seed and unfermented wine. Today, Dijon mustard comes in all strengths and colors (yellow or brown when made with vinegar or white wine, red when made *aux quatre fruits*, green *aux trois herbes*).

Then there is cassis, or blackcurrant juice to which wine and a little *marc* have been added. Cassis and white wine are the ingredients that make up the *apéritif* now known as *Kir*, after the famous Canon Kir, mayor of Dijon, who died in 1968. This drink was known long before Kir's time, but he always served it at official receptions. He was very well known in the region, and his small figure, in a black *soutane*, was often seen in the post office or in local stores. He had wide sympathies; he was a Catholic priest with communist leanings, yet with a great affection for the United States, which caused him

to keep the flag of Dallas in his mayoral office and to talk frequently of being an honorary citizen of that city. He liked being asked about the correct proportions for a *Kir*, and always avoided committing himself. A *Kir impérial* is cassis with champagne, and some cafés serve a *communard*, which is cassis with red wine. White wine or champagne is also served with strawberry liqueur.

Finally, there is gingerbread, again a product of the Dijon region. *Pain d'épices* and *nonnettes* (a fortunate mixture of honey and almonds) are commodities that conjure up the thought of medieval fairs and the belief that no man was really famous until his effigy had been constructed in Dijon gingerbread.

130

Charolais, a Burgundian breed of beef cattle named for the town of Charolles, graze in a field near Pouilly-en-Auxois, preceding overleaf. The crop in flower behind them is rape. One of the largest cattle markets in Europe is in Saint-Christophe-en-Brionnais, above, which specializes in Charolais. It is open one morning a week and attracts buyers and sellers from all over the continent. By dawn, deals are sealed over a drink in a café, left, in the market, and when the drinking and dealing are done, a proper midday meal can be had—at 9 A.M.

ALTHOUGH Burgundy was always a favored land, it was also one with the same rural poverty as in other parts of France. Some traditional recipes recall these years of poverty. A *daube* was not the very special meal that interested the characters of Virginia Woolf's *To the Lighthouse*, but instead a convenient food for the vineyard workers to take with them for midday. In general, the chuck or neck of beef was first marinated and then placed in a dish that had been lined with pigskin, accompanied by a large veal bone, and allowed to cook for three or four hours. When cold, it was kept in its jelly and cut into slices, thereby lasting for several days.

A *soupe aux beursades* was a simple concoction of cooking fat, boiling water, and bread. In more recent but still fairly primitive times an agricultural worker might well begin his day with a combination of lard and bread, washed down with a glass of light wine.

There are, however, many Burgundian soups that are rather more appealing to us today. *Potage de Morvan* consists of cabbages, potatoes, and lardons; *soupe au vin* is made from carrots, onions, turnips, and white of leek, which are lightly fried before being covered in red wine and then cooked in beef stock with tapioca; and a rarity from the Mâcon region, *potage Brémont*, is made from milk and fresh walnuts.

The *potée bourguignonne*, a frequent preparation these days, is a remarkable achievement. Two pounds of shin of beef cut into small cubes are cooked with a small chicken, a good piece of slightly salted pork, an uncooked garlic sausage, a cabbage heart, potatoes, leeks, celery, and turnips. After about five hours, the liquid is served poured over slices of bread; the meat and vegetables are served separately.

The most famous Burgundy dishes are undoubtedly *bœuf bourguignon* and *coq au vin*. Curiously, the former does not exist in some of the early books on *la cuisine bourguignonne*, and, even more curiously, there are recipes that recommend that the cooking be done in champagne and Madeira.

One of the secrets of *bœuf bourguignon*, or *bœuf à la bourguignonne*, is that after the marinated beef (topside) has cooked in wine for about four hours with a calf's foot, onions, *lardons*, herbs, and mushroom stems, the meat should be removed and the liquid passed through a fine sieve. Then the cooking should be resumed for another hour, with the calf's foot cut into small pieces and the mushroom caps added. Another version of the dish uses oxtail, finely sliced, with the addition of carrots and grapes (*queue de bœuf vigneronne*). It is also possible to use sirloin and white wine, but this dish (*aloyau braisé à la nivernaise*) should be accompanied by carrots, and the sauce served separately.

The *coq au vin* and other versions of chicken were so common that farmhands used to insist that they should not be served more than three times a week.

Game is also cooked in wine, and various recipes are attached to Burgundian folklore because of the old tradition whereby the *seigneur* would allow the villagers to hunt on his lands at Easter. *Râble de lièvre à la Piron* recalls a well-known family from the Dijon region, while *civet de Capucin* suggests the good living that was often associated with the religious orders. The former is marinated for two days in *marc* with shallots and herbs, the latter for only one day in white wine with *marc* and shallots and herbs. The former, if served during the wine harvest, can have grapes to accompany it; the latter is usually served with boiled potatoes. *Lièvre à la royale* is probably a poacher's dish and can rarely be found nowadays, since it requires drawing the unskinned hare and salting the inside. The whole is then covered in clay and cooked in a bright wood fire for an hour and served with mushrooms.

PROBABLY the essential reason that wine has become an integral part of Burgundy cooking is that the Catholic population became so bored with the interminable fish dishes. It was not until the 1830s that any sea fish other than salted herring reached the area in reasonable condition, and that was cod. So ways of making fish more interesting were sought, and doubtless the Saône valley, or the area of other rivers such as the Doubs, were the source of various forms of *pochouse* or *pauchouse*, which probably recalls a *patois* name for a *pêcheur*, or fisherman.

You take a variety of fish such as pike, perch, eel, carp, and crayfish. Some modern recipes suggest that you simply remove the heads, but the more traditional recipe requires you to make a stock with the heads, onions, and white wine. This you sieve and pour over the fish as they cook in butter. You can add *marc* and flambé the whole. Finally, remove the fish and reduce the sauce and then stir in a spoonful of cream. The presentation is very important. Arrange *croûtons* rubbed in garlic in a circle on the dish, place the fish in the middle, and pour the sauce over them before serving.

Eggs played an important part in the folklore of Burgundy, especially around Easter, but as with fish it was always thought necessary to make them more interesting by cooking them in wine, like *œufs en*

Among the riches of Burgundy, opposite (clockwise from top left), are simple and sophisticated foods and scenes, all utterly French: pâté de poisson cressonière has a watercress sauce and a tomato carved into a rose; fishing on the Saône is best at dawn; an exotic entrée is made of cockscombs and a partridge egg, with a casserolette d'écrevisses; quinces ripen on the tree; a Swiss chard dish with Fourme, a blue cheese, is from *the Restaurant Troisgros in Roanne; the café is Chez Lulu in Chauffailles; lamb kidneys are cooked en brochette with bacon and mushrooms; an assortment of cheeses—goat's-milk cheeses for spring and summer, cow's-milk cheeses for the rest of the year; and an array of Burgundian candies, most of them fruit-flavored.*

meurette, which caused Madame de Sévigné to become so tipsy that she felt obliged to make a special confession. *Œufs en bourguignonne* is a similar recipe but involves poaching the eggs directly in the wine and keeping them warm in the oven, while turning the wine into a *roux* with butter and flour.

Eggs can also be cooked with Dijon mustard. For *œufs à la dijonnaise*, cut hard-boiled eggs lengthwise; mix the yolks with mustard, cream, chopped shallots, and herbs; pour this mixture into the whites, adding butter and a drop of vinegar; and put the eggs in a hot oven for ten minutes. When cooking with mustard, remember that the longer it cooks, the more it is liable to lose its flavor.

In Burgundy, ham was the traditional dish at Easter. On great family occasions it was customary to serve a whole ham. This was a sign of the real Burgundian approach to the cuisine. It is often cooked in white wine, as in the *jambon persillé*, but it can also be cooked with other sauces, such as the *saupiquet des amognes*, which depends on a peppery sauce, sometimes known as *sauce espagnole*.

In addition to the Burgundians' attention to the taste of food, they show great concern with display.

Homemade cheese dries in the open air, above, on a small farm in La Fourche, near Charolles. In Beaune, below, the pâtissière *is Mme. Bazeron, and her delicacies are* gougères, *puffs of cheese pastry, which often accompany a glass of Burgundy. The brother and sister Moindrot, below right, of tiny Thoisy le Desert, with their morning bread delivery—a* couronne *and a* pain de campagne. *The Canal de Bourgogne, opposite, near Bovey, is used today primarily by fishermen and tourist barges.*

The village of Pommard clings to the edge of its famous vineyards, left, and the Clos de la Commaraine (upper left), the château that bottles the wine from these vines. A well-trained horse, top, plowing a vineyard in Pruzilly where Julienas is produced, stops on its own if the plow hits a vine root. On the Louis Latour estate, above, near Beaune, the vendangeurs pick the grapes in the fall. Later, in another vineyard near Mâcon, natives pick over the harvested vines for late-ripening grapes from which they make their own wine.

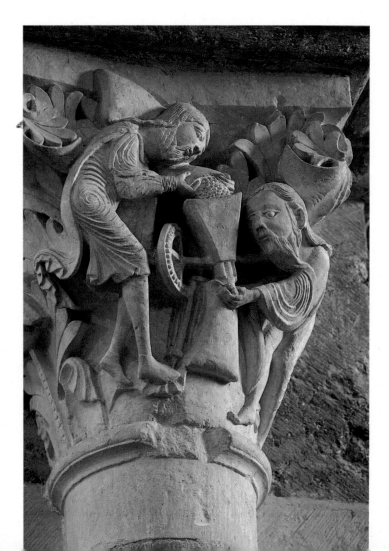

The cellar of the Hostellerie de la Poste in Avallon, above, is known for its wines from other regions as well as its Burgundies. Nearby, in the Romanesque basilica of Vézelay, left, the subject of a stone carving is the crushing of the grapes. Tasting his wine, opposite top, André Noblet-Adnot, master of the cellar of the great Domaine de la Romanée-Conti, near Beaune, demonstrates the basic steps: studying the color, sniffing the bouquet, and, finally, tasting a small sample by swirling it around in his mouth as he inhales. Meanwhile he keeps the cork in his left hand to assess its moisture. M. Leblanc, below, a traditional vintner of Pernand-Vergelesses, tastes a pressing of his excellent white wine.

Jambon persillé, *opposite, is a familiar* en gêlée *dish in which ham—cooked in wine, onions, shallots, garlic, cloves, and herbs—is layered in a bowl with chopped parsley and set in the cooking liquids. The recipe of Marc Chevillot of the Hôtel de la Poste in Beaune also includes lemons, carrots, leeks, and tomatoes. The white Burgundy Bourgogne Aligoté is the usual accompaniment. A* charcuterie *in this part of France, right, posts the dates of its annual closing (in the bottom right corner)—not in August, when the tourists arrive, but during the quieter fall.*

Good restaurants serve impressive salads containing lamb's lettuce (*mâche*), celery leaves, purple *Roquette*, endives, *salade frisée*, and other leaves. Quail is presented surrounded by grapes. A tart of poached pears and custard and grated almonds looks as if it is posing for a photographer.

The Burgundian writer Henri Vincenot claims that in matters of cooking it is necessary to dream up recipes and menus. He cites a friend of his, a doctor, who had the idea of injecting kirsch liqueur beneath the skin of a hare as it was hanging, just to see how it affected the taste of the *civet*.

If you are worried that so much wine, cream, *viandes en sauces*, and other rich food is liable to upset you, and perhaps bring on high blood pressure or gout, the Burgundian will recommend that you take garlic to prevent the former, and will tell you that in Roman times those who suffered from gout were excused from paying taxes because they were an élite. Perhaps it is best not to ask if either is true. You wouldn't want to make yourself conspicuous.

GOUGÈRE

This is a *choux* pastry made with cheese. It is eaten cold or lukewarm throughout Burgundy and is an excellent accompaniment to Burgundy wines. You can make it a marvelous appetizer by garnishing the *gougère* as you would a *vol-au-vent*: with a *sauce marinère*, with sautéed mushrooms, with a *sauce Nantua*, with kidneys Rossini, with fresh vegetables—whichever you prefer.

9 tablespoons butter (125 g)
Pinch of salt
2 cups flour, sifted (250 g)
5 large eggs
½ pound Gruyère cheese, thinly sliced (225 g)
Salt, freshly ground pepper
1 egg, beaten

In a saucepan, combine the butter, salt, and 1½ cups of water. Bring to a boil, remove from the heat, and add the flour all at once. Mix with a wooden spoon. Return to the heat and stir until the compact mixture dries out and comes away easily from the pan, 2 or 3 minutes.

Preheat the oven to 350°F. Remove the pan from the heat and add the 5 eggs one by one, mixing each one until well blended. Add the Gruyère, and season with salt and pepper.

Butter a baking sheet and arrange the pastry in a ring or in little balls. Glaze with the beaten egg and bake for about 40 minutes, until golden. (The circular arrangement takes longer to cook than the little balls.)

for 6 people / photograph on page 134

ESCARGOTS AU CHABLIS   *Snails with Chablis*

4 dozen live snails, or 2 7½-ounce cans of imported snails, drained, and 48 snail shells
Handful of coarse salt
¾ cup vinegar (200 ml)
2 cups Chablis (½ liter)
2 cups good chicken stock (½ liter)
1 large bouquet garni—see Appendix
2 shallots
1 clove garlic
Salt
¼ cup *marc de Bourgogne* (60 ml)
About 1 cup fine dried breadcrumbs (125 g)

FOR THE SNAIL BUTTER
1½ cups butter, softened (350 g)
1 clove garlic, finely chopped
2 shallots, finely chopped
1 tablespoon chopped parsley
Salt, freshly ground pepper

The basic method of preparing snails never varies. If using live snails for this recipe, feed them nothing but a few tablespoons of flour for a week; this will purge them of any poisonous plants they may have been eating. When ready to cook them, wash several times, soak in the coarse salt and water acidulated with vinegar for 2 hours, then wash once again in plenty of clean water. Blanch them in boiling water for 5 to 6 minutes.

In a saucepan, combine the snails with the Chablis and the stock. Add the bouquet garni, shallots, garlic, salt, and the *marc*. Simmer, so that the liquid is barely trembling, for 3 hours. Allow the snails to cool in the cooking liquid.

If using canned snails, combine the Chablis, stock, bouquet garni, shallots, garlic, and salt in a saucepan. Bring to a boil and simmer for 20 minutes. Add the snails and cook over medium-low heat for 10 minutes. Remove the pan from the heat and allow the snails to cool in the liquid. Place a snail in each shell.

Meanwhile, prepare the snail butter. Combine the garlic, shallots, parsley, and butter; season with salt and pepper.

Preheat the oven to 350°F. Put some snail butter in each

shell and arrange the shells in a flameproof gratin dish. Sprinkle with the breadcrumbs and a few drops of Chablis. Bake the snails for a few minutes until heated through; increase the heat to about 425°F and bake until the butter starts to sizzle. Serve immediately.

Serve a hazelnut sorbet after eating the snails. It is said to get rid of the lingering garlic taste and to help digestion.

for 4 people / photograph opposite

ŒUFS EN MEURETTE OU ŒUFS À LA BOURGUIGNONNE *Eggs in Red Wine Sauce*

6 eggs
½ bottle red Burgundy
1 bouquet garni—see Appendix
1 onion, sliced
Sliver of garlic
Salt, freshly ground pepper
2 teaspoons sugar
2 tablespoons butter, softened (25g)
2 tablespoons flour (20 g)
3 slices of white bread, trimmed and fried in butter

Pour the wine into a saucepan and add the bouquet garni, onion, garlic, pepper, and sugar. Simmer for 20 minutes or more until the liquid has reduced by half, then strain and return to the pan.

Put the pan back over a gentle heat, then break the eggs one by one into a small bowl and slip them into the simmering liquid. Cover the pan, remove from heat, and leave it for 3 minutes. Carefully remove the eggs with a skimmer and keep warm without letting them cook any further.

Make *beurre manié* by working the softened butter and flour together into a paste. Skim the sauce again to remove any bits of egg white. Taste and add salt and pepper if necessary. Return the liquid to the heat and add the *beurre manié*, stirring gently until it thickens.

Trim the eggs (cutting away any irregular bits of white around the edges). Place them on the bread in soup plates and pour over the hot red wine sauce.

for 3 people

COQ AU VIN *Cockerel Stewed in Red Wine*

1 4-pound capon (1¾ kg)
5 to 6 tablespoons butter (60 to 75 g)
¼ pound streaky bacon, diced (125 g)
12 button onions
½ pound button mushrooms, cleaned and quartered (250 g)
¼ cup flour (30 g)
2 cloves garlic, crushed
1 bottle red Burgundy
1 bouquet garni—see Appendix
4 to 5 tablespoons *marc de Bourgogne*
Salt, freshly ground pepper
3 tablespoons chicken's blood or pig's blood (optional; if you cannot obtain this, the dish is still worth making)
½ pound *croûtons*, painted with melted butter and toasted—see Appendix (200 g)

Have the chicken cut into 8 pieces and reserve the liver separately. Season the pieces with salt and pepper. Melt 2 tablespoons of the butter in a large casserole and brown the bacon and onions. In a separate pan, melt 2 tablespoons butter and sauté the mushrooms.

When the bacon and onions are nicely browned, remove them with a slotted spoon and reserve, and put the pieces of chicken into the same casserole.

Sauté the chicken pieces until golden. Sprinkle with the flour and let it brown a little, adding more butter if necessary. Add the garlic and the wine. Bring to a boil and then add the sautéed mushrooms, the reserved bacon and onion mixture, bouquet garni, *marc*, and salt and pepper.

Cover and simmer for 45 minutes. Remove the chicken, mushrooms, onions, and bacon and keep them hot in a deep dish.

Strain the sauce into a saucepan, taste it for seasoning, and place it over a low heat.

Cut the chicken liver into small pieces and sauté them rapidly in about ½ to 1 tablespoon of butter, then purée them in a blender together with the blood. Put the puréed liver mixture in a saucepan and pour the boiling sauce slowly into this purée, whisking.

Cover the pieces of chicken and vegetables with the velvety sauce and serve hot with *croûtons*.

for 6 people

JAMBON PERSILLÉ *Ham Jellied with Parsley*

2 pounds uncooked ham, in 1 piece (1 kg)
½ pound veal shin (shank) (250 g)
2 calves' feet, chopped
2 sprigs each of fresh chervil, tarragon, and thyme
5 onions, 1 stuck with a clove
2 shallots and 1 clove garlic
2 bottles dry white wine, preferably an Aligoté
Generous handful of chopped parsley
Salt
2 tablespoons white wine vinegar

A day in advance, soak the ham overnight in cold water
to cover. Simmer the ham in a large pan of unsalted
water for 1 hour. Drain, rinse in fresh water, drain
again, and put the ham into a large saucepan with the
veal, calves' feet, herbs, and seasonings, except the
vinegar and parsley, and cover with the wine. Bring
to a boil, reduce the heat, cover, and simmer. Cook,
allowing at least 30 minutes per pound, until the ham
is tender enough to be crushed with a fork. Crush all
the ham with a fork, and mix it together with the
other meat and fat.
Place half of the crushed ham mixture into a bowl,
sprinkle with half the chopped parsley, then more
ham, and finally the rest of the parsley.
Strain the cooking liquid and add salt if necessary. Add
the wine vinegar and pour the hot liquid over the
ham. Put it in a cool place and/or refrigerate until it
sets; the jelly should be translucent.
Serve the *jambon persillé* straight from the bowl or
turned out. It is eaten accompanied with a salad.

for 8 people / photograph on page 140

SUPRÊME DE BROCHETON
À LA BOURGUIGNONNE
Supreme of Pike, Burgundy Style

4 whole pike, about ½ pound each (250 to 300 g)
4 tablespoons butter (50 g)
6 shallots
½ pound mushrooms, minced (250 g)
2½ cups Chablis (½ liter)
Salt, freshly ground pepper
½ cup *crème fraîche*—see Appendix (125 ml)

Preheat the oven to 400°F. Butter a deep, oven-proof
dish and add the shallots and the minced mushrooms.
Clean, wash, and dry the pike and lay them on the
other ingredients in the dish. Season with salt and
pepper, moisten with the white wine, and place in
the oven. After 7 or 8 minutes lower the temperature
to 350°F and leave the dish in the oven for another 12
minutes or so, basting the fish frequently.
When the fish are golden brown, add *crème fraîche* to the
sauce. Mix and correct the seasoning.

for 6 people

POUSSIN À LA MOUTARDE *Chicken with Mustard*

1 very small chicken (400 to 500 g)
2 to 3 tablespoons Dijon mustard
½ cup *crème fraîche*—see Appendix—or heavy cream
   (125 ml)
Salt, freshly ground pepper
1 tablespoon butter (15 g)

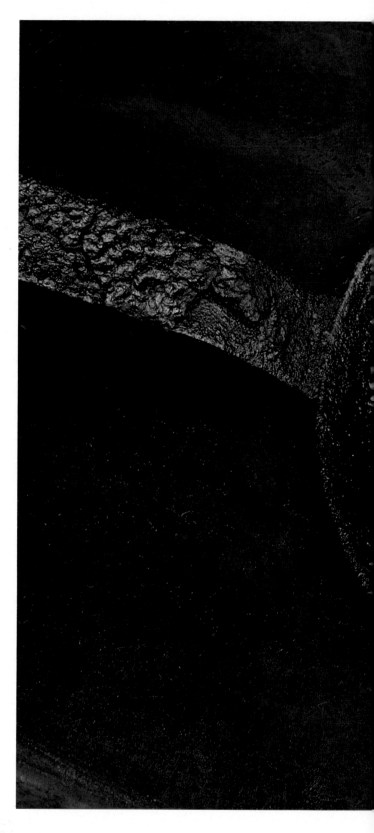

Preheat the oven to 425°F. Truss the chicken and cover it all over with a thick layer of mustard. Bake in a small gratin dish until the mustard turns golden brown, about 40 minutes.

Heat the *crème fraîche* in a small pan. Take the chicken out of the oven and remove any surplus mustard; pour on the *crème fraîche*. Bake for 10 minutes more. To serve, place the chicken on a hot dish. Whisk the sauce, taste it for seasoning, and whisk in the butter just before serving.

for 2 people / photograph below

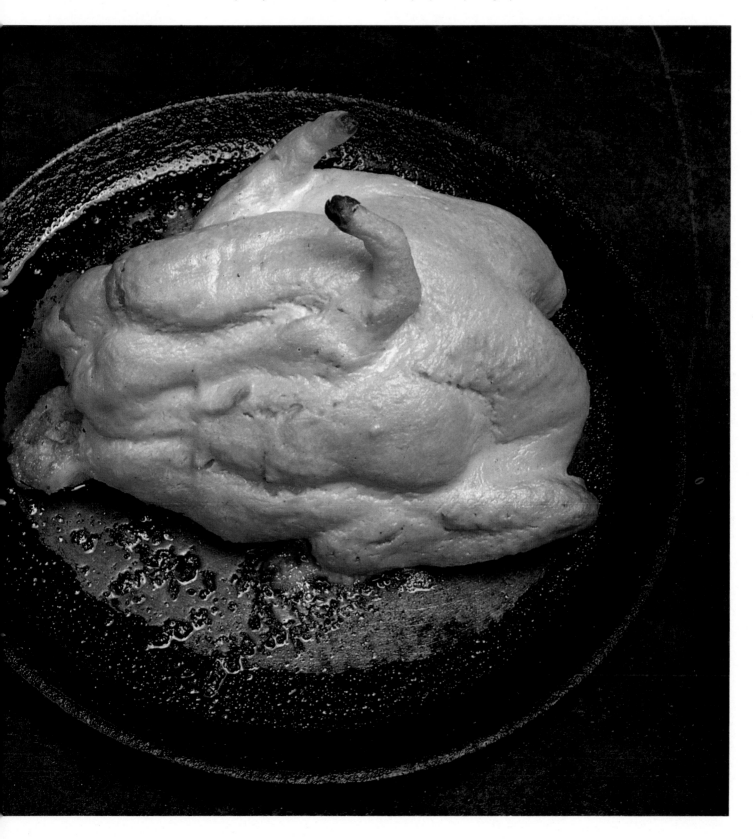

LYONNAIS

LYONNAIS

THE MOST obvious reason for Lyon's reputation as a leading gastronomic center of the world is that it is so well situated —it has access to the very best food supplies. It is near the Dauphiné, one of the first regions of France where potatoes were successfully cultivated (in the seventeenth century); it is near the Charolais for beef, the farms of Bresse for poultry, the Auvergne for lamb, the lakes of the Dombes and Bourget for carp and frogs, Savoy for mushrooms, and innumerable rivers for fish.

And this is not a recent phenomenon, the result of modern marketing. Before the end of the nineteenth century, travelers were enchanted by the animated markets by the Saône. The cheeses alone formed an unbelievable list: white cheese and *tomes* from the Dauphiné, Mont-d'Or from nearby, *tête de moine* from farther east, the red cheese of the Mâconnais and the Cévennes, the blue cheese from Gex (drier than what is known as Bleu de Bresse) and from Septmoncel in the Jura, goat cheeses from the Beaujolais, Saint-Marcellin, and *rigottes* from Condrieu that had been soaked in white wine and preserved in vine leaves. On a Sunday, the *canuts*, or silk workers, would take their

At the versatile L. Barbet café-restaurant in Chaumont, north of Lyon, Mme. Barbet whiles away a summer afternoon over a newspaper, preceding overleaf. Lyon, above, a lively port at the confluence of the Rhone and the Saône rivers, was the meeting ground of international merchants. Over the centuries, a distinctly lyonnaise culture and

cuisine developed, one product of which is Ypocras, opposite, a spiced honey wine made according to a recipe from the Middle Ages. Saffron, two kinds of anise, clove, cinnamon, ginger, and cardamon are combined with Madeira wine and a spoonful of honey to create a concoction that, the Lyonnais claim, stimulates digestion.

weekly walk to the Mont Cindre, in the Saône valley, where they would gather dandelions for salad, or in autumn, rose hips for jelly. There was watercress from the Ozon valley, and cherries and apricots from Vienne and Ampuis. And it is still a weekend pastime to fish for crayfish near the Vivarais, between the Rhône and the Loire.

In addition to all these resources, Lyon is surrounded by the finest of wine countries. The old saying is that Lyon has three rivers, the Rhône, the Saône, and the Beaujolais, and another saying describes Beaujolais as the *café-crème* of the Lyonnais. To the south is the equally famous Côte-Rôtie, and all around lie literally dozens of local wines many of which are excellent but, because they do not travel well, are not widely known. They include perhaps the most tantalizing of white wines, the Château Grillet, said to be the equal of the greatest wines of Bordeaux and Burgundy, but jealously kept away from the intrusive purchaser.

Lyon has always been great and proud enough to withstand the influence of Paris. When the Revolution and Empire decreed centralization, it was often taken for granted that what Paris did was best, in cooking as in everything else. With the educational reforms of the Third Republic, cooking classes for girls and special schools for chefs were organized by the Paris administration. Regional cooking was in danger of becoming relegated to the rank of the quaint. But Lyon, sufficiently rich and independent to preserve its traditions, was the exception.

Then, because its population grew and changed, it was able to maintain a gastronomic culture that renewed itself and developed. Lyon was originally the home of a vast fair, and always a center and a refuge for travelers, so its cooking was dominated by inn and hotel keepers. Just as the wealthy traders and silk manufacturers organized themselves in companies and guilds, so the arts of cooking were protected by a hierarchical system. In pre-Revolu-

tionary days a man who aspired to be a *rôtisseur*, or specialized cook, was apprenticed for four or five years. Then, if he passed very severe tests and satisfied his examiners, he became a *compagnon*. After four or five years at this rank, in order to work independently and to be his own master, he had to create some new masterpiece of cooking. Some of the names of these highly skilled *rôtisseurs* are still remembered, and their menus arouse astonishment and envy today.

But with the industrial revolution Lyon became the home of new social classes. There were different brands of the bourgeoisie, with their aspirations and pretensions, in terms of food, and there was a large working-class population, sufficiently cohesive to forge its own culture in cooking as well as in other matters. It is true that there was great poverty, and frequently the silk workers could afford only soup three times a day—the *soupe de farine jaune*, for example, made from flour, water, and milk. With luck, it would contain small pieces of browned pork or onion, and as rice became more common, it sometimes replaced the flour. But even the poor had their festivities, and how else could

Regional dairy farmers often make their own cheeses and sell them in local markets. Cheesemaking is a painstaking process with several steps, opposite. First, a culture added to the milk causes it to curdle (foreground). Then, the farmer pours the cheese into faisselles, *or perforated molds, adds salt, and lets them drain for a day or two. Once drained, the* faisselles *are overturned onto straw mats, so that air can circulate around the cheeses as they age. A crust gradually forms—the darker the crust, the older the cheese. The nearly white cheeses on the lowest mat are just out of the mold; the darker cheeses above them are about one week old; and the cheeses in the wooden crate (top) are from three to six weeks old. Some regional cow's-milk cheeses, right, include a large, round Tomme de Savoie, with smaller Saint-Marcellins of different ages and sizes in front and on top of it. In the foreground, Chavignols of three different ages are pierced with straws in order to speed their drying and make them easier to handle.*

they celebrate, other than with food and drink? Special dishes, often based on pork (the pig is the most economical of animals, as its entire carcass is edible), became part of Lyon's traditions.

In the middle of the nineteenth century, small eating-houses, called *mâchons*, became a regular part of Lyon life. Workers and middle classes mingled at mid-day, often eating pork and cheese delicacies. The *mâchon*'s modern and still-thriving equivalent is known as a *bouchon*, specializing in meals of sausages and wine. By the end of the nineteenth century, Lyon was famous for its enormous cafés, each with a vast hall usually packed with customers.

Many of the great Lyon dishes are served in the luxury restaurants of the Place Bellecour, or in more humble dwellings in the Croix-Rousse or in the montée des Carmes. They are classless. A recent guide to good restaurants in the city lists no fewer than 168. Some of them maintain the old tradition of being run by women chefs—another example of how Lyon has distinguished itself from Paris.

When eating in one of the more traditional restaurants, it is a good idea to begin with the *gras-double* or the *tablier de sapeur*, both tripe dishes. If the tripe is cut into bigger pieces, say four by three and a half inches, the pieces have the form of an apron. In English this dish is sometimes called erroneously, "fireman's apron." The correct translation would be "sapper's apron"—and *sapper* is a military term, meaning "leather apron": Marshal Castellane, military governor of Lyon during Napoleon III's rule, had been an officer in the engineers, where it was customary to wear a leather apron to protect the uniform, and being a great lover of tripe he gave his title to this dish.

Several pork dishes are made from shaven pig's

skin tied into small packets, called *couennes*, and then poached in stock before being fried in lard with parsley and pepper. *Cochonailles lyonnaises* consist of a pig's head, chine, ears, ribs, trotters, and a *couenne*. Soak these in water overnight before boiling them for at least an hour with onions, carrots, parsley, and other herbs and seasonings. After the mixture has boiled for thirty-five minutes, add a pork sausage. Serve with a hot potato salad and an onion sauce. There is no attempt to make a special dish out of the pig's trotters (a famous French gourmet so appreciated them that he had all the handles of his cutlery shaped in the form of trotters). But *cochonailles lyonnaises* combine three popular ingredients of the region—pork, potatoes, and onions.

Nostalgia may not be what it once was, but there is nothing like the nostalgia of eating what one's mother or grandmother used to cook, and this may explain the present popularity of these *plats de famille*. There is also the pleasure of eating in the same way as did the working class of past times.

LYON sausages have always been famous. In an English cookbook of 1865, they were recommended for breakfast. Nowadays the best sausages are made from leg of pork that has been stuffed into the *rosette*, the long pig's gut measuring about twenty inches. The meat is salted twenty-four hours before being cooked. To it are added small pieces of pork, taken from the firmest parts of the flesh, that have been soaked in *marc* (a spirit distilled from the skins and pips of grapes after the wine has been made) and pepper and other seasonings. Another form of sausage is the *andouillette*, which in Lyon is a tripe sausage based on veal rather than pork. Edouard Herriot,

153

who was mayor of Lyon from 1905 to 1957, used to say that there were only two things that left an unmentionable taste in the mouth, politics and *andouillette*, and it is perhaps because of this opinion that the Lyonnais started to use veal.

Naturally the Lyonnais don't make *saucisson* or *andouillette* at home nowadays. The standard of the *charcuteries* is very high, and they vie with each other in their sale of a wide variety of products. They also sell *boudin*, a form of blood sausage, and a Lyonnais specialty, *boudin blanc*, which is made from pork, onions, and eggs, without the blood. This last, which is served poached, grilled, or fried, can be prepared in various ways. It is sometimes cooked with truffles, and sometimes with a white wine that derives from a chalky soil. It is usually served with mashed potatoes, but these days it can also be served with fried apples. *Andouillettes au Saint-Véran* (a white wine from the Mâconnais) and *andouillettes moutarde* can be found quite easily. Sausages cooked inside brioche is a common dish, and one that you would never confuse with a hot dog.

The particular characteristic of these dishes is that they are usually served in the Lyonnais as a first course, or *entrée*.

The same applies to the Lyon salad bowl. This is a far cry from the *hors d'œuvre variés* or *crudités* that are usually part of Parisian menus. For a Lyon salad, you begin by cooking a sheep's trotter in stock for an hour and a half, by broiling a chicken liver, and by marinating a couple of herrings. Then, as the sheep's trotter cools, remove the meat and dice it, adding it to a highly seasoned dressing with olive oil, pepper, and vinegar. Add to this the crushed liver, the boned and filleted herrings, and three sliced hard-boiled eggs, and season with chives, parsley, and other herbs. Sometimes sheep's trotters dominate the "salad," as in the *salade de clapotons*, where they are split open and allowed to marinate for half a day in a mixture of vinegar and mustard before being cooked for one and a half hours in boiling water, together with carrots, onions, and a small quantity of flour, and then served with mayonnaise. Even when the salad consists of lettuce, endives,

In the village of Collonges-au-Mont-d'Or, just outside of Lyon, the three-star restaurant affectionately and universally called Chez Bocuse is located. Here chef Paul Bocuse works a kind of culinary magic on the essentially hearty fare of the region. To prepare jambon cuit dans le foin, *below, he first*

soaks a ham in water for twenty-four hours to draw out excess salt. Then he simmers it with two pounds of new-mown hay until the ham has taken on a delicate and fresh bouquet. In the village of Les Allymes, Mme. Badollat, opposite, bakes bread for the village.

dandelion, lamb's lettuce (*mâche*), or various forms of artichokes, it is customary to add either pork lardons or *grattons* (cracklings), or slices of liver, or lightly smoked sausage called *cervelas*. A traditional salad, named after the Ile Barbe, the site of a fifth-century abbey near the Mont-d'Or, consists of cold potatoes and peppers, mixed in a well-peppered oil sauce with diced ham, sliced lobster tail, olives, and truffles.

Lyonnais cooks have always rejected the contention that onions play an overwhelming role in their cooking. But even they acknowledge the importance of onions in such dishes as the *gras-double*, and it is a fact that as lunchtime approaches, the odor of onion predominates in the streets near the rue Edouard Herriot and in Le Vieux Lyon, areas with many restaurants. A traditional dish of the silk workers was a form of onion soup. It was customary for this soup to be served last, because it was assumed that poor workers would prefer to end their meal with the most substantial dish (if indeed they had more than one dish).

Onions now play a vital role when it comes to sauces and to the cooking of potatoes. *Sauce soubise* is a simple onion sauce, launched into fame by the great aristocratic name it carries. But in the Lyonnais it should be made differently from the onion sauce that is found in other regions, such as Picardy. First blanch the sliced onions, then lightly cook them in butter, taking care that they do not become browned. Next add a white sauce (a *béchamel*), and cook the two together for about twenty minutes. After this, sieve the mixture and bring it to the boil. You can then add fresh butter and cream. The sauce can be used in a variety of ways—with sausages, for example. With the addition of mustard, it becomes a *sauce Robert*.

Pommes de terre lyonnaises consist of potatoes cooked in salted water and then peeled and cut into small pieces; to these you add a *sauce soubise* or, more simply, fried onions, and mix them together. *Pommes de terre Louise* consist of grated raw

In cardon à la lyonnaise, *below left, bone marrow, a feature of many regional dishes, is poached, then combined in a cheese sauce with Swiss chard. In* loup en croûte à la sauce choron, *below right, a* loup, *or sea bass, is stuffed with lobster mousse, then wrapped in a pastry crust. Prepared by Paul Bocuse, it is served with* sauce choron, *a rich mixture of*

tomatoes, wine, egg yolks, vinegar, and butter. Far simpler, but no less formidable, is the gratinée lyonnaise, *opposite. Onion soup was the staple of silk workers in Lyon; and baked with bread and cheese in classic fashion is still an immensely satisfying and popular dish.*

156

Lyonnais cooks have exported a host of dishes to the rest of the world, and one of the best known is quenelles de brochet à la lyonnaise, *above. Properly prepared, the* quenelle *is a velvety dumpling in which the flavor of the pike is subtly lightened but never lost. The* quenelles, *a mixture of*

ground pike, butter, flour, eggs, and milk, opposite, are prepared the day before the dish is to be eaten. To finish the quenelles, *they are poached and then covered with a béchamel sauce, sprinkled with Gruyère cheese, and lightly browned in a hot oven.*

potatoes, mixed with chopped onions, flour, parsley, seasoning, and two or three eggs. Fry the whole (measuring about one inch in thickness) lightly in oil until it is browned, and then carefully turn it and fry the other side in the same manner.

The potato was "the truffle of the poor," and Stendhal claimed that in Lyon he discovered twenty different ways of cooking potatoes, at least ten of which were unknown in Paris. In the neighboring province of the Bourbonnais, where the potato is also abundant and important in the diet of poor people, there is a potato dish called *le pâté de pommes de terre*, which is known in the Lyonnais as *pommes de terre à la pâte*. A simple method of preparing this dish is to quarter the potatoes and put them into hot lard. Add onions and herbs, sauté briefly, and cover the mixture three-quarters of the way up with water. After about half an hour, crush the whole together and serve. A more complex recipe suggests rolling out two sheets of pastry. Into one of them you put fried onions with lardons and thinly sliced raw potatoes. Moisten the edges of the pastry with egg and milk, then cover with the other sheet of pastry. Make a hole in the top, and cook in a hot

oven for about an hour and a half. Before serving, add melted butter through the hole.

Sometimes potatoes were accompanied by a pork chine. The workers from the Dauphiné brought with them the idea of adding milk or cream; those from Savoy preferred the addition of meat stock; those from the Forez added garlic and egg and made the whole into a sort of pancake.

It is, in fact, quite difficult to be sure of the exact origin of a dish. There is an argument about whether the Lyonnais used leeks before the inhabitants of the north, and the *tarte aux poireaux* or *soufflé aux poireaux* (more frequently to be found in Lyon today) is also claimed as a creation of Picardy.

Even the most undeniably Lyonnais dish, *quenelles*, which seems to have appeared in the nineteenth century, may owe its name to the German dumpling, or *knödel*. It was a much-prized dish in a very Catholic city where fish was greatly in demand and where people tended to get bored with the carp and pike that came from neighboring rivers and pools. *Quenelles* are made from puréed pike (although these days about a third of the mixture can be veal) that is mixed with a *panade* (a sort

A typical nineteenth-century bourgeois dining room, above, has been recreated in the Musée des Arts Decoratifs in Lyon. Left, the Relais Gourmand, an exclusive national association of excellent restaurants, has hung its seal of approval at the Orsi, in Lyon. Mme. Badollat, opposite, with her husband Maurice, is called "la tante" in her village of Les Allymes. She cooks in her café-restaurant, is the village bread baker, and sells slices of her famous tâtre, a kind of pizza.

of thick, unsweetened custard) and then poached. Crayfish, truffles, or a tomato paste can be added and the whole baked in a hot oven. But it is common in Lyon to serve the *quenelles* with a Nantua sauce, although Nantua is in Bresse (which is theoretically part of Burgundy rather than the Lyonnais). This is a wine sauce with crayfish. The Lyonnais usually add mushrooms (for which there are a good many different names in the region), or they may well serve the *quenelles* with a simple cream sauce, adding cheese. When people visit Lyon, they usually buy as a present *quenelles* from a *charcuterie*. There is often a wide range of stuffings, and the shops compete with each other as to which has the most attractive—shrimp, mussels, mushrooms, pistachio nuts, a cream sauce; some have them all.

Naturally there are many dishes that are presented as being *à la lyonnaise*. Cod *à la lyonnaise* usually means cooked in vinegar, as does the *poulet au vinaigre de Roanne; côtelettes de veau à la lyonnaise* means cooked with Parmesan cheese; kidneys and sweetbreads *à la lyonnaise* means with cream and cognac; *gratinée lyonnaise* is an onion soup with cheese. The *jambon au foin* is more directly associated with Lyon, and with a number of lyonnais restaurants, although these days the ham is usually cooked with a variety of aromatic herbs rather than being poached gently in a large quantity of water along with fresh hay.

Poularde en demi-deuil (chicken in partial mourning) is a chicken with truffles, which became customary eating on a Sunday, usually after the races, in one or two famous restaurants. Place the truffles, sliced fairly thickly (mushrooms can be substituted), under the chicken skin, between the skin and the breast, in the form of a pattern. Their black color should be visible through the skin, thus conveying the impression of partial mourning. Stuff the chicken with sausage meat, white of egg, cream, and breadcrumbs; then carefully wrap it and put it in a cool place, but not in a refrigerator, for twenty-four hours. Cook it in a large pot, with carrots, leeks, turnips, onions, cloves, and herbs, with a large spoonful of flour to about one and a half gallons of water. As appearance is all-important, the chicken should be served on the vegetables, which have been puréed in a blender. Sometimes this dish is known as *poularde à la Mère Fillioux*, after the restaurant where it originated.

When it comes to cheese, Lyon is well placed. But traditionally, cheese, mixed with cream and white wine, or a cream cheese, mixed with finely chopped shallots and garlic, was to be found on the tables of the bourgeoisie or on those of the *canuts*. For sweets, Lyon revels in cherries (those from Vienne, south of Lyon, were famous in Saint Petersburg in the years before 1914) and in pears. In the bizarre folklore of the region, pears arranged in a tart were said to look like agricultural workers doing handstands, or, as they said in the nearby province of Bourbonnais, like oak trees, *piqués comme chênes*, and sometimes the Bourbonnais *patois* is applied to this tart, *piquenchâgne*. In these days when there is a cult of the regional past, to call a dish by this old name gives it an additional luster, even in a town famous for its cream, ice cream, and chocolate.

The Lyonnais consists of large urban centers and extensive suburbs; but the countryside is real and unchanged. Lyon itself is impressively modern, with its efficient transport, industries, and multiple commercial activities. But the visitor has only to wander through Le Vieux Lyon to find a unique world of traditional and specialized cooking reflected in a host of restaurant offerings.

GRATINEÉ LYONNAISE   *Onion Soup*

Gratinée is easy to make, but takes some time to cook because the onions require at least 45 minutes of slow cooking to become tender and digestible.

2 pounds onions, finely sliced (900 g)
6 tablespoons butter (75 g)
2 tablespoons vegetable oil (30 ml)
4 tablespoons flour (45 g)
2 quarts hot beef stock (2 liters)
3 cups dry white wine (¾ liter)
½ cup port (125 ml)
Salt, freshly ground pepper
12 slices French bread
1 tablespoon olive oil (15 ml)
3 cloves garlic
¾ cup grated Gruyère and Parmesan cheese, combined (75 g)

Heat the butter and oil over low heat in a large saucepan, put in the sliced onions and cook until translucent. After 30 minutes sprinkle on the flour, stirring it in well, and then add the heated stock and white wine. Season lightly with salt and pepper. Let the soup simmer very gently for 30 to 40 minutes, then taste for seasoning and add the port.

While the soup cooks, make the *croûtons*. Preheat the oven to 350°F. Lay the bread slices on a cookie sheet or piece of aluminum foil and heat them in the oven for 15 minutes, until they are dry and toasted. Brush with oil on both sides and rub with a cut clove of garlic.

Pour the soup into heated bowls, float the *croûtons* on top, and sprinkle generously with cheese. Place the bowls under a very hot broiler and serve when the top is melted and golden brown.

for 6 to 8 people / photograph on page 157

SAUCISSON EN BRIOCHE   *Sausage in Brioche*

1 large, fresh or smoked, pure pork sausage, weighing about 1¾ pounds (800 g)
1 egg, beaten
Dijon mustard

FOR THE BRIOCHE
3 cups flour, unsifted (450 g)
½ teaspoon salt
½ teaspoon sugar
2 packages dry yeast (7 g each)
½ cup warmed milk (110 ml)
3 eggs, well beaten
12 tablespoons butter, softened and cut into bits (175 g)

Prepare the brioche dough a day ahead. Sift the flour and salt into a bowl. Dissolve the sugar and yeast in the warmed milk. When frothy, add to the flour mixture with the eggs. Mix into a dough with a wooden spoon and gradually work in the butter. Cover and leave to rise for 2 hours. Punch down, cover and leave overnight on the lowest shelf of the refrigerator.

To cook the sausage, slit the skin here and there to prevent it splitting and place it in a pot of cold water. Bring slowly to a boil and simmer for 45 minutes. Remove, allow to cool and drain on a cloth, then carefully remove the skin with a sharp knife.

Preheat the oven to 375°F. Roll out the brioche dough into a 1-inch thick rectangle large enough to enclose the sausage. Place on a greased baking sheet and brush the edges of the pastry with water. Wrap the sausage in the dough, overlapping the long sides and then folding the ends over. Brush the dough with the beaten egg and bake for 1 hour, until the pastry is golden.

Transfer the cooked brioche to a plate and serve it in slices about ¾ inch thick, with Dijon mustard.

for 6 people / photograph opposite

GALETTE LYONNAISE   *Lyonnaise Potato Galette*

2 pounds baking potatoes (900 g)
3 medium onions, sliced
10 tablespoons butter (150 g)
Grated nutmeg
Salt, freshly ground pepper

Peel the potatoes, boil in salted water until tender, and drain. Let them steam for a few minutes, then mash, until fairly smooth.

Melt 3 tablespoons of the butter in a large pan and sauté the onions until golden, then add half the remaining butter and the mashed potatoes. Season well with nutmeg and salt and pepper and stir thoroughly. Transfer to an enamelled cast-iron gratin dish, smooth down, and dot the top with the remaining butter. Brown lightly in the oven or under the broiler. These potatoes are delicious with roast meats or steak.

for 4 or 5 people

ROBERT FRESON

PHOTOGRAPHE

JE AIME...

154 WEST 57 STREET
NEW YORK 10019 N.Y.
TÉL. 581.29.89

MOULIN DE VILLIERS
86210 ARCHIGNY
TÉL. (49) 86.81.03

JAMBON CUIT DANS LE FOIN   *Ham Cooked in Hay*

Serve this chilled at a summer party—the flavor is extraordinary and very delicate; the only hard part is finding the new-mown hay.

If you live in the middle of a town and can't get hay, you can use aromatic herbs—rosemary, sage, wild thyme—instead. It will taste different but still very good.

1 smoked raw ham, weighing about 9 pounds (4 kg)
2 pounds new-mown hay (1 kg)

Soak the ham in water to cover for at least 24 hours to remove the salt. Rinse thoroughly, and put the ham in a large pan with plenty of water. Add the hay, and simmer for 4 to 4½ hours with the water just trembling; it mustn't boil. The hay is infused in the water and its flavor permeates the ham. When cooked, take the ham out of the pan, peel off the skin, and serve, hot or cold, in slices.

for 12 people / photograph on page 154

CARDON À LA LYONNAISE   *Cardoon, Lyon Style*

Cardoon is a plant of the artichoke family, whose edible part is not the button-shaped flower but the ribs of the leaves. After you have removed the hard stalks, the fibrous parts, and the ends, there will remain only about 2 pounds of ribs.

1 good-sized head of cardoon, weighing about
   7 pounds (3 kg)
4 cups boiling water (1 liter)
1 tablespoon flour (10 g)
3 tablespoons vinegar (45 ml)
1½ teaspoons salt (10 g)

FOR THE MARROW SAUCE
14 tablespoons butter (200 g)
1 tablespoon flour (10 g)
2 cups beef stock (½ liter)
¼ pound marrow (100 g)
1¼ cups grated Gruyère cheese

Cut the cardoon in pieces and toss them in the boiling water. Dilute the flour in the vinegar and add this mixture to the water—this will prevent the cardoon from discoloring. Cook until tender, about 1 hour; drain.

While it is cooking, make the sauce. Melt the butter on low heat and blend in the flour. Add the beef stock, stirring constantly. Let simmer and reduce for 30 minutes.

Preheat the oven to 450°F. Cut the marrow in thick strips and poach for 5 minutes in salted boiling water.

In a gratin dish, arrange the drained cardoon, add the marrow, pour over the reduced sauce, sprinkle liberally with Gruyère, and bake for 15 minutes, until the cheese melts.

for 6 people / photograph on page 156

CÔTE DE BŒUF À LA MOËLLE   *Rib of Beef with Marrow*

Bone marrow can usually be obtained from a good butcher, albeit with some difficulty. Ask him to save marrowbones for you and to saw them into short lengths. The marrow can then be extracted with a very long thin knifeblade or marrow spoon.

1 rib of beef on the bone, weighing about 2 pounds (1 kg)
6 good-sized slices of beef marrow
Salt, freshly ground pepper
Vegetable oil

FOR THE BEAUJOLAIS SAUCE
5 tablespoons butter (60 g)
1 tablespoon shallots, chopped
1½ tablespoons flour (20 g)
2 cups Beaujolais (½ liter)
Salt, freshly ground pepper
1 small sprig of thyme
½ bay leaf
1 clove garlic

Season the beef with salt and pepper and rub it with oil. Grill or broil for about 10 minutes per pound for rare meat, 15 minutes per pound for medium.

Meanwhile, make the sauce. Heat the butter in a medium saucepan. When it starts to sizzle add the shallots and cook until golden. Sprinkle with the flour and gradually add the wine. Season with salt and pepper, add the herbs and garlic, and boil for 10 minutes.

In a separate saucepan, gently poach the pieces of marrow in boiling salted water for about 1½ to 2 minutes. Remove them carefully from pan and drain. Stir the pieces of marrow into the sauce when ready to serve it.

When the rib of beef is ready, put it on a heated dish, and pour on the Beaujolais sauce, containing the pieces of marrow.

for 4 people / photograph opposite

GALETTE PEROUGIENNE *Perugian Pastry*

This pastry-cake with butter is found in various regions of France in a number of different forms.

1 cake fresh, compressed yeast (14 g)
⅓ cup lukewarm water (100 ml)
14 tablespoons butter (200 g)
1 egg
Peel of 1 lemon
Pinch of salt
½ cup sugar (100 g)
1⅓ cups flour, sifted (200 g)

Put the yeast in the lukewarm water to soften for about 10 minutes. In a bowl, mix about 8 tablespoons of the butter with the egg, lemon peel, salt, and about 2 tablespoons sugar. Add the dissolved yeast mixture, then little by little add the flour, mixing it into a stiff dough. The homogeneous dough is ready when it separates by itself from your fingers. Let the dough rise for at least 2 hours at room temperature.

Preheat the oven to 450°F. Roll out the dough into a thin sheet. Trace a large circle. Make a ridge around the edge of the pastry to prevent the butter topping from overflowing onto the oven surface. Place the remaining 6 tablespoons of butter in small knobs on top of the pastry. Sprinkle liberally with the remaining sugar. Bake for 8 to 10 minutes, until browned.

for 6 people / photographs above, left, and opposite

GAUFRES GRAND-MÈRE BOCUSE
Grandmother Bocuse's Waffles

3⅓ cups flour, unsifted (500 g)
1 tablespoon sugar (15 g)
Pinch of salt
8 egg yolks
1 cup plus 2 tablespoons butter, melted (300 g)
1 cup milk (250 ml)
4 egg whites
1 tablespoon baking powder
¼ cup rum (optional) (60 ml)

Mix the flour, sugar, salt, egg yolks, and melted butter together in a large bowl. Add the milk, a little at a time, to thin the mixture down; the batter should be fairly liquid—add a little water if necessary. In another bowl, beat the egg whites until they hold their shape and fold them into the batter very thoroughly. Add the baking powder at the last moment and also the rum, if you are using it.

Grease and heat the waffle iron. Pour a generous spoonful of the batter into the middle, close the iron, and cook for not more than 2 minutes.

The waffle should be cooked through and a pale golden color. Serve it sprinkled with sugar or with honey, jam, or cream, whichever you prefer.

for 8 people / photograph opposite

TÂTRE DES ALLYMES   *Onion Flan*

The *tâtre* is like a large pizza covered with onions and *fromage blanc*, which is a no-fat fresh cheese. (A substitute can be made by combining ½ cup yogurt with ½ cup low-fat ricotta cheese and then allowing the mixture to rest in the refrigerator for 24 hours.)

1 recipe *pâte brisée*—see Appendix
5 onions, sliced
2 tablespoons oil (30 ml)
2 eggs
½ cup *fromage blanc* (125 g)
½ cup heavy cream (125 ml)
Salt, freshly ground pepper
Pinch of nutmeg

Cook the onions slowly in the oil in a large pan until softened. Beat the eggs thoroughly into the *fromage blanc* and the cream. Season it with salt, pepper, and nutmeg and add the onions.

Preheat the oven to 350°F. Roll the pastry out until ⅛ inch thick and place in a round 9-inch flan ring or tart pan; pinch up the edge to form a raised border, which will contain the filling. Pour in the cheese and onion mixture and bake for 35 minutes. Eat while hot.

for 6 people / photographs at left and above

169

PROVENCE

PROVENCE

PROVENCE's air is laced with the intermingling scents, stronger and more clearly defined than anywhere else, of herbs that grow wild on the stony hillsides—thyme, oregano, mountain savory, rosemary, fennel, wild lavender—bringing aromatic support to the food of Provence and, mysteriously, reflected in the bouquets of the local wines, the best known of which is still Châteauneuf-du-Pape. The outdoor markets are colorful, abundant, and varied, the produce truly fresh, and the atmosphere delightfully joyful. The market of Toulon—running the length of the Cours Lafayette from the main boulevard to the indolent promenade of the port—shaded by plane trees, vibrant with dappled light and the vendors' chants, is the most beautiful.

The high-spirited, playful Provençal cuisine (the Provençaux like to describe it as *spirituelle*—"witty"), with its staples of tomatoes, garlic, saffron, sweet and hot peppers, salt anchovies, olives, olive oil, and the native wild herbs, although certainly unique, is much closer to that of other Mediterranean countries than to any other regional French cuisine. It is family cooking, not restaurant cuisine; the professional

The tapestry of Provençal colors and textures is marvelously varied; in a cultivated landscape in the Vaucluse, preceding overleaf, fruit trees, lavender, grapevines, and olive trees thrive in sunny fields. Medieval villages, like Gordes, above, were built right into rocky peaks to take advantage of natural fortifications. The produce of Provence, opposite,

includes such herbs and spices as (in basket) rosemary, wild mint, thyme, cade, carob, jujube, marjoram, juniper berry, and sage; cherry tomatoes (in bowl); green and black cracked olives, called cachado in Provence; almonds (foreground); and (in bottles at back) a bitter apéritif made from the gentian root, olive oil, and herb-flavored vinegar.

cook who can bring the right homely touch to it is very rare indeed. It is the only part of France that has always approached vegetables with respect and imagination, reserving a place apart on the menu for the vegetable entrée (between the fish and the roast for a festive meal or between the *hors d'œuvre* and the main course for a simple lunch).

Garlic's vogue, today, has taken a distinctly upward swing. In the last century most writers on cooking tended to apologize for its inclusion in a recipe, suggesting that it could be eliminated or at least used with such discretion that no one would perceive its presence.

Jules Breteuil, the nineteenth-century author of *La Cuisine Européenne*, affixes this note to his recipe for *gigot à la provençale*: "This dish can be supported only by those who are accustomed to meridional cuisine, in which garlic plays an obligatory part in nearly all preparations." It is unlikely that he had ever prepared or tasted the dish that he describes—a leg of mutton (or lamb), pierced with a dozen whole garlic cloves and twice as many salt anchovy fillets, roasted and accompanied by a full quart of whole, peeled garlic cloves, first blanched three times over in fresh batches of boiling water and the cooking finished in a cup of bouillon.

In fact, this is one of the most wonderful ways of serving roast lamb. The garlic garnish, though used in surprising abundance, is rid of its strong taste by repeated blanchings, and innocent guests rarely fail to ask what the lovely, mysterious vegetable accompaniment is.

The use of salt anchovies, first soaked, filleted, rinsed, and dried, to flavor meats is traditional but perhaps less appreciated today than in the past; a mixture of Provençal herbs—thyme, winter savory, oregano, marjoram—pounded into a paste with a clove of garlic and a pinch of coarse salt and loosened with a little white wine or olive oil, poured into deeply pierced vents, the remainder rubbed over the surface of the leg, can advantageously replace the anchovy flavoring.

Three or four heads of fresh garlic, or about half as much as Breteuil calls for, are enough, and the repeated blanchings are unnecessary—partially cooked in salted water for ten minutes or so and simmered for another five to ten minutes in a bit of bouillon, the cloves and their bouillon may be added to the sauceboat with the degreased roasting juices, deglazed with white wine, and the juices that flow from the joint as it is carved. The garlic cloves should be intact but of a melting puréelike consistency. If a bay leaf and a couple of leaves of fresh sage have been added to their first cooking water, the water may be saved for supper to be poured, boiling, over crusts of bread that have first been anointed with olive oil. This is the simplest version of the famous *aïgo boulido*, the Provençal cure-all, a soothing nourishment for invalids and comforting to nervous stomachs, tired from gastro-

The sizes, shapes, and colors of olives in Provençal markets are astonishing; an olive-stand in the Toulon market, below left, has just a fraction of the choices. Dorade, a Mediterranean sea bass with a delicate flavor and exceptionally tender flesh, is for sale, below center, in the market in the old quarter of Nice. Also at the Nice market, below right, are sacks of chickpea flour (foreground), kidney beans, lentils, and split peas.

On the small farm in the Vaucluse, above, the soil is plowed and ready for a winter crop. Two women, right, wheel home a load of wood for their evening fire.

nomic excesses; for sturdier nourishment, a beaten mixture of eggs, olive oil, and grated cheese can be whisked into it over gentle heat without approaching the boil.

Provençal eating habits loyally respect the seasons; people shop daily and the freezer is held in suspicion. In mid-summer, when the abundant tomatoes are at their sweetest and have their greatest depth of flavor, when fresh basil and hyssop abound and the market is flooded with tiny, freshly picked green beans, a sort of culinary abandon takes over: The taste of all fresh things is so pure and so intense that the less one does to them, the better they are. Lunch is served in the shade of an arbored terrace, and the terrace is lighted for dinner. Full-bodied wines do not take kindly to the heat, and the light Côtes de Provence reds and rosés, not always the most distinguished of wines, are quaffed cool. With a *bouillabaisse*, the Marseillais will drink a white wine from Cassis, but the Toulonnais (who, to the horror of the Marseillais, add potatoes and mussels to their *bouillabaisse*) will more likely accompany it with a rosé or a cool young red from neighboring Bandol.

In early autumn, the first game to arrive is thrush, roasted on spits before an open fire and, like the woodcock, never gutted. Partridge, pheasant, woodcock, boar, and hare follow, the last nearly always prepared as a *civet*—a red wine stew that is thickened with the animal's blood just before serving; the gamy bouquet of an old Châteauneuf is its perfect accompaniment. Green olives are picked at the beginning of October, and prepared either as *olives cassées* to be eaten before Christmas (each olive is given a tap to break the skin before it is soaked in a dozen changes of water in as many days to draw out the bitterness, then plunged into an herb-flavored brine, with an accent on fennel), or as *olives à la picholine*, to serve throughout the remainder of the year (a couple of months later, some ripe olives are preserved as black olives and the remainder are transformed into the year's supply of olive oil).

During the grape harvest, everyone who makes wine draws off a portion of the unfermented juice and boils it down to concentrate the natural grape sugars before seeding it with yeasts by adding some of the fermenting wine. The result is a sweet dessert wine called *vin cuit*, which is kept by all Provençal families for special, traditional meals—it always accompanies the thirteen desserts of the Christmas Eve supper, for instance.

The little violet artichokes are back for a brief season during October and November, eaten *à la poivrade*—raw with a vinaigrette sauce—when young and tender, before the chokes have formed, and, when more advanced, prepared *à la barigoule*. Wild mushrooms begin to appear after the autumn rains; they are all sautéed *à la provençale*—in olive oil with the addition of chopped garlic, parsley, and a squeeze of lemon—the ideal way to prepare the *lactaires délicieuses*, the commonest of the mushrooms of the region, and *girolles (chanterelles)*. There are probably better ways of preparing *cèpes*, and the lovely, most delicate of all mushrooms, Caesar's *amanita*, is, sadly, annihilated by this robust treatment.

Provence is less celebrated than the Périgord for its truffles, but Valréas, a village in the north of Vaucluse, is an important truffle center. These magical parasites with their heavenly scent, growing beneath the earth near the roots of oak and hazelnut

A briny plateau de fruits de mer, opposite, served on a bed of cold seaweed in a bistro in Nice, includes oysters, mussels, palourdes (a kind of clam), sea urchins, and crabs, with fresh lemon. Other Provençal treats, right from top, are la socca, a chickpea-flour pancake eaten salted or sweet; the ingredients of a soupe de la mer; a serving of it, with croûtons, spicy rouille sauce, and cheese added; and blood-colored mushrooms called sanguins, which grow wild all over the region.

La soupe au pistou, *above, is a minestrone invigorated,* à la provençal, *with a heady paste made of fresh basil, garlic, Parmesan cheese, and olive oil. M. Rousselet, chef and owner of Les Bories, near Gordes, prepares the soup with vegetables that his mother, opposite, gathers in the restaurant's garden.*

trees, begin to appear in mid-November and find their greatest use in the region at Christmas time, but they are ripest, richest, and least expensive in January and February. Here, they are not wasted on elegant decoration but are instead thrown into omelettes or fresh pasta, sautéed with potatoes or savored by themselves. A truffle merchant, explaining his favorite preparations, said: "They are expensive, so we don't eat them during the week but, in season, we often cook up a pound of them in a bottle of Châteauneuf for the Sunday meal."

Spring comes early. The almond trees are in flower by the beginning of February and, depending on the year, artichokes reappear shortly after and the young broad beans make their first appearance; for the two months to follow, a platter of tender, young broad beans is placed on every table along with the inevitable olives and *saucisson sec* to begin lunch; they are hulled at the table and dipped into salt and eaten with bread and butter—or, sometimes, bread and oil.

The winter and early spring months are the season for *daubes*: beef, mutton, octopus, old fowl, and others. The Marseillais *pieds et paquets* is also a *daube*, made of lamb's trotters and packages of lamb stomach, each enclosing a stuffing of green bacon, chopped garlic and parsley, and a pinch of herbs from the hillsides. A *daube* is always made in the same way (with variations), and the rules are strictly respected (with variations), or so the practitioners believe.

Beef and lamb *daubes* will be improved if you first lard the pieces of meat with strips of pork fat tossed in finely chopped garlic and parsley and then marinate the pieces of meat for a few hours in the wine that will be used to moisten them. In an earthenware pot, alternate layers of meat—intermingled with cubed lean green bacon, squares or tied scrolls of blanched and rinsed pork rind, and a sprinkling of salt—with layers of a mixture of chopped aromatics (onions, garlic, leeks, mushrooms, peeled and seeded tomatoes), beginning and ending with chopped aromatics. Embed a bouquet garni or two in the assemblage (a stalk of celery, a sprig of parsley, thyme, bay leaf, and a strip of dried orange peel—a recurrent element in the Provençal bouquet). Press it all down, and pour wine over so that the contents are just covered. (Traditionally, red wine is used for mutton or octopus, red or white for beef, and white for *pieds et paquets*, but any bottle ends of any color can profitably be disposed of in a *daube*.) Cover the *daubière* tightly (the lid may be sealed with a flour and water paste), slowly heat it and keep at a bare, beneath-the-boiling-point murmur for eight or nine hours. Traditionally, the *daubière* is embedded in ashes in the fireplace overnight.

Boiled potatoes usually accompany *pieds et paquets* or an octopus *daube*; a *macaronade*—parboiled macaroni, layered with sprinklings of grated cheese and moistened with *daube* cooking juices, heated in the oven long enough to melt the cheese—accompanies the beef and mutton *daubes*. A beef *daube* is served the second day, chilled in its aspic. Arrange the pieces of meat in a bowl, pour the sauce over, and after refrigerating overnight, unmold it and decorate it as your fancy dictates. If there are leftovers, melt the sauce free of the meat, chop the meat with parboiled and squeezed chard or spinach, mix it with *brousse* (fresh sheep's-milk cheese, similar to ricotta), and use it to stuff ravioli.

Toward the end of March, tiny tender shoots begin to push up from the bases of tortured, prickly, intertwining vines of wild asparagus. The shoots are thicker than a matchstick but never as thick as

put again to cook with a ragout of sausage meat, tomato, white wine, and breadcrumbs. They are called *à la suçarelle*, for, to eat them, you suck on the snail, the hole at the tip permitting it to pop into the mouth with the stuffing and sauce; it is important not to suck with too much enthusiasm, lest you choke.

CULTIVATED asparagus appears on the market at this time also. The green variety —from the Vaucluse, the Bouches-du-Rhône, and the Var—are very good indeed, well peeled and served hot, accompanied by fruity olive oil, homemade wine vinegar, salt and pepper, with which each person makes his or her own sauce; the purple-tipped, short but thick-stalked Niçoise asparagus has the finest flavor of all.

By May, the broad beans begin to be a bit advanced for eating raw and will soon be replaced on the *hors d'œuvre* platter by the red-orange–fleshed, richly flavored *charentais* melons from Cavaillon (criminally doused with port wine in restaurants),

Épaule d'agneau farcie au thon, *below, a lamb shoulder stuffed with green and black olives, bacon, tuna, hard-boiled eggs, and herbs, may be served cold, with a salad, or hot, with garlic purée and a sauce flavored with fresh thyme.*

a pencil, and their flavor is the essence of asparagus with something wilder thrown in; the tips are snapped free from the stems at the tender point and, most often, rapidly sautéed, without prior blanching, in olive oil before being incorporated into an omelette.

Throughout April, the natives scatter to the hillsides in search of the wild asparagus and, if a rain has preceded, snails are collected also—*petits gris*, smaller, but similar to the familiar Burgundy snails, and a smaller, white-shelled snail, known locally as *limaçon*. Both are briefly starved before being given a salt and vinegar bath to "de-slime" them, well rinsed, and cooked in a white wine *court-bouillon*, flavored with wild fennel and the other hillside herbs. The *petits gris* are often served straight from the *court-bouillon* as one of the elements to accompany an *aïoli* (a heavily garlic-flavored mayonnaise). They may also be stuffed with a snail butter and reheated like Burgundy snails, or removed from their shells, dipped in batter, and deep-fried. The little white snails usually have the tips of their shells snipped after their time in the *court-bouillon* and are

180

often accompanied, as in Italy, with thinly sliced raw ham. Meanwhile, the broad beans have reached the ideal stage for cooking. Peel them first, and then parboil them for a few minutes with a bouquet of the tender spring shoots of wild mountain savory before tossing them briefly in butter. Alternatively, you may sweat them in olive oil with little artichoke hearts, small onions, and a few drops of water—or some shredded lettuce, which will lend sufficient moisture—with the same bouquet of savory, to create a delectable vegetable ragout called *barbouiado*. At a still more advanced stage, as the flesh begins to harden but before it loses its tender green cast, you can transform broad beans into a sublime purée and serve them, reheated and generously buttered, either as a garnish for roast lamb or, spooned into butter-stewed artichoke bottoms, as a separate course.

Morels (wild mushrooms), both blond and black, appear in April and May, more often in the Alpes-Maritimes than to the west. They are of great delicacy and are best butter-stewed or creamed, but in Provence they usually suffer the same treatment as the *oronge* (Caesar's *amanita*). Fresh anchovies begin to swarm, and it is the moment to put up the year's supply in salt: The heads are torn off, the bodies are salted down for a few hours to rid them of excess water, and then they are packed in layers with coarse salt in jars.

Typical of Provençal *charcuterie* are the delicious *saucissons d'Arles*, made of a mixture of pork and donkey meat, and *caillettes*, of which there are many variations—those from the region around Avignon are lighter by virtue of containing a large amount of parboiled and squeezed chopped chard or spinach, mixed with garlic-flavored pork liver, spleen, and flesh. Balls of the mixture are wrapped in caul and baked to be served cold as an *hors d'œuvre*; for special winter occasions, they are served hot with a truffle sauce.

Many Provençal preparations are either celebrational or ritualistic in character. Typical of the celebration dishes is the *grand aïoli*; in addition to the poached salt cod and boiled potatoes and carrots that accompany the *aïoli* at many family luncheon tables every Friday, squid stews, boiled octopus, sea snails (very similar to whelks), *petit gris* snails, hard-boiled eggs, boiled artichokes, beetroot, salsify, asparagus, cauliflower, chickpeas, and green beans count among the elements that may make up a *grand aïoli*. A rather special celebration, the *aïoli monstre*, is organized each summer in villages throughout Provence.

The Christmas Eve supper is the most remarkably ritualistic meal of the year. It is strictly a family dinner and strictly Lenten (the truffled turkey is eaten the following day), consisting of a series of

Pieds et paquets *(literally, feet and packages) is a dish for which Marseilles is famous. Packages of lamb stomach are stuffed with salt pork, which has been flavored with onions, garlic, and parsley. The resulting* paquets *are then simmered with lambs' feet in a tomato and wine sauce.*

rustic fish and vegetable dishes, often with snails and *aïoli* or simply raw celery with *anchoïade* (a thick anchovy and garlic vinaigrette—sometimes a paste) to begin. Eel, octopus, and salt cod are typical of the fish, usually prepared in a sauce such as *raito* (based on red wine, tomatoes, anchovies, and aromatics) or a *capilotade* (a *roux*-thickened caper sauce sharpened with a dash of vinegar). The vegetables are usually prepared *au gratin*, and the thick white ribs of Swiss chard in a white sauce are typical.

The desserts, of which the ritual obligatory number is thirteen, are accompanied by *vin cuit*. One may be a prepared dessert, such as the typical sweet chard or spinach tart (permitting the green parts of the leaves, left over from the chard-rib gratin, to be used). The rather dry olive-oil biscuit known as *pompe à l'huile* is traditional, as are nougats; the remainder of the thirteen desserts are made up of fresh fruits and *mendiants*, the dried fruits and nuts so called because the basic four, *les quatre mendiants*—almonds, hazelnuts, raisins, and dried figs—resemble in color the robes of the four monastic mendicant orders—the Augustinians, the Carmelites, the Dominicans, and the Franciscans.

FOR TRAVELERS anxious to discover the spirit of Provence in its food, one restaurant recommends itself above all others—Avignon's Chez Hiély, up one flight at 5, rue de la République, the town's main street. Here the local *caillette* mixture has been transformed into a *terrine aux herbes*, which is accompanied by a juniper-flavored chicken-liver mousse; other regional appetizers are the *cassolette de moules aux épinards* (a gratin of mussels and spinach in white wine sauce), the *petite marmite du pêcheur* (angler fish, among others, in a light, creamy saffron-flavored sauce), and the lovely, creamed ragout of fresh egg noodles, sole, and shellfish, surrounded by a sauce of puréed sweet red peppers.

Among the main courses, turbot in red wine with leek *julienne* is wonderfully delicate, *pieds et paquets à la provençale* is always on the menu (and has been for thirty years), and the perpetual, but delicious, grilled *pièce d'agneau des Alpilles*, accompanied by a perfect potato gratin, is an ideal choice, especially if one is tempted to relax and enjoy a bottle of great wine with it. The cheese trolleys (one with a large array of local goat cheeses, the other with a more classic selection) are spectacular, and the dessert trolley (from which one is encouraged to test a large selection) is famous. The wine list carries all of the best wines from Provence, including the solid and subtle, beautiful red Bandol from the Domaine Tempier, Château Simone from the Palette *appellation*, outside Aix-en-Provence, and some twenty Châteauneufs-du-Pape from half as many growers, reaching back to 1961.

In the heart of Toulon, the restaurant Au Sourd, to the side of the opera, in the rue Molière, provincial in spirit—even to the faded artificial flowers that have sprouted from protruding wall vases for years—is in appearance like many an anonymous bistro serving honest but unimaginative food—except for anything that comes from the sea. There is always a large selection of freshly caught bass, dorades, pageots, rougets, sards—all of the noble varieties from the Mediterranean—to be grilled to order. But above all, this restaurant offers the most glorious tray of bivalves and other living marine delicacies to be found anywhere (the selection is necessarily somewhat diminished in the months without an "r").

The patron, a passionate lover and scholar of all things edible from the sea and a practicing diver, supplements the tray with rarities for which he dives in the clear waters off the island of Porquerolles. The amorphously shaped leather-hided little *vioulets*, whose outer surfaces form a rich garden of other microscopic sea life, reveal a soft and delicate lemon-tinted flesh with a bit of lemon in the iodiny sea flavor when they are split open; sea urchins, whose red corals are among the most opulently flavored of sweet things (often added to fish sauces also, which dish then takes the name of *oursinade*); oysters, mussels, clams, *moules rouges* (very small mussels whose shells are covered with a furry seaweed and whose sweet flesh is red), *dattes de mer* (small bivalves the same size, shape, and color of fresh dates), *amandes de mer*, *palourdes* or *clovisses*, and *praires* (all hard-shelled bivalves, clamlike but smaller and each very distinct in flavor); there are others still.

Some days a *soupe aux favouilles*—the little crabs that are constantly escaping from their crates in the markets—will appear on the menu, and others an *omelette aux orties de mer*, the little jellyfish that cling to the rocks. The patron will tell you that you should never order a *bouillabaisse* in a restaurant because *bouillabaisse* is more an ambiance or atmosphere than a culinary reality—it must be shared among *copains* in a cabin or on the seashore, and it must be cooked in a large pot over a roaring bonfire. And then he will explain *le coup de la bouillabaisse* when *les copains* are entertaining *les "éstrangers"*: With your back to your guests, throw a handful of salt into a ladle of the fish broth, then pass the ladle, first to friends who dip in their fingers and taste approvingly, then to the Parisians who, with a grimace, will remark that it seems a bit salty; with a crushed look on your face, throw a few old wine corks into the pot of *bouillabaisse*, boil them for a couple of minutes, and pass around another ladle of broth. Miracle of miracles, it is perfectly seasoned, and your guests will return home to tell their friends about the inexplicable but true alchemy of corks in the *bouillabaisse*.

Some sweets and fruits of Provence, opposite: glazed apricots, peaches, mandarins, and figs on a lace-covered plate; a wicker basket (foreground) of jujubes and black truffles; a large basket (center) containing (clockwise) black and green olives,

Provençal garlic, quinces, and figs, a bowl of fruits soaked in Cointreau, and a dish of juniper berries; and (top) grapes, almonds, and two kinds of melon.

At Moulin de Mougins, a three-star restaurant in Mougins, just north of Cannes, a dessert specialty is apple tart—above, just before and just after baking. The tart is baked to order at the restaurant and served hot. Another Provençal dessert, below right, is navettes de Saint-Victor, one of the traditional thirteen desserts of Christmas and named after the third-century martyr who was cut to pieces for refusing to deny his faith. Gratin de courge, below left, is a vegetable dish in which parboiled squash is covered with a béchamel sauce and breadcrumbs and baked. Provençal breads and pastas, opposite, include fougasse, the flat, pierced loaves, and raïoles, the meat-and-herb-stuffed ravioli-shaped pastas.

SOUPE AU PISTOU

A *soupe au pistou* is a minestrone with a heady paste of fresh basil, garlic, Parmesan cheese, and olive oil stirred into it at the moment of serving. *Pistou* is the Provençal word for "pestle."

The result is much better if fresh, newly shelled white beans are used. Onions are often added and, in parts of Provence, a large chunk of diced pumpkin is considered essential for the smooth, voluptuous texture it lends to the soup as it cooks into a purée.

The following recipe is a Niçoise version. The French beans and the diced *courgettes* (small zucchini) should be added at the same time as the pasta to retain their texture and flavor.

2 pounds fresh white haricot beans, shelled (1 kg) (or an equivalent amount of dried white beans, partially cooked)
1 pound potatoes, peeled and diced (450 g)
¾ pound carrots, peeled and diced (375 g)
1 pound very ripe tomatoes, peeled, seeded, and diced (450 g)
½ pound leeks, white and tender green parts cut into rounds (275 g)
Salt
1 pound small zucchini, diced (450 g)
¾ pound very thin, small green beans, trimmed (375 g)
¼ pound short macaroni or spaghetti, broken up (125 g)

FOR THE PISTOU
Coarse salt, freshly ground pepper
6 cloves garlic
25 (or more) fresh basil leaves
1 cup freshly grated Parmesan cheese (100 g)
½ cup olive oil (125 ml)

Start the fresh white beans cooking in a pan with 4 quarts of water. Bring to a boil and simmer for 30 minutes.

Add the potatoes, carrots, tomatoes, and leeks to the haricot beans and season with salt. Let simmer for about 45 minutes, until all the vegetables are practically melting. Add the zucchini, green beans, and pasta and cook for 20 minutes.

While the soup is cooking, make the *pistou*. In a mortar, grind together a good pinch of coarse salt, pepper, the garlic, and the basil. Pound carefully at first, then more roughly, until the leaves and garlic are reduced to a rather coarse purée. Add some of the cheese and pound to a paste, loosen with a bit of the olive oil, stirring and pounding. Add more cheese, then pound, more oil, and so forth, until both are used up. (You can also make the *pistou* in a food processor or blender, adding the ingredients the same way.)

Serve the hot soup from its pot and present the mortar of *pistou* at the same time so each guest may season the soup to taste.

for 8 people / photographs on pages 178 and 179

BŒUF À LA GORDIENNE   *Beef Stewed in Red Wine*

3 pounds stewing beef (1½ kg)
6 tablespoons olive oil
⅓ pound lean streaky, unsmoked bacon, cut into lardons (150 g)
2 shallots, chopped
Salt, freshly ground pepper
1 calf's foot, split and blanched (optional)

FOR THE MARINADE
About 4 cups red wine (1 liter)
¾ cup wine vinegar (200 ml)
2 onions, sliced
3 carrots, cut into fine rounds
2 cloves garlic, crushed
Several pinches of crumbled dried herbs
1 bouquet garni containing a strip of orange zest, parsley stems and root, bay leaf, celery rib, leek greens, savory, oregano, thyme, and marjoram

The night before, cut the beef into cubes and marinate in a bowl with the marinade ingredients.

About 5 hours before serving, remove the meat from the marinade and pat dry, reserving the marinade. In a large casserole heat the olive oil and sauté the bacon and the shallots. When the fat starts to run from the bacon, add the beef and brown all over. Strain the marinade and add the vegetables to the casserole. Stir them around and let them brown a little; add the bouquet garni and the liquid from the marinade. The beef should be just covered with the liquid; if necessary, add more wine. Season well with salt and pepper.

Cover the pot, using a sheet of oiled parchment paper and then the lid to seal it hermetically. Bring the mixture to a boil, reduce the heat, and simmer for 3 hours or longer. Discard the bouquet garni.

To serve hot, skim off any fat from the top. To serve cold, add a calf's foot to the other ingredients.

The traditional accompaniment to *bœuf à la Gordienne* served hot is *macaronade*, a long macaroni. Cook it in boiling salted water until just tender (about 15 minutes) and drain. Transfer to a buttered oven dish and sprinkle layers of the macaroni with Parmesan cheese or a mixture of Parmesan and Gruyère. Moisten with a ladleful of the gravy from the beef and heat through in a hot (400°F) oven for about 10 minutes.

for 6 people / photograph opposite

187

LOUP DE MER "AUGUSTE ESCOFFIER" *Sea Bass in Lettuce Leaves*

1 sea bass, weighing about 2 pounds (1 kg)
Salt, freshly ground pepper
⅓ cup flour (50 g)
5 tablespoons butter (60 g)
1 or 2 large heads of lettuce
4 shallots, finely chopped
1 tablespoon dry vermouth
¼ cup heavy cream (60 ml) or 4 tablespoons butter
   (50 g) (optional)
Small pieces of fried bread

FOR THE FUMET

¾ cup dry white wine (200 ml)
1 pound head, bones, and trimmings from the fish,
   plus others if possible (500 g)
1 onion, finely sliced
1 celery rib, finely sliced
1 carrot, finely sliced
1 bouquet garni containing thyme, bay leaf, parsley,
   and leek greens
Salt, freshly ground pepper

Have the fish cleaned, scaled, and cut into 8 slices. (Ask
   the fishmonger for the fish head, bones, and trimmings and, if possible, some extra of these for the
   fumet. They must be from delicately flavored white
   fish such as sole, turbot, whiting, or angler fish.)

Make the *fumet*: in a saucepan combine the wine, fish
   head, bones, trimmings, onion, celery, and carrot.
   Cover with water, add the bouquet garni, and simmer
   for 30 minutes. Season with salt and pepper toward
   the end of the cooking; strain this somewhat reduced
   stock through a cheesecloth placed over a sieve.
Season the fish with salt and pepper and dust with the
   flour. Heat 3 tablespoons of the butter in a frying pan
   and sauté the fish on both sides for 5 minutes.
Bring a large pan of salted water to a boil and blanch the
   best leaves of the lettuce for about 30 seconds.
   Remove quickly, drain well, and spread them out on
   a cloth. Wrap each slice of bass in 2 or 3 leaves.
Melt the remaining butter in a sauté pan just large
   enough to hold all the fish pieces side by side. Sweat
   the shallots gently for 4 or 5 minutes, then moisten
   them with about ¾ cup of the *fumet*, and add the fish
   and the vermouth. Cook gently over a very low heat
   for about 8 minutes; do not boil. Remove the fish
   parcels and reduce the sauce over high heat.
If you prefer, add the cream to the reduced sauce for
   a more velvety consistency, or remove the sauce from
   the heat and whisk in about 4 tablespoons butter,
   cut into small pieces (this will bind the sauce, giving
   the same smooth body as a *beurre blanc*).

for 4 people / photograph opposite

ARTICHAUTS À LA BARIGOULE
Artichokes Stuffed with Garlic and Parsley

12 violet (or small globe) artichokes
3 cloves garlic
6 sprigs of parsley
Salt, freshly ground pepper
2 generous sprigs of fresh thyme
About ¼ cup olive oil
White wine

Using a stainless-steel knife, remove the stalks and
   tough outer leaves of the artichokes, cut the tops off
   almost halfway down, and remove the chokes with a
   teaspoon. Put the artichokes into a bowl of acidulated water (1 teaspoon lemon juice to 1 quart of
   water) to prevent them from discoloring.
Place the artichokes side by side in a large shallow
   flameproof earthenware casserole, just large enough
   to hold them. Chop the garlic and parsley and stuff
   the centers with the mixture. Season, and sprinkle
   with thyme leaves and the olive oil. Add enough white
   wine to the casserole so that it comes halfway up the
   sides of the artichokes, sprinkling a little into the artichokes as well. Cover, and simmer for 1½ hours,
   removing the lid toward the end of the cooking so that
   most of the wine can evaporate. Grind on additional
   pepper before serving.

for 6 people / photograph at left

GARDIANE D'AGNEAU   *Lamb Stew with Olives*

2 pounds lamb neck chops or shanks (1 kg)
¼ cup olive oil (60 ml)
Salt
2 onions, finely sliced
5 or 6 cloves garlic, lightly crushed
1 bouquet garni containing thyme, bay leaf, celery rib,
    parsley, leek greens, dried strip of Seville orange rind
Handful of green and black (or both) olives, blanched
1½ pounds potatoes, peeled and thickly sliced (750 g)

Heat the oil in a casserole and brown the pieces of lamb
in it. Season with salt, add the onions and garlic and,
a few minutes later, the bouquet garni, the olives,
and the potatoes. Add enough boiling water to almost
cover and simmer, covered, for 1½ hours. Serve from
the casserole.

for 4 people

TIAN DE COURGETTES ET DE TOMATES   *Zucchini Gratin*

2 pounds small zucchini, sliced into rounds (1 kg)
2 pounds tomatoes, sliced (1 kg)
6 tablespoons olive oil (90 ml)
2 onions, sliced
2 red or green peppers, seeded and sliced into rounds
2 eggplants, thinly sliced
1 clove garlic, crushed
4 to 5 pinches of savory and thyme, mixed
Salt, freshly ground pepper
½ cup freshly grated Parmesan cheese or fine bread-
    crumbs (or a mixture of both) (50 g)

Preheat the oven to 350°F. Heat 3 tablespoons of the
olive oil in a large frying pan. Add the onions and

brown them slightly. Add the peppers, eggplant, and
garlic. Season with salt and pepper, and cook gently,
stirring occasionally, until softened.

Place the cooked vegetables in the bottom of a baking
dish. Arrange the zucchini and tomato slices on top,
overlapping in rows. Sprinkle with savory and thyme.
Season with salt and pepper, sprinkle with 2 tablespoons of the olive oil, and bake for 30 minutes.
Remove the dish from the oven, sprinkle the top with
the Parmesan, drizzle with the remaining olive oil,
and bake for 15 minutes. You can also scatter breadcrumbs and cheese over the top.

for 6 people / photographs below and opposite

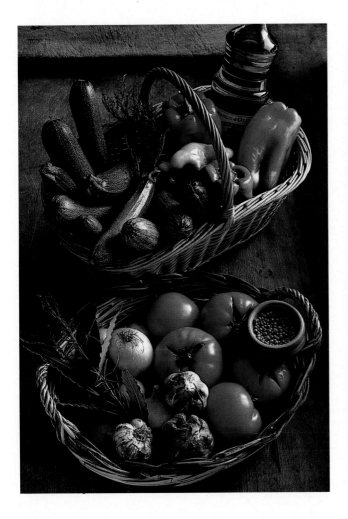

LANGUEDOC

LANGUEDOC

THE CUISINE of the Languedoc? Ah, yes, great, great! The *cassoulet*, the *brandade de morue*, the oysters of Bouzigues ... well, all the glories of this famous region. A lyrical but slightly vague response is often evoked by such a question. Here is why.

The nub of the matter is that no one knows—or no two people agree on—what are the boundaries of this gastronomic area. A vacationing couple, spending a first night in Albi, snugly installed in an *auberge* within the ancient fortifications, had the daring idea of asking the proprietor outright whether they were or weren't in the Languedoc. She advised them amiably to consult the lady in the bookshop across the road. They did, and received a great deal of assertion and lamentation. The assertion was that Albi most certainly was in the Languedoc, and that every right-minded person now acknowledged this. But she lamented that many decades had passed when the matter was so clouded by doubt that the *Guides Michelin* had omitted the city because they didn't know which volume to put it in.

Is there, then, no book on the Languedoc cuisine that would supply

Some authorities believe that there is such a thing as Oc cuisine. The concept seems somewhat artificial; nevertheless it must be acknowledged that one of the references for this chapter is a cookbook written in Oc (it is *Nostra Cózina*, by Dóttór Charles Vidal, Editions Occitania, Paris and Toulouse, 1930, and it is almost comprehensible to anyone who reads French, but not fully so). And it is true, of course, that there are broad distinctions, based on differences in climate and produce, to be made between the cooking of the north of France and that of the south. If you take the south as a sort of gastronomic entity, you will find common factors that give it some cohesion. But you will also find important subdivisions. The cooking of the Landes is plainly distinct from that of, say, Nice and its environs. And the olive oil that is fundamental to the cooking of Provence gives way to the goose fat of the southwest. In this context, the importance

Moules grillées, below, prepared at Les Frères Runel in Montpellier, are usually eaten as a first course. Chopped garlic, shallots, and parsley, left, are mixed with butter, then spread on the mussels in their half-shells. They are then sprinkled with breadcrumbs and briefly broiled. Other fruits de mer, opposite (clockwise from top), are Bouzigues oysters, bizoux (sea potatoes), tellines (tiny clams), palourdes, cockles, and, above them, escargots de mer.

the necessary definition of the area? Apparently there isn't. So be guided by the concoction offered here. It is generously drawn, and with good reason.

One reason is that the very name "Languedoc" (which equals *langue d'Oc*, meaning "the language of Oc") implies quite a sweeping territorial claim. "Oc," which appears in graffiti all over the south of France but is not a pop group as one might think, was the language of the south of France. "Oil" was what was spoken in the north. (The mysterious monosyllables reflect two different ways of saying what is now *oui*, meaning "yes.") In the sixteenth century, the north emerged as the dominant power, and those parts of the south that were still independent, such as Provence, were incorporated into the kingdom of France, which assumed the shape that France has today. The Oil version of French became the sole official language. People in the south went on speaking Oc; but as a language or group of languages, it went into decline. Efforts to revive it, dating from the end of the last century, have been associated with nostalgia for the ancient "Occitan civilization" and with political pressures for the French rulers in Paris to pay more attention to the south. In this situation, the region called Languedoc is proclaiming by its very name that it is the heartland of the south, of that *Occitanie* that has no official existence but that is definitely alive.

of the Languedoc is clear. Its great extent, the variety of its terrain, and its central position between Gascony and Provence, straddling both the olive-oil and the goose-fat areas, combine to give it a certain eminence. The same factors make it hard to sum up its gastronomic features in a few pages.

THE FRENCH Mediterranean coast is conveniently, although not precisely, bisected by the Bouches-du-Rhône. To the east lies the coast of Provence, long known as the Côte d'Azur; to the west, the coast of the Languedoc, until recently not much known at all; and in between, the mysterious area of the Bouches-du-Rhône itself, of which the Camargue is the most fascinating part. As for the edible fish and *fruits de mer* (the convenient French term that embraces marine mollusks and crustaceans and a range of edible oddities such as sea urchins and *violets de mer*), there is little to distinguish the Languedoc coast. It is, however, noteworthy that for much of its length it has large saltwater lagoons that are well adapted to the culture of oysters and other bivalves, notably mussels. Driving west from the Bouches-du-Rhône along the coast, you run into long tracts of road that are almost lined with stalls offering

dégustation de fruits de mer, these "fruits" being the product of the "beds" at Bouzigues, one of the major oyster-producing towns in France. Consuming the oysters and mussels, and clams too, of Bouzigues at roadside stalls is a great pleasure, and inexpensive.

One phenomenon that is noticeable all along the Languedoc coast is that the local names for fish are frequently of Catalan origin. So, indeed, are many of the fishermen. In the Roussillon, by the Spanish frontier, this is no surprise, since the indigenous population is Catalan. What is less well-known is that in the past, and especially in the eighteenth century, Catalan fishermen established themselves on the French Mediterranean coast in relatively large numbers. Part of the explanation for this is that the people of the Languedoc were really more interested in viticulture and commerce than in fishing.

Wine is indeed the main product of the land, although it is little used in traditional Languedoc cookery. This part of France produces very large quantities of wine, much of which is the rather weak *vin ordinaire* that has to be mixed with stronger wines from North Africa or Italy or elsewhere to produce an acceptable *vin de table*. This is not to say that the wines of the Languedoc are without interest. On the contrary, there are many small areas

A sampling of the dozens of petits pâtes de Béziers, opposite. They come in many sizes and shapes, are made from various doughs—from flaky pâte brisée to a crustier shell— *and can be stuffed with seafood, sweet and sour meats, or herb fillings. In the harbor of Sète, below, a commercial fisherman's nets are left on a dock after the day's work.*

autumn, carts laden with what looks like solid gold are a familiar sight, and they do indeed represent gold for the farmers, since the new strains of corn have very high yields, and much of the land in the south and southwest of France is ideally suited to their cultivation. But the gold perceived by the eye only becomes gold in the farmers' pockets after it has been transmuted into goose or duck.

The goose is of great importance in the western part of the Languedoc, which is one of the several *foie gras* areas of France (*foie gras* being the enlarged liver of a goose that has been force-fed, during the early winter, up to the point at which further cramming has no effect) and which is also part of the *confit* territory, a more interesting matter.

A CONFIT consists, in its ideal form, of large pieces of goose (*confit d'oie*) or duck (*confit de canard*) preserved in its own fat. The same technique may be used for chicken, for example, but a subtle difference in nomenclature is apparent—it is not *confit de poulet*, but *poulet*

Gigot de lotte, below, isn't a lamb dish, but fish, baked with vegetables and herbs. Eggplants, tomatoes, red peppers, and onions, left, are first sautéed with garlic in oil and then put in a baking dish as a bed on which to cook the fish, which is barded with garlic as in the preparation of gigot.

where little-known wines of real merit are produced. The Minervois is one such; parts of the Roussillon provide others; and the *appellations contrôlées* of, for example, Banyuls, Maury, Lunel, Muscat de Frontignan, and Muscat de Mireval are further examples. The last two names are of fruity dessert wines that have a certain renown. But, although wine lovers could spend many happy weeks exploring the resources of the region, they would traverse many large areas in which what is produced is just plain wine, and nothing more can be said to its credit.

A crop that has been increasing in importance in relation to the grape is corn. If you stop for a picnic in a cultivated area of the Languedoc, the odds of your being in the midst of vineyards are very high. The next likelihood is that you'd be in the middle of cornfields.

Corn has a long history in the south of France. Ever since it was brought back from the New World, it has been grown there to some extent; and it used to play a significant role in providing food for human beings (as it still does in northern Italy, for example, where *polenta* remains a popular food). Nowadays, it is almost all grown for animal fodder. In the late *en confit.* One may have other things *en confit* too, but the *confit* method of presentation is, by common consent, best when applied to goose and duck, which render their own fat.

There seems to be no good reason why the technique should be used only in the southwestern quarter of France. It is an ideal method of preservation, and why it should be practiced in so restricted an area is a mystery.

The fat from one fattened goose is more than enough to make a *confit* of all the meat. You can therefore use it either for general cooking purposes or for making something else *en confit.*

Goose fat, alone or as part of a piece of *confit d'oie*, has a natural role to play in *cassoulet*, one of the two dishes for which the Languedoc is most famed. It is, essentially, a dish of haricot beans and meats, cooked slowly, flavored with garlic, and so substantial that it is only with difficulty that it can be accommodated in a menu without a serious risk that the meal will stop there, for no one will have room to eat anything else.

In gratin de sole et langoustines, *below, the sole and the prawns are enriched with mussels, truffles, and mushrooms, right, baked in a cream sauce flavored with* blanc de blanc, *dusted with grated Gruyère, browned under the broiler, and served with puff pastries.*

The history of *cassoulet* is a subject of debate. The earliest theory ascribed it to the Arabs, who were said to have introduced the culture of white haricot beans to the south of France in the seventh century A.D. and to have taught the inhabitants how to make a *ragoût de mouton aux fèves blanches*, which could be taken as the ancestor of *cassoulet*. The idea exists that it could only have evolved after the discovery of the New World, since the bean that is so important in its composition is *Phaseolus vulgaris* —the French or kidney bean—which originated in Central and South America and only became familiar to Western Europeans in the sixteenth century. However, it does seem entirely plausible that Arab influences introduced to the south of France a dish that was the forerunner of *cassoulet* and that it was from this dish that the French finally evolved *cassoulet*, substituting the new and preferable beans from the New World and discarding mutton in favor of goose, pork, and lamb.

Whatever the truth of the matter, there is no doubt but that the western Languedoc is the home of *cassoulet* and that the question that is most debated is whether that of Castelnaudary, that of Toulouse, or that of Carcassonne is the most authentic or the best. If the simplest version of a dish is usually the earliest, then Castelnaudary wins on that score. The good people there (the smallest and friendliest of the three contesting cities) traditionally make it with beans and garlic (other seasonings and herbs too, but garlic is the vital one), pork rind, pork meat (fresh, salted, in sausage form—any or all of these), and (perhaps) a modest portion of *confit d'oie*. At Carcassonne they add lamb and, in season, partridge. At Toulouse they add lamb, and always include *confit d'oie* and sausage.

There is, incidentally, a certain mystique about the "crust" that forms on top of the dish during the final cooking. Everyone seems to agree that this should be broken at least once and reincorporated in the mixture below. But arguments about how many more times, and in what circumstances, it should be broken lead into the sort of gastronomico-theological discussions in which adversaries denounce each other as "heretics," and which are best avoided.

However, religion has played an important part in shaping food habits in the Languedoc, and in differentiating the eastern part of the region from the western part. Perhaps the most famous schism in the region was that produced by the so-called Albigensian heresy, the proponents of which are still honored, five centuries after they were suppressed and massacred, as *les cathares*. Their heresy consisted in taking a cool look at the world around them, discerning much wickedness, and drawing the conclusion that the Devil, not God, must have been the Creator. If this heresy had prevailed, it would have had grave implications for gastronomy. What did survive, however, in the realm of dissent, at a later stage and despite fierce repression, was a Protestant movement that was also political, the Roman Catholic Church and the royal government in Paris being perceived as a joint threat to the "land of Oc," i.e., the south. This movement was strong in the Cévennes and in the area around Montpel-

The game birds that thrive in many parts of the region find their way to the table. Larks wrapped in pork rind, above, are cooked en brochette *and served six to a customer. Wild guinea hens (top) are stuffed, wrapped, and baked. A rare pâté, below, is made from the meat of thrushes. Turkeys and guinea hens, below left, are raised for the table as well. To make* lièvre en saupiquet, *opposite, the hare is marinated in a mixture of wine, vinegar, garlic, and some of the hare's own liver. It is stuffed with the rest of its liver and other organs chopped and combined with onions, garlic, herbs, and bread-crumbs—all moistened with its blood. The meat is well-larded and baked.*

lier, where at one time the Protestants used to hold highly visible and provocative feasts on Fridays, constructing menus that contravened the rules that governed that day of abstinence from meat.

WHILE no detailed records survive of the effect of these extraordinary feasts, it must have been diminished by the existence in the Languedoc of one of the most satisfactory fast-day dishes ever contrived: *brandade de morue.*

Salt cod, in the Middle Ages and indeed until quite recent times, had an importance that it would be difficult to exaggerate. Even on the Mediterranean coast, where fresh fish was to be had, it became established as a staple food, and there were countless ways of preparing it. *Brandade de morue* is, many would say, the best. It is in effect an emulsion (like mayonnaise) made from salt cod, and the result is superb, especially in Nîmes, which is *the* city for this dish.

Mention of Nîmes brings us to the eastern extremity of the Languedoc, namely, the west bank of the Rhone, and also provides us with a convenient point of departure for considering the importance of snails in the area. Nîmes has a number of special dishes, and the nîmois method of preparing snails is one.

The snails may be procured either in the state of hibernation (which is convenient, because they have fattened themselves in preparation for it) or in active condition. In the latter event, it is necessary to starve them briefly and then feed them lettuce and aromatic herbs for two weeks. Such precautions are not necessary if the snails are taken in an appropriate habitat, which, so far as the Languedociens are concerned, would be vineyards (as in Burgundy) or what are called the *garrigues.*

Jacques Cambon, whose interesting work on *Gastronomie Languedocienne* was published in Montpellier in 1965, relates the story of the acquisition by the Montpelliérains, in the distant past, of the barony of Caravette, which is right in the heart of the *garrigues*, a region of dry limestone plains characterized by sparse vegetation—dwarf oak trees, thyme, and lavender—and given over to sheep, who may safely graze there, for it is a wild and unpopulated part of the country. Cambon points out that it is precisely in the barony of Caravette, to the north of Montpellier, that one finds the best snails, and he gives a picturesque description of how their excellence is celebrated, at Saint-Guilhem-le-Désert, by the annual "procession of snails."

The *garrigues* are matched in suitability for sheep by the upland regions known as "les Causses." These are also limestone plateaus, about 350 feet in altitude, cleft by canyons and spotted with char-

The foods and sights of the Languedoc are as varied as the region. A vineyard in October, above, with its toolshed, is near Pezeras. Opposite (clockwise from top left): a chapel belltower in the Camargue at twilight; a lone farmer heading home; the bitter-tasting liqueur Suze advertised from a farmhouse wall; in the market at Carcasonne a fermière *offers her own fresh* chèvres; *two types of olives—green* lucques *and black* picholines—*along with walnuts and almonds, from the Camargue; trout in a Toulouse fish shop; pumpkin and other squash on sale in Carcasonne; three regional cheeses —Roquefort, Mezel, and Cabrol; and several* chèvres *—plain, with pistachios, and with pepper.*

acteristic depressions of which the smallest are *cloups* and the larger ones *lavognes*. The limestone absorbs rain like a sponge, so that the Causses are arid on the surface, although much watery activity goes on below, for which the people of Roquefort have good reason to be grateful.

The limestone of the Causses has many "faults" and natural caves. The village of Roquefort is perched on a hillside that contains the most famous and valuable of these. The caves, which you can walk into, constitute a system of remarkable complexity and size, in which the temperature and other conditions remain stable the year round. These conditions are ideal for a microorganism known as *Penicillium roqueforti*; and it was discovered long ago that cheeses stored in the caves would be invaded by this microorganism and would, if all turned out well, become particularly delicious "blue" cheeses. "If all turned out well" refers to the fact that originally the production of Roquefort blue cheese was rather a hit-or-miss affair. Now it is all scientifically controlled. In the biggest caves, which belong to the biggest producers ("La Société"), a sophisticated

guide will show you around, pointing out where the cheeses arrive (all of pure sheep's milk, but no longer all from sheep of the Causses, their supply being inadequate and reinforcements from Corsica and the Pays Basque being necessary), how they are carefully inoculated with the precious microorganism, how they are stored and turned and wiped and generally given tender loving care, and finally packed in whole cheeses or halves for dispatch to destinations all over France and indeed all over the world. The "added value" is, of course, considerable. Roquefort is an expensive cheese; and the cachet bestowed by the name is jealously guarded and protected against imitation.

You may, however, ask whether the caves at Roquefort are unique. Given the extent of the Causses and the number of fissures and caves in the landscape, are there not other places where similar conditions prevail and "Roquefort" can be made? The answer is yes, but it can't be called Roquefort and is known instead as Bleu des Causses. It costs just a little less. And at its best, it is equally delicious.

After the vendage, *local people bring the residue of the grape pressings to a traveling still, preceding overleaf, to be distilled into a formidable, colorless alcohol, which is used in many home-brewed concoctions.* Crème d'Homère, *left, is a flan made with eggs, honey, white wine, cinnamon, and lemon zest. Among the pâtissier's* specialties, opposite, *are slotted galettes aux fritons, fat buns called* couques, *a round cake called* un soleil, *and anise-sprinkled* gateaux.

PETITS PÂTES DE BÉZIERS *Small Béziers Pastries*

The stuffing for these little pastries is made of chopped roast mutton, but you can also use leftover leg of lamb. They are suitable as an appetizer for a dinner.

1 recipe *pâte brisée*—see Appendix
½ pound roast mutton, chopped (250 g)
¼ cup rendered pork fat (or lamb-kidney fat) (60 ml)
Handful of raisins
2 teaspoons brown sugar
Salt, freshly ground pepper
Grated lemon peel (optional)

Preheat the oven to 425°F. Mix the chopped meat with the fat, raisins, brown sugar, salt, and pepper.

Roll out the pastry fairly thin and cut into 6 large squares or rounds and 6 slightly smaller ones. Place a large spoonful of stuffing in the center of each larger piece of pastry. Shape the pastry into a potlike shape, with high sides. Cover with the smaller piece of pastry, dampen the edges with water, and pinch them together to seal. Bake for 30 minutes. These pastries are eaten hot.

The little cakes of Pezenas are made in the same way, except that a little grated lemon peel is added to the stuffing. The form of pastry is different, however; the ingredients are sealed in a purse shape.

for 6 people / photograph on page 198

SOUPE À LA CITROUILLE *Pumpkin Soup*

This soup is a specialty of an area called the Lauragais, midway between Albi and Toulouse. This recipe is taken from *The Cuisine of the Languedoc*—part of a four-volume survey by Philip and Mary Hyman.

½ pound dried white beans, soaked overnight in water to cover and drained (250 g)
1 salted ham hock, soaked overnight in water to cover
2 onions, finely sliced
1 bouquet garni—see Appendix—including 10 black peppercorns
3 pounds fresh pumpkin, peeled and cut into large pieces (1½ kg)
2 small potatoes, peeled and sliced
3½ ounces tightly packed pork fat back, chopped to a paste (100 g)
3 cloves garlic
2 cups milk (½ liter)
Salt, freshly ground pepper
Toasted crusts of bread

Put the beans in a pan with 6 cups of water, the ham hock, onions, and bouquet garni. Bring to a boil and simmer for 1 hour. Add the pumpkin, potatoes, fat back, and garlic, and simmer for 1 hour.

Just before serving, remove the bouquet garni and discard it. Take out the ham hock and cut the meat off the bone. Cut the ham into small pieces, put it back in the soup, and add the milk. Bring to a boil, season with salt and pepper, and serve with toasted crusts of bread.

for 6 people

BROUILLADE AUX CHAMPIGNONS *Scrambled Eggs with Mushrooms*

¾ pound fresh wild mushrooms--see Note (350 g)
2 or 3 tablespoons goose fat or butter mixed with oil
1 or 2 cloves garlic, finely chopped
Handful of parsley, finely chopped
Salt, freshly ground pepper
10 eggs

Clean and slice the large mushrooms; smaller ones may be left whole. Heat the goose fat in a heavy frying pan and sauté the mushrooms until they have released their juices and the juices have evaporated. Season with salt and pepper and add the garlic and parsley.

Cover the pan while you beat the eggs in a bowl, then remove the lid and pour the eggs over the mushrooms. Stir and scramble, keeping the eggs runny. Serve at once with salt and pepper.

Note: If you have no means of obtaining fresh wild mushrooms, you can add a few dried *cèpes* soaked for 30 minutes in warm water to your cultivated mushrooms to improve their flavor. Alternatively, use preserved *cèpes* in jars, draining well before use.

for 4 people / photograph opposite

CASSOULET DE TOULOUSE

FOR THE BEANS

1½ pounds dried white beans, soaked overnight in
    water to cover and drained (700 g)
¾ pound salted spareribs or pork belly, soaked over-
    night in water to cover (300 g)
½ pound fresh pork rind, tied in a bundle and parboiled
    for 1 minute (250 g)
2 carrots, peeled
1 onion, stuck with a clove
2 medium tomatoes, peeled and chopped
1 bouquet garni—see Appendix
2 cloves garlic, crushed

FOR THE SAUTÉ

1 tablespoon rendered goose fat
About 1 pound boneless shoulder of lamb, cut into
    chunks (400 g)
2 onions, chopped
3 cloves garlic, 2 of them chopped
2 tomatoes, seeded and chopped
Salt, freshly ground pepper
1 small bouquet garni—see Appendix
6- to 8-inch-long piece of Toulouse-type sausage (fresh
    pork sausage), cut into 6 to 8 pieces
Lard (for frying)
6 to 8 thick slices garlic sausage
2 pieces, about 1 pound, preserved goose or duck
    (*confit*) (450 g)
1¾ cups dried breadcrumbs (160 g)

Put the beans into a large pot with the other bean
    ingredients and 2 quarts of water and cook until the
    beans are tender, 1½ to 2 hours.
Meanwhile, prepare the sauté. Heat the goose fat in a
    large frying pan, add the lamb, and brown the meat
    over a medium heat. Add the onions and the chopped
    garlic and brown them lightly, then spoon in enough
    liquid from the bean pot to barely cover the meat.
    Add the tomatoes, salt, pepper, and a small bouquet
    garni. Cover and simmer slowly for 1½ hours. Brown
    the Toulouse sausage in a little lard and add
    it with the garlic sausage to the pan with the lamb
    and simmer for 10 minutes.
Preheat the oven to 350°F. Remove the bouquet garni,
    whole carrots, and onion from the bean pot and discard.
Remove the meat and pork rind from the bean pot and
    cut them into large chunks. Rub the inside of a large
    earthenware pot with the clove of garlic, and place
    half of the beans in the pot. Add all of the meat (in-
    cluding the lamb and the preserved goose) and cover
    with the remaining beans. Bring the *cassoulet* to a boil
    on top of the stove, then sprinkle the surface lightly
    with breadcrumbs.
Transfer the pot to the oven and bake for 1½ hours,
    breaking the crust that forms and stirring it in, then
    sprinkling lightly with more breadcrumbs every 15
    minutes so that you will have broken and stirred in 5
    to 7 crusts; leave the last crust to brown before serving.

for 8 to 10 people / photographs on page 195 and opposite

MORUE À LA MINERVOISE   *Salt Cod with Olives and Anchovies*

2 pounds dried salt cod, rinsed and soaked in cold
    water, which should be changed every 6 hours or so,
    for 24 hours (1 kg)
3 tablespoons olive oil (45 ml)
2 ounces small black olives, pitted (50 g)
3 anchovy fillets
2 sprigs of fresh thyme
2 sprigs of parsley

FOR THE SAUCE

1 onion, chopped
2 tablespoons olive oil (30 ml)
1 rounded tablespoon flour (15 g)
1 clove garlic, crushed
1 cup strong full-bodied red wine (in the Languedoc
    region, the wine used would be Minervois) (250 ml)
Salt, freshly ground pepper

First prepare the sauce. Brown the onion lightly in olive
    oil. Sprinkle with the flour, add the garlic, and gradually
    add the wine and about 1 cup of water, stirring well.
    Season and simmer gently for 45 minutes.
Drain and dry the cod and cut into large cubes. Heat the
    oil in a sauté pan and sauté the cod until golden,
    but do not brown. Cover with the sauce and add the
    olives. Simmer gently for 20 minutes. Chop the
    anchovies and add them to the cod. Sprinkle with
    thyme and parsley and serve with boiled potatoes or
    cornmeal dumplings.

for 6 people

FOIE DE PORC SALÉ   *Dried and Salted Pig's Liver*

One of the most interesting pig's liver preparations to be found anywhere in France, it is quite easy to make and requires only patience and a well-ventilated kitchen or a back porch for perfect results.

1 2-pound whole pig's liver (1 kg), which will weigh about 1 pound 2 ounces when dried (500 g)
Coarse salt
Freshly ground pepper

Place a layer of coarse salt in a glass or stoneware platter large enough to hold the liver. Put the liver on top of the salt and pour on enough salt to bury it completely. Leave for 18 days, remove the liver from the salt, and wash it in cold water.
Place the liver in a large bowl with cold water to cover and soak for 24 hours, changing the water once or twice. Drain the liver and dry with a clean towel. Season it generously with freshly ground pepper. Place the liver on a clean cloth and roll it up to form a sausagelike shape. Wrap string tightly around the outside of the cloth and tie the ends of the cloth off as close to the ends of the piece of liver as possible. Hang the liver in a well-ventilated place, or outdoors in the shade, to dry for at least 1 week before unwrapping and cooking.
To serve as a salad, slice the liver and fry rapidly in olive oil. Add to sliced radishes, hard-boiled eggs, and artichoke hearts. Deglaze the pan with a few drops of wine vinegar and sprinkle over the salad. Add more olive oil to taste.

for 6 to 8 people / photograph opposite

GIGOT DE PALAVAS   *Turbot, Gigot Style*

1 good-sized piece turbot or ling (2 pounds), cleaned and scaled (1 kg)
¼ cup olive oil (60 ml)
3 onions, minced
3 green peppers, seeded and cut into strips
½ pound eggplant, sliced (250 g)
10 cloves garlic
1 pound tomatoes, seeded and quartered (500 g)
Salt, freshly ground pepper
½ pound zucchini, sliced (250 g)

Preheat the oven to 350°F. In an oven-proof baking dish heat the oil and sauté the onions, until golden. Add the green pepper strips and cook until softened. Add the sliced eggplant. Crush 3 cloves of garlic and add them along with the tomatoes. Season with salt and pepper and cook over low heat, without stirring, so that the vegetables reduce gently. Add the zucchini and cook gently for 20 to 25 minutes. Stud the turbot with garlic slivers (like a leg of lamb) and place it on the bed of vegetables; add salt and pepper.
Bake, turning the fish over regularly, so that it cooks evenly. Baste it with the vegetable juices and cook until done, 20 to 25 minutes. (When tested with a fork the flesh should flake readily and no longer be translucent.) Serve from the same dish in which it was cooked.

for 6 people / photograph on page 200

CRÈME D'HOMÈRE   *Wine and Honey Cream*

1⅓ cups sweet white wine (⅓ liter)
⅔ cup pale honey (150 g)
6 eggs
Pinch of ground cinnamon
Strip of lemon peel
Sugar (for caramel)

Preheat the oven to 300°F. Put the wine into a pan with the honey, cinnamon, and lemon peel and bring slowly to the simmering point. When the honey has dissolved completely, set aside to cool a little while you beat the eggs.
Pour the liquid slowly onto the beaten eggs, whisking all the time. If you leave out 1 or 2 of the egg whites, the texture will be creamier and lighter.
Coat a large mold or several smaller molds with caramel: sprinkle the mold with sugar and heat in the oven or over low heat until the sugar is brown and bubbling. Increase the oven temperature to 325°F. Fill the molds with the egg and honey mixture and bake for 30 minutes for small molds, a little longer for one large mold.
When cool, turn out and serve. This cream can be accompanied by dry cakes, such as the *croquets* of Limoges.

for 6 people / photograph on page 208

PAYS BASQUE

PAYS BASQUE

IN AINHOA, a dignified Basque village in which the twentieth century is represented by a filling station and little more, an evening mist drapes the hilltops. You are warmly welcomed in the inn, served an appropriately early evening meal (Basque air, freshened by Atlantic breezes, accelerates the appetite), and the Basque fare is quite tasty. However, inspection of the menu indicates that the local specialties are not very numerous. By the time you have had a couple of Basque soups, a *pipérade* (a scrambled-egg dish with garlic, onion, peppers, and a little *jambon de Bayonne*), chicken or fresh tuna *à la basquaise*, some of the local bread, also with *jambon de Bayonne* and with Basque *charcuterie*, and a good wedge of *gâteau basque*, there aren't a great many Basque dishes left to try, unless you're able to penetrate farmhouses, make yourself understood, and sample some of the more obscure peasant dishes, such as *Etchke Biskoxa* or *Arrouchquilla*.

Yet Basque food is well worth exploring. Though the range is small, everything is harmonious and straightforward. Basque cooking enhances the flavor of the trout of the local rivers, the salmon of the Adour (one of the few French rivers in which salmon are still to be

Salmon run up the Adour river in the spawning season, and, when freshly caught, *left*, are prepared simply. For saumon grillé, *chef Rouzard at the Caravelle restaurant near Tarbe marinates thick salmon steaks in olive oil, then grills them briefly, turning each steak carefully and leaving a cross-hatched pattern. He finishes the dish by baking the salmon, opposite, on a bed of fennel, parsley, laurel, and thyme.*

had), the mutton, the lamb, and the vegetables. And the scenery and architecture are superb, which adds greatly to the pleasure of eating.

The whole question of who the Basques are and how they have come to stay in the same area for as long as they have (they have been there for as far back as records stretch), preserving what is in many ways a medieval style of life, is a mystery that seems to be more pronounced on the French than on the Spanish side of the frontier. Visits to bookstores bear this point out. The foods and cooking of the Basque people in Spain have been the subject of not just a few books, but many; and these include a whole volume of the *Enciclopedia Vasca*, 550 pages of culinary lore and gastronomic subtleties (seven different recipes for *piperrada*, the Spanish Basque name for *pipérade*) and many an enticing picture in full color of Basque festivities.

If you keep to the French side of the frontier, you find nothing comparable. In fact, it seems that nothing deals exclusively with the cuisine of the Pays Basque. One book combines it with the Béarn; another with the Landes and Gascony; a third with southwest France.

The obvious explanation is that the Basques are far more numerous and occupy far more territory in Spain than in France. But can this be enough to account for so great a difference? The Basque people and their language are indeed puzzling phenomena, and the origins of their culture are impossible, in the present state of our knowledge, to discern.

The coastal region of the Pays Basque has been changed almost beyond recognition, especially as a result of the annual tide of French vacationers that washes into the area for six weeks or so; but

to travel even a dozen miles inland is to step back into a world that has changed very little since the Middle Ages. Too little, say those Basques who feel that their corner of France has been unfairly neglected in economic planning, which it has been. On the other hand, you can see why the officials of Paris, contemplating the tiny Basque-speaking area, and the Basques' determination and efforts to preserve their social structure, system of land tenure, language (despite its having no official status), and customs, would hesitate to try to transform a seemingly unchangeable pattern. An examination of the natural resources of the Pays Basque, in farming terms, could only reinforce their hesitation.

The raw materials available to Basque cooks are limited today in much the same way they were centuries ago; and as a result of the dynamism (or perhaps inertia) of the Basque cultural tradition, they continue to do much the same things with this limited range of produce. Limited, yet variegated nevertheless—for the Pays Basque comprises within its small confines very different types of land.

First, there is the coastal strip, running from just south of Bayonne to the Spanish frontier. (Bayonne, incidentally, is the capital of the Pays Basque, although it lies just outside the linguistic frontier. One Basque's explanation for this is that on market days Bayonne temporarily has a majority of Basque-speakers.) This coastal strip is a gateway to the riches of the Atlantic Ocean or, more specifically, to those of the Bay of Biscay. Second, there are the mountain valleys, whose small rivers yield excellent trout and that provide space for market gardening and for growing the red peppers, long and thin and moderately piquant, that appear in so many

Basque dishes. Third, there are the mountains, still partly clad in forest, where sheep and pigs roam in ideal conditions. And, finally, there are some small plains, such as the one around Saint-Palais, where normal agriculture can be practiced, and it is possible to drive for as many as ten miles through fields of corn, the crop most suited to local climatic conditions.

Let us turn to the sea and seafoods. Saint-Jean-de-Luz, the main fishing port, specializes in tuna fishing. The Luziens seem to have had a long-standing penchant for large fish, and for whales too. However, they also fish for anchovies and sardines in inshore waters. Much of their catch is destined for the canning factories, which they have set up on a cooperative basis. Even so, the Basque coast is an excellent place for fishing for fresh tuna, which is most often served *à la basquaise*.

The term *à la basquaise* doesn't seem to be used in any of the early French cookbooks. It isn't mentioned in Gouffé, or in Urbain-Dubois. Even *La Grand Cuisine Illustrée*, by Salles and Montagné (editions around the beginning of this century), leaves out any mention of the Pays Basque. Indeed, it seems to have been only with the publication of Austin de Croze's *Plats Régionaux de France* (1928) that the term and the region were put on the gastronomic map, although the strength of Basque traditions is such that we can assume that dishes had been being made *à la basquaise* for centuries. What, then, does the term mean? Something cooked in (or, perhaps, first cooked and then covered with) a thick sauce ranging in color from grayish-orange to a vivid red and having as its main constituents both tomatoes and the piquant red peppers of the Pays Basque. These peppers are cultivated in various parts of the region, but most noticeably at Espelette, a major Basque village that has the distinction of being responsible for one of the most popular postcards of the area, showing a typical Basque house in the village, festooned with strings of the red peppers hanging out to dry in the sun. Plastic sachets of coarsely ground or flaked red pepper can be bought anywhere in the region.

Ttoro, *opposite, is the Basque version of* bouillabaisse. *At the Hôtel Bakea in Biriatou, on the Spanish border, chef François Bakea makes a spicy* fumet *with tomatoes and chili peppers, to which he adds mussels, langoustines, and several kinds of fish. In the Pays Basque, where one is never far from the mountains or the sea, the catch of the day may be fish or fowl, or both, such as salmon and woodcock, top right. At center right, the indispensable bouquet garni, here with bay leaf, parsley, thyme, and scallions. Bottom right, alevins d'anguilles, an unusual dish made of baby eels, here served at the Pablo in Saint-Jean-de-Luz.*

223

Thon à la basquaise, made with slices of freshly landed tuna, is a very tasty dish and is available at any of a score of small, unpretentious, but good restaurants in Saint-Jean-de-Luz and Biarritz.

THE BASQUE fishing community is responsible for one of the best-known French Basque dishes: the soup called *ttoro* (*tioro* on the Spanish side of the frontier). In its very simplest form, this soup is made with herbs, bread, olive oil, and the water left from cooking salt cod (*morue*, not to be confused with *cabillaud*, which is fresh cod); and salt cod is, or was, for everyone, not just for the fishermen's families. However, the soup commonly contains fish, for example, conger eel or angler fish; and, like *bouil-*

Jambon de Bayonne, opposite, is one of the Pays Basque's best-known products. The hams are cured in a pickling mixture that includes wine, and they might be lightly smoked. Despite their name, most come from Orthez, and producers have formed an association to protect the purity of the curing process. A farmer's wife, below, gathers fresh hay for her goats and rabbits.

labaisse in the Mediterranean, its humble and common-sense origin (make something easy with what is left over from the day's catch) has been overlaid by the addition of what are now expensive ingredients, such as langoustines (Dublin Bay prawns) or even oysters. The one-star restaurants, surprisingly numerous in the Pays Basque, are apt to tell you that they need forty-eight hours' notice if you want to have *ttoro*, a requirement that in itself tells us much about the history of this simple fisherman's dish.

Another dish, perhaps more interesting, is the *soupe de poissons à la Biarrotte*, which is based on what are called "*poissons maigres*," that is, fish that are not much good for anything but the soup pot, and calls for the goose fat that is typical of the whole of the southwest of France, plenty of sorrel, and lettuce. It is good. So is the Spanish Basque *marmitako*, a soup that has bonito, a fish revered in the north of Spain, and potatoes as its main ingredients and that really is a fisherman's dish, although it is eaten by others too.

"Progress" has seemed to threaten the future of Saint-Jean-de-Luz, since the charming little port, well adapted to provide berths for the delightfully colored and relatively small fishing boats of the Basque fishermen, cannot take the larger vessels that are now being used and that have to discharge their catch at Bayonne, or even in Spain. However, another aspect of progress, improved roads, has ensured that these same catches can be swiftly transported to the canning establishments of Saint-Jean-de-Luz, so it looks as though they will be able to go on canning for the indefinite future. And the inshore fisheries should suffice to guarantee the natural continuation of the town as a picturesque and active fishing port.

Let us, however, leave the fishermen and consider the Basque pig and its most famous product, the *jambon de Bayonne*. This is ham that has been salted with *sel de Bayonne* (which, in fact, comes from underground sources between Mouguerre and Briscous) and rubbed with the local red pepper. It may be eaten raw, in very thin slices like those of Parma ham, or chopped up and used in cooking. It turns up as part of the garnish in many dishes, for example, fried trout. It is an excellent product, whose reputation extends far outside France. However, the demand for it is so great in relation to the local supply of pigs that something like 90 percent of the hams are "imported" to Bayonne from other regions to be given the treatment. It is a pity that the Pays Basque can't conveniently accommodate more pigs, since those that root around in the wooded hills are by common consent particularly healthy members of the species and make very good eating. Like most of the regions of France,

the Pays Basque has its own range of *charcuterie*. A particularly appealing offering, to some tastes, is blood sausage with tiny pigs' tongues embedded in it. Sliced, it gives the impression of two pink eyes staring out of a round black face.

The pigs have taken us up into the foothills of the Pyrénées, where there are few Basque towns. The geography of the area accommodates villages, and even some large ones. These villages are attractive and impressive: large houses, a style of architecture that has changed little over the centuries, a sense of pride and continuity that has caused most of the houses to be built with stone lintels over the doors on which are inscribed the names of the men who had them built and the dates of construction. To each house belongs some land, for household farming; and to each village belongs much more land for communal use. Real estate is not broken up among surviving kith and kin when the owner dies. It passes intact to the principal heir. This system keeps the units "right" in size. It also encourages children who are not heirs to property to emigrate; and scores of thousands of Basques have left their country for destinations in Latin America and elsewhere (elsewhere including the Church, which absorbs a relatively high proportion of them).

I F YOU VISIT the Basque Museum in Bayonne, and persuade the attendant to unlock the glass case of publications and to extract for you a faded pamphlet called *Usoak et Panthières en Pays Basque*, by André Ospital, you will find yourself puzzling over an enigmatic cover picture. A man wearing a Basque beret is standing, legs astride, on a thinly camouflaged platform raised high above the countryside. He seems to be poised to hurl a white disk into the air. Inside the booklet is the explanation. He is indeed about to hurl a white disk aloft; and his purpose is to project it upwards at a flight of wood pigeons making their annual migratory flight to the south.

The story goes that many hundreds of years ago, a young monk was idly flinging flat white stones into the sky, when he noticed that if a stone rose toward a flight of these birds, they would instantly descend almost to ground level, flapping their wings, under the misapprehension that they were being attacked from below, in characteristic fashion, by a sparrow hawk. It quickly dawned on him that if he had helpers below in the valley, with nets, they

M. Justin Daréet of Saint-Maur par Mirande, opposite, raises much of what he eats and would never be seen without his béret Basque. *The* foie de canard aux pommes, *top right, is gently cooked in port wine. Still pink, it is sliced, bottom right, and served on toast with stewed apple slices.*

Oeufs Grand-père Rouzard, *above, is a simple but elegant dish in which an egg is poached in* sauce Périgueux, *or truffle sauce, and served with the sauce on sautéed* foie de canard escalopé. *M. Rouzard of the Caravelle, near Tarbes, named it after his father, who gave him the recipe. Opposite, a slice of Rouzard's* dodine de foie de canard à l'Armagnac, *a duck liver terrine, is steeped in Armagnac and served with a sprig of watercress.*

would snare many of the birds; and thus was born the cooperative Basque sport of pigeon hunting.

The hunters and the birds have maintained the same patterns, of cunning cooperation and fatal panic, ever since. Although the number of migratory birds seems to be diminishing, it is still possible in the season, which is the autumn, to obtain a fine *salmis de palombes* in the Basque villages. The pigeons are quartered, then browned in hot olive oil. Small onions and diced *jambon de Bayonne* are lightly fried, then set aside. A white *roux* is made in the pan, deglazed with a cup of red Bordeaux, and diluted with a quart of bouillon. The pigeon pieces, onions, and ham, including the scraps of rind, go into the sauce and are simmered very gently

for an hour and a half. The pigeon pieces are served on slices of bread fried in a mixture of oil and butter, with plenty of the sauce.

On a chilly evening this would be a good dish to eat by the fire sitting on a piece of furniture also to be seen in the Basque Museum. It is a high-backed wooden bench for two; but a shelf folds down from one half of it to convert it into a seat for one with a TV-type table at the diner's elbow. The other ingenious item of Basque furniture found in the museum is a splendid kitchen/dining table that incorporates an immense drawer. Why was it so big? It was the larder, the attendant explained. Movement between table and larder had been eliminated by this masterly piece of design.

Another booklet in the Basque Museum relates to the curious history of the chocolate makers of Bayonne. The explanation for why Bayonne acquired fame as a source of fine *chocolaterie*, as for so many minor gastronomic mysteries, goes back several centuries, to the time when chocolate first came to Spain from the New World. Among those who worked on the new product were Spanish Jews, who having been persecuted first in Spain and then in Portugal, arrived in southwestern France, where they had commercial links. From the early seventeenth century, they were making chocolate in the region of Bayonne. At first, they could work only for French *chocolatiers*, but after the French Revolution their efforts to establish themselves as chocolate makers in their own right were successful. A great vogue for chocolate had swept France in the eighteenth century, and the Jewish producers' prior and expert knowledge of the qualities of the various kinds of cocoa bean and of the techniques of manufacture stood them in good stead. The reputation of houses such as Biraben, one that survives to the present day, grew rapidly.

An amusing anecdote illustrates the fame of Bayonne chocolate. When, at the end of the Carlist War in 1876, the defeated Carlist army straggled out of Spain into the Pays Basque, there was much confusion in Bayonne. One of the leading *chocolatiers* left his shop in the charge of a young employee while he went to view the hubbub; and this youngster was soon confronted by a noble of the Carlist army, doing the one bit of shopping that he could fit in before heading north. Bayonne chocolate was the natural choice. The noble scooped up a sackful of chocolate bars from the window display, threw the lad four *douros*, and galloped off. Returning later, the owner of the shop was shaken to find that all his dummy chocolate bars, of wood, had disappeared.

The other chocolate story of the Pays Basque is set in World War II. Sugar was in very short supply in France, and *chocolatiers* were compelled to use

has eighteen different varieties, of which the pistachio version is the prettiest and possibly also the most delicious. A study of the variety of patterns suggests that behind the scenes the nougat manipulators fall into two schools, the Proto-Iberians, who specialize in whorls reminiscent of certain cave paintings, and the modernists, who insert cunning little rectangles of color and have evidently been under Cubist influence. But visual excitement of this order, although clearly in tune with the Basque temperament, is not an essential feature of their confectionery. The macaroons found in Saint-Jean-de-Luz are demurely normal in appearance, but they may be the best to be found anywhere.

A subdued appearance is also characteristic of one of the stock items on Basque menus—the *gâteau basque*, a wholesome confection rather like a shallow pie. The ingredients are simple: flour, eggs, sugar, butter, milk, and a little grated lemon peel. Some add rum. With or without the rum, it is very good. So is the Basque pumpkin bread, which can serve as the symbol of the impact of New World foods on this ancient community, for it requires both cornmeal and pumpkin, and, preferably, a little rum from the West Indies. It is a sweetish bread, which goes very well with fresh fruit. The combination of flavors is a delightful one to retain when you leave the Basque country.

Pétite tarte aux pommes à la crème, *opposite, is prepared according to Michel Guérard's recipe.* Tarte à l'orange, *right, is a popular dessert at the Caravelle restaurant near Tarbe. A selection of nougat* tourons, *above, includes coffee-and-vanilla (top), pistachio (center), and fruit (foreground).*

substitutes. All of them but one—Polit, of Arnéguy. This fortunate man had his factory on the Spanish bank of the Nive, where it forms the frontier with France, and his shop on the French bank. The two were joined by a footbridge. The business that he did, using Spanish sugar to make his chocolate, was enormous; indeed, he couldn't increase his output sufficiently to cope with the demand!

There is plenty of other evidence that the Basques have a sweet tooth. The most eye-catching items in Basque confectionery shops are the vividly colored displays of *touron*, as they call the famous nougat of Spain (*torron* in Spanish). The nougat is in the form of long flattish loaves cut open to exhibit the intricate patterns inside. White, green, and brown are the main (but not the only) colors. One shop

OMELETTE À LA PIPÉRADE

Pipérade (see recipe below)
6 eggs
2 tablespoons chopped parsley
Salt, freshly ground pepper
1 generous tablespoon rendered goose fat or lard
4 small slices ham

Beat the eggs in a bowl with the parsley and season with salt and pepper. Heat the fat in a large frying pan until hot and pour in the beaten eggs. When they start to set, add the *pipérade* and stir it into the eggs. Fold the omelette before it is completely set. Serve with the slices of ham, nicely browned in a separate pan.

for 4 people

PIPÉRADE

4 large red, yellow, and green peppers
¼ cup olive oil (60 ml)
1 large onion, sliced
4 large tomatoes, peeled and cut into chunks
1 clove garlic, sliced
½ chili pepper
1 bay leaf
1 sprig of fresh thyme
Salt

Skin the peppers by broiling under or over a direct flame until the skin puffs up and blisters. Place in a brown paper bag to steam for 5 or 6 minutes. Peel and core the peppers and cut them into strips.

Heat the oil in a heavy pan, add the onion, and sauté until softened. Add the pepper strips, tomatoes, garlic, chili, bay leaf, and thyme. Cook gently, stirring for a while, then cover the pan and simmer for 30 minutes, until all the excess liquid has evaporated. Add salt to taste.

for 4 people

MOULES AUX AMANDES *Mussels with Almonds*

4 pounds mussels (2 kg)

FOR THE STUFFING
1 clove garlic
2 sprigs of parsley, chopped
4 tablespoons butter, softened (50 g)
½ cup fresh white breadcrumbs (30 g)
2 or 3 tablespoons white wine
¾ cup ground almonds (or whole almonds, chopped fairly fine) (100 g)
Salt, freshly ground pepper

Make the stuffing: pound the garlic and parsley together, then add the softened butter. Soak the breadcrumbs in the white wine until soft and squeeze them dry; add them to the garlic mixture. Mix in the almonds and season, working everything together into a paste.

Preheat the oven to 425°F. Clean and scrape the mussels under running water. Put them into a large saucepan with a lid and shake them over a brisk heat until they have opened. Allow them to cool a little and then remove the top shells. Arrange the mussels on a large dish or two smaller ones and put a little almond mixture onto each mussel. Bake the mussels for 5 or 6 minutes.

These mussels are eaten sizzling hot with a *pousse rapière*—in other words, a shot of the following concoction: fill a glass with ice, put in a measure of Armagnac, add a slice of orange, and fill with sparkling dry white wine, very well chilled.

for 4 people / photographs at left and opposite

SAUMON GRILLÉ   *Grilled Salmon*

4 thick slices fresh salmon, about ½ pound each (250 g)
½ cup olive oil (not too strong) (110 ml)
Salt, freshly ground pepper
Oil (for greasing paper)
4 bay leaves
4 sprigs of parsley
8 sprigs of fennel
2 lemons

Marinate the salmon in the olive oil for about 1 hour, turning it over occasionally. The cooking is done in two stages. First, drain the salmon and broil gently, turning the steaks several times. Don't overdo it, the slices should be just cooked through. The flesh near the bone should be pink, not red.

Preheat the oven to 400°F. Cut two rounds of parchment paper (or aluminum foil) for each slice of salmon, oil them, and put a little bouquet of the herbs on one. Place the salmon on top, season it well, and cover with the second piece of parchment paper, folding the sides up to seal them. Bake the *papillotes* for 5 minutes and serve with lemon wedges.

Steamed potatoes, sprinkled with melted butter and chopped parsley, finish off the dish.

for 4 people / photographs on pages 220 and 221

CHIPIRONS EN SU TINTA   *Squid Stewed in Their Ink*

2 pounds squid (1 kg)
2 onions
2 cloves garlic
4 tablespoons olive oil (60 ml)
½ cup fresh breadcrumbs (30 g)
Salt, freshly ground pepper
1¼ cups white wine (¼ liter)
2 large tomatoes, peeled and chopped
Pinch of chili powder
A little potato flour or arrowroot
Dash of Armagnac (optional)

Clean the squid. Cut off the head and tentacles, which should be separated from the hard part in the center (the stomach), and set aside. Cut off the black spot (the mouth) on the lower head. Remove the bone from the stomach, cut open the bodies, and throw away the entrails but keep the ink sacs, being careful not to damage them. Pull off the dark outerskin of the stomach and set the stomach aside.

Make a stuffing. Cut the heads and tentacles of the squid into little strips. Chop 1 onion and cook it in 2 tablespoons of the oil until softened, together with 1 crushed clove of garlic and the squid strips. Let them cook gently for 30 minutes. Add the breadcrumbs, salt, and pepper, and then fill the squid with this mixture and fasten the ends shut with toothpicks.

Heat the remaining 2 tablespoons of olive oil in a sauté pan and lightly brown the squid together with the remaining onion and garlic, finely chopped. Add the white wine, tomatoes, and chili powder, and simmer, uncovered, for about 30 minutes.

Pour the ink into a cup, mix in a little potato flour, and stir it into the sauce, which will turn quite black. Add a dash of Armagnac, season with salt and pepper, and simmer, covered, for 1 hour. Taste for seasoning before serving—it should be a particularly strong and highly flavored dish.

for 4 people / photograph below

TTORO *Basque Fish Soup*

FOR THE FUMET

1 head of a conger eel and trimmings and heads of a
  silver hake, *rascasse* (hogfish or hogsnapper), or
  angler fish
2 tablespoons olive oil (30 ml)
2 onions, sliced
1 bouquet garni—see Appendix
2 cloves garlic, crushed
1 tomato
½ chili pepper
2 cups dry white wine (½ liter)

FOR THE SOUP

1 whole (1 pound 2 ounces) angler fish, cleaned (500 g)
1 whole (1 pound 2 ounces) conger eel, cleaned (500 g)
1 whole small *rascasse*, cleaned (hogfish or hogsnapper)
2 whole small gurnard, cleaned (sea robin)
4 raw langoustines or jumbo shrimp, cleaned
2 pounds mussels, cleaned (1 kg)
2 to 4 tablespoons olive oil
2 tablespoons flour
Salt, freshly ground pepper

To prepare the *fumet*, chop the fish heads and trimmings.
  Sweat them in a large covered pan, by cooking gently
  in the olive oil with the onions, bouquet garni, and
  garlic.
When the onions just begin to brown, add the tomato,
  chili, white wine, and 5 cups of water. Cover and
  simmer for 1 hour. Strain the *fumet* through a fine
  sieve and return to a boil—it should be deliciously
  velvety.
Preheat the oven to 450°F. To make the soup: cut the
  fish into thick slices. Sprinkle them with salt and dip
  them in flour. Heat the oil to sizzling in a large frying
  pan and fry the fish slices on both sides. Drain well
  and arrange in the bottom of a large casserole
  (preferably flameproof earthenware). Add the
  langoustines and mussels and pour on the boiling
  fumet, which should just cover everything. In the
  oven, bring the soup to a boil, and cook for 5 minutes.
  Season with salt and pepper.
Sprinkle the soup with chopped parsley and serve with
  croûtons of fried bread rubbed with garlic.

for 4 or 5 people / *photograph on page 222*

PASTIZA   *Basque Cake*

FOR THE PASTRY
2 cups flour (275 g)
¾ cup plus 2 tablespoons butter, softened (200 g)
1 whole egg
2 egg yolks
2 cups powdered sugar (200 g)
Zest of 1 lemon
Pinch of salt
Flour (for dusting)

FOR THE FILLING
1¼ cups milk (¼ liter)
3 egg yolks
1 cup sugar (200 g)
3 tablespoons flour (30 g)
3 tablespoons rum (45 ml)

Prepare the pastry. Place the flour in a bowl and make a well in the center. Put all the remaining ingredients for the pastry in the well and mix them together with your fingers, gradually drawing in the flour. You should have a supple dough similar to a sweet flan pastry. If it seems too stiff, work in 1 or 2 tablespoons of lukewarm water. Form into a ball and refrigerate for at least 1 hour.

Meanwhile, prepare the custard filling. Heat the milk until boiling in a saucepan. Beat 2 of the egg yolks with the sugar until light and pale. Whisk in the flour and then gradually add the boiling milk, whisking all the time. Return the mixture to the pan and stir over a low heat until it thickens. Flavor with the rum and let cool, whisking occasionally.

Sprinkle a clean dish towel with flour and work two-thirds of the pastry into a large round, ⅛ inch thick. Work the remaining pastry into a 9-inch round.

Preheat the oven to 350°F. Butter and flour a 9-inch cake pan with a removable base. Line it with the pastry, which should be large enough to hang over the edges. Pour in the custard and wet the edges of the pastry. Cover with the remaining pastry and pinch the edges together. Make a design on the top with a fork; brush with the remaining beaten egg yolk. Bake for about 50 minutes, keeping an eye on it to see it does not burn. When it is nicely golden, cover the top loosely with a sheet of aluminum foil to protect it. Serve cold. You can use a different filling such as apricot purée or cherry jam and cherries.

for 8 people / photograph opposite

ORANGES SOUFFLÉES   *Orange Sorbets with Meringue Topping*

FOR THE SORBET
6 oranges
Juice of 4 oranges
Juice of 1 lemon
1 cup sugar (200 g)

FOR THE MERINGUE
2 egg whites
A few drops of lemon juice
½ cup powdered sugar (50 g)
1 tablespoon Cointreau

Cut off the tops of the oranges and keep them to use as lids. Scoop the insides out of the oranges and chop in a food processor or blender. Strain into a bowl, with the juice of 4 more oranges and the juice of 1 lemon. In a heavy pan, dissolve the sugar in ½ cup water and heat gently until the sugar has completely dissolved. Allow to cool and mix with the orange juice.

Fill the empty oranges with the mixture and freeze. If there is more than enough, freeze the rest separately.

Twenty minutes before serving, preheat the oven to 450°F and make the meringue. Beat the egg whites with a few drops of lemon juice until stiff, then gradually add the powdered sugar, beating all the time.

Remove the oranges from the freezer, arrange them in an ovenproof dish, and surround them with ice cubes. Pour a little Cointreau into each one and spoon some of the meringue on top. Bake for 3 or 4 minutes, until the meringue is golden. Serve at once with their lids.

for 6 people / photograph below

BORDELAIS

BORDELAIS

IF YOU were to visit the province of the Gironde and the wine-producing area known as the Bordelais, of which Bordeaux is the capital city, late in the year when the grapes have been stripped from the vines and crushed to make wine and the vine prunings gathered for fuel, and if you were invited to sit at the table in the kitchen of a small château, such as the Château Cissac in the Médoc region, to lunch with the proprietor and perhaps the cellar master —the *maître de chai*—who supervises the vintage, your meal would surely include a boned rib steak, grilled over the smoking vine twigs, and with it a generous portion of those brown-capped, succulent wild mushrooms known as *cèpes*.

The steak would arrive covered with chopped shallots, and the *cèpes* would be dusted with finely chopped parsley and garlic. The proprietor of Cissac, Louis Vialard, is an authority on Bordelais cooking and has appeared on French television to show cooks how to prepare local dishes, in particular a true *entrecôte bordelaise*, a traditional dish whose origins are based entirely on the produce of the region and the habits of local industry. Few, if any, restaurants will go to the trouble of

In one of the thousands of acres of vineyards in the Bordelais, preceding overleaf, a vigneron *and his plowhorse turn the rich soil of the Sauternes-producing Château de Suduirant. The city of Bordeaux, top, on the river Garonne, grew and prospered around the wine trade and is one of the gastronomic centers of France. Oysters from Arcachon,* opposite, are a specialty of Bordeaux cuisine and can be served with crépinettes truffées—*pork sausages studded with truffles. Both the oysters and the* crépinettes *take a sauce made with wine vinegar and shallots. A dry white Bordeaux is the expected drink.*

obtaining vine prunings (*sarments*) to grill their steaks, so that the *entrecôte bordelaise* is found only in its natural habitat—the vineyard.

According to historian Christian Guy, the original dish was made, long ago, with the meat of vineyard rodents (apparently very tasty) that had grown plump and winy from their environment: "The ancestor of the steak *à la bordelaise* is steak *tonnelier* (cooper). It is made with rats fattened in the winemaking plants of the Gironde. After they have been cleaned and singed, covered with a light layer of oil and a lot of coarsely chopped shallots, they are grilled on a fire made from the remains of casks or vine shoots." It is likely that the *entrecôte* steak, an English invention, began to figure in French cooking after its introduction in the late eighteenth century, to become a specialty in a region not particularly noted for its beef.

It is important, explains Vialard, that your steak be grilled over *two* different species of vine, the Cabernet Sauvignon, which gives a searing heat, and at the last moment a bunch of twigs from the Merlot vine, a refinement that creates smoke, which adds flavor to the steak. The steak, about two inches thick, must be grilled on both surfaces until you see juice appearing on the surface. Then you toss in the Merlot prunings, give it a second or two, and your steak is almost ready—all but the final touch—the addition of chopped, raw shallots sprinkled over the meat. The shallot is to Bordeaux what garlic is to the south, and purists say you shouldn't mix garlic and shallots together—it must be either one or the other. As with most regional recipes, there are many variations, in the Bordelais from vineyard to vineyard—some add poached beef marrow as a garnish.

STRICTLY speaking, the dish is really an *entrecôte maître de chai*, for that known in restaurants as *entrecôte bordelaise* is usually a steak served with a wine and shallot sauce and is probably a nineteenth-century invention of Paris chefs. The shallot symbolizes the cultivated, the *cèpe* the wild, produce of the Bordelais. At the end of August and until November, in the woods of the Gironde, and the forests of the Landes to the south of Bordeaux, the brown-capped, fat-stemmed *cèpes* push their way through the humus of last year's oak and chestnut leaves. The *cèpes* are difficult to detect for they are well camouflaged, and their arrival is eagerly awaited by an army of *cèpe* hunters. In Bordeaux the *cèpe* rules. Doctors say that they are pestered for certificates for "sick leave" because everyone wants time off to go mushroom picking, or to hunt game through the forests.

In some districts game stocks are becoming seriously depleted, or perhaps the birds are more cunning; partridges, quails, pheasants, larks, thrushes, and buntings of the Landes forests are not falling to the guns as they did in the past. In these days of stiff competition, even the mushroom hunters often return empty-handed, although some have a particular knack for finding the elusive fungi, almost a nose, you might say; one man was envied for discovering a fine crop on the Bordeaux golf course, for the value put on these spongy, superior mushrooms (known to botanists as *Boletus edulis*) is such that early arrivals in the markets fetch the equivalent of $2 per *cèpe*.

The experienced *cèpe* gatherer takes a wicker basket—plastic bags being unacceptable—and searches for the delicacy in the oak woods or pine forests, according to the type of *cèpe*. There are two principal varieties, the *vrai cèpe de Bordeaux*, also called the *cèpe de chêne*, and the less-esteemed subspecies, the *cèpe des pins*.

An immaculate foie gras de canard, *below, comes crated from the farm. When prepared* à la bordelaise, *opposite, it is baked for twenty minutes, and the fat is drained off. Then it is baked again, this time for ten minutes, with unripened, peeled grapes, which have been macerated in cognac.*

Cèpes, *above, are the edible boletus mushrooms that grow wild and are an element of the cuisine nearly as important as is wine. Cooked with garlic, they are authentically* à la bordelaise; *with shallots, they are* à la provençale. *Traditionally, however, Paris restaurants will serve the dish with shallots and call it* à la bordelaise.

One does not pull a *cèpe* by the root, but slices through the base of the stem with a sharp knife. The rules of the game are no less exacting when it comes to the cooking, and on this everyone is an expert. The general opinion is that you first get rid of excess moisture by lightly grilling the *cèpes*. You then separate the cap from the stem, make an incision in each cap with the point of a knife, and poach the *cèpes* in plenty of peanut oil, preferably in a casserole. This liberates the brown dye, which is tannin. You then drain the *cèpes*, and refry them in fresh oil in a frying pan until they take on a natural, brownish color. A few moments before you have finished the cooking, you toss in the finely chopped stalks, with parsley and just a touch of garlic, "enough so that you want more." Some cooks prefer to cook a whole clove of garlic in the oil along with the *cèpes* during the preliminary frying. Notice that there is no mention of shallots—in *cèpes bordelaise* the mushroom, curiously enough, is never married to its likely partner.

Ingredients in many local dishes reveal a delicate balance between north and south. Butter is rarely employed for cooking, and oil is preferred, as in the south; garlic is a southern influence, while shallots are northern, perhaps introduced from the Channel Isles and from Brittany. Likewise, several fish dishes are northern in style—such as the *alose* or allis shad from the Loire and the Seine, cooked in Bordeaux over *sarments*, and served with a purée of sorrel, or stuffed with sorrel, which is said to soften, by chemical action, the fish's tiny bones. There was once a minor industry in Gironde caviar, when sturgeon were caught in the estuary, but no one has seen a sturgeon for at least ten years: it is rather like the frequent reference to *"fromage du pays"*—there are no indigenous cheeses in the Bordelais.

Not typical of Bordeaux cooking, yet a "specialty of the region," is that curious dish *lamproie à la bordelaise*. Lampreys are eel-like fish found in the estuaries of large rivers, which travel upstream like salmon, to spawning grounds where they are easily trapped. This recipe has much in common with Lyonnais recipes such as the *matelote d'anguilles* and the *meurette*, in which river fish are cooked in a rich, red wine sauce with tiny onions and chopped ham; it is possible that *lamproie* is Bordeaux's ver-

Artichokes, above, are cultivated in many regions of France; in the Bordelais they are grown along the banks of the Garonne. Asparagus, too, is grown in most of the country. Argenteuil

asparagus, above, is sold during the season in the Marché Saint-Michel in Bordeaux, the largest market of the city.

sion of a Lyonnais dish. Cooks used to prepare the lampreys by hanging them, alive, from a nail driven into the wall and letting them bleed to death, for you need the blood to thicken the sauce. *Courage, mon brave!* for you now have to remove the poisonous, cartilaginous cord that runs down the lamprey's back. Failure to do this may have resulted in the death of Henry I, who died of a surfeit of lampreys.

The lampreys are stewed with leeks, mushrooms, onions, chopped ham, and a bottle of red wine. It is not, as you will have gathered, an everyday dish. The people of the Gironde say that canned lamprey is better than fresh lamprey, which it ought to be since a can of *lamproie à la bordelaise* can cost the equivalent of $20.

The finesse that characterizes the cooking of Bordeaux is well complemented by the infinitely subtle variety of its wines. Bordeaux is, of course, the premier wine-growing region of France, though you would get an argument from a Burgundian, and in Bordeaux one doesn't mention the word "Burgundy." The region contains about 35,000 growers, producing 3,500 different *crus*, or growths, of red and white wines—nowhere else in the world are

wines of such quality produced in such variety. Indeed, one of the great *premier cru* red wines, the Graves of Château Haut-Brion, is within city limits.

AT CHATEAU Cissac, in the parish of Pauillac in the Médoc, Louis Vialard produces an excellent *cru bourgeois* red wine, and the estate is but a cork's throw from the famous Château Lafite. "My vines touch the backside of Lafite," says Vialard cheerfully, a jibe at the austere and strict hierarchy of Bordeaux's wine system. Lafite heads the list of the five estates that produce the *premiers crus*—the aristocrats of Bordeaux wines, classified by a committee of brokers in 1855 and assessed, pragmatically, by the prices the wines were fetching on the market—then, as now, you get what you pay for. The other estates are Château Margaux, Château Latour, Château Haut-Brion, and Château Mouton-Rothschild, the last admitted to the *premiers crus* in 1973. These are all red wines, and three of them are in the little commune of Pauillac.

During the vintage when the wines are being made, Vialard is a constant presence, ever watchful,

245

nursing his wines through every stage of production. "I live with my wines, they are part of me. When I die, the wine will not be the same. Mind you, I'm not saying they will be less good—but simply not the same." No less attention is paid than at Lafite to the production of the wines, yet the Lafites will become aristocrats, for which connoisseurs will pay large sums. The disparity is due in part, Vialard explained, to the slope of the ground that provides drainage for the vine roots, but mainly to the proximity of the river. The Gironde keeps the vines cool and moist in summer and warm in winter. The quality of the great wines is the result of the precise geography of the estates in relation to the river, and the Gironde's microclimate. "I can show you the spot," said Vialard, "to within a few yards where the favorable conditions cease." Château Lafite is owned by the Rothschilds, who keep no fewer than eighty thousand bottles of this legendary wine in their private cellars, and their grapes are small, black, and sweet. Standing on the dry, stony soil among the vines, eating the grapes and spitting out the seeds—when you consider that it takes approximately one vine plant to produce one bottle of wine—is, it seems, the ultimate in hedonism.

Fishing on the Garonne, top, a well-equipped fisherman baits his hooks for shad, eel, and many other fish. Another rig, left, is permanently anchored near the bank and uses nets that are baited and lowered, then raised when the time is right for a good catch. Alose à l'oseille is shad, opposite, stuffed with sorrel that has been sautéed in butter and to which shad roe has been added. The fish is marinated in oil and white wine before it is baked.

THE CUISINE of Bordeaux is not without its luxuries. The Gironde borders the Dordogne, a source of truffles. The Landes produces preserved duck and goose—the *confit d'oie* that made Stendhal shudder—and the ortolan bunting, a tiny bird that you are advised to eat whole, your head covered by a table napkin so that outside influences cannot distract your attention from the flavor. *Fois gras*, the plump liver of specially fattened geese and ducks fed on corn, is cooked rare, *à point*, dressed with a *demi-glace* sauce of finely chopped truffles. This dish was served, preceded by a *tourin à l'ail*, and followed by *confit de canard* with *cèpes*, at a luncheon for eight hundred guests at the *ban de vendanges* in the church cloisters in Saint-Émilion. The *ban* proclaims the start of the grape harvest, and the menu is as representative and typical of the region as you would find anywhere in the Bordelais.

Geographically, Bordeaux is on a level with Parma

In the Marché Saint-Michel in Bordeaux, below, the fresh fish for sale are (from top) rougets barbets, sardines de Royan, and live eels. Grilled eels make a quick lunch at a Bordeaux café, opposite. The recipe—anguilles grillées avec persillade—includes garlic and shallots with the parsley, and the wine is a vin du pays, *perhaps a Graves sec.*

in Italy, so it is not surprising that oil rather than butter is important in the kitchen, and that garlic is used in Bordelais dishes. The cooking of Bordeaux has the best of both worlds, and has for centuries exploited the produce of that vast area called Aquitaine: In terms of variety Bordeaux is still the richest region in France.

The term *à la bordelaise* is open to varied interpretations. To the people of the Gironde, it means a dish containing chopped parsley and either shallots or garlic. It may also refer to any dish served with *cèpes*, or to meat with a red wine and shallot sauce. *À la bordelaise* in the classic repertoire means a meat dish with a garnish of artichoke bottoms, potatoes, fried onion rings, and parsley and has nothing whatever to do with Bordeaux culinary traditions.

The city was the birthplace of one of France's most celebrated chefs, Alphonse Dugléré, who presided over the kitchens of the famous Café Anglais in Paris during the mid-nineteenth century. Dugléré is credited with having invented *potage Germiny* and *sole Dugléré*—the latter a rather prosaic dish with onions, tomatoes, and a *velouté* sauce sharpened with lemon juice. Whether or not this chef from Bordeaux also created *tournedos Rossini* is disputed, since Rossini himself claimed it as one of his own more inspired inventions.

The flatness of the land and the crisp, clean air give the impression that Bordeaux is on the sea, yet the city is far from the oyster beds and sand dunes of Arcachon. The maritime atmosphere is due, in part, to the broad expanse of the Gironde that splits into two rivers—the Dordogne and the Garonne—just north of Bordeaux. The Garonne flows through the city and beneath the seventeen arches of the Pont de Pierre, where the elegant, eighteenth-century façades of riverside buildings from the Quai Richelieu sweep past the Bourse to the Quai des Chartrons, the center of the Bordeaux wine trade. In the mid-1930s an English journalist, visiting Bordeaux, doubted that anyone would find it a beautiful city, but Stendhal, writing exactly a century before, found Bordeaux "unquestionably the most beautiful city in all France."

IN THE CITY markets one is impressed by the variety, but above all the abundance—towering pyramids of green beans, tomatoes, artichokes, and scrubbed potatoes. Inside the modern Halle des Capucines, you notice the care with which products are offered for sale: bunches of tiny white radishes the size of a child's thumbnail; mushrooms with skins as soft and pure white as the mold on a Camembert; translucent yellow haricot beans; big bunches of thyme, basil, and rosemary, and carrots with plumes of feathery leaves.

A farmers' market, the Marché Saint-Michel, offers animals to raise, among them piglets and ducklings, above.

The French are anxious to preserve their regional dishes, and you will find those of the Gironde as specialties on restaurant menus. Even the humble but excellent garlic soup, the *tourin à l'ail*, is featured in such restaurants as La Tupina and the Gironde in Bordeaux. One day, someone will write a book on trade and industrial cooking, and the vineyards will be accorded a large chapter. It was the grape-pickers who introduced the *chabrot*—when you have all but finished the last few spoonfuls of *tourin* in your plate, you add a glass of red wine, which turns the colorless soup a delicate pink. The habit has all but disappeared, but today the vineyard kitchens continue to prepare the old recipes for the workers, especially at the time of the *vendange*. *Soupe de vendanges*, really a *pot-au-feu*, is made in a two-gallon cauldron in which you throw fifty-five pounds of beef—usually the shoulder or *plat de côtes*, and the shin, *gite* or *jarret*, with onions, leeks, turnips, and sometimes cabbage. The soup is eaten separately with lots of bread. Then the meat arrives, served with gherkins, tomato sauce, and mustard.

A brief glance at the Gironde region might give you the impression that the entire area is devoted to cultivating grapes to make wine, but the southern boundaries are encroached upon by the pine forests of the Landes, a source of timber and resin, and a produce that adds much to the versatility and character of Bordeaux cooking. Guidebooks apologize for the monotony of the forests, through which straight roads run with little relief for over a hundred miles, past timbered farmhouses that look as if they had been transported, in their entirety, from Normandy. The forests were planted in the early nineteenth century, and attracted a variety of wildlife and game, which in France means one and the same thing. Wild boar, deer, hares and rabbits, wood pigeons, larks, figpeckers and ortolans, snipe and wild duck are found there. Local innkeepers made *salmis* of game and *civets* of stewed venison. The Landes shepherds, copying the technique of Pauillac, began to rear milk-fed lamb, and today this near-white, exceptionally tender meat comes from lambs a mere six to eight weeks old, seasonal from January to Easter. The forests taper to a point at Arcachon, which is renowned for some of the finest oysters in France, and for the highest sand dune in Europe, the 375-foot Grand Dune de Pyla. One comes to Arcachon not for the sand—although the town has been a seaside resort since the last century—but for the *fruits de mer*.

The Arcachon basin is all but surrounded by oyster cultivators, and the basin itself is a vast oyster park. The oysters and other mollusks, clams, cockles, and mussels, are kept in concrete pens of running sea water, after being harvested from the park. The oysters are contained in a plastic basket, known as a *bourriche*, and graded according to size, from no. 6 for the smallest upward to no. 0, the largest and best. When you ask for oysters in a restaurant, what you will get is usually a no. 3, and in the region of production you can eat them all year round.

In 1970 the entire oyster stock was hit by an epizootic parasite that killed every oyster in the basin. The oysters—Portuguese *plates* and *creuses*—had to be replaced by a hardy and fast-growing Pacific oyster, the *japonaise* or *gigas*, and the cultivators produced a hybrid with natives from Charente

A farmer at the Bordeaux market, above (from left), has a prize hen to sell; an old woman does a little business in flowers; and an elderly shopper takes home a new duck.

Below, M. Céville, in his bleu *workingman's coat near the town of Bontoc, and a ninety-one-year-old* fermière *in Le Merle.*

and Brittany. According to an oyster fancier in Bordeaux, it wasn't disease that killed the oysters, but "some idiot who thought he could get rid of the weeds that pestered the culturists, and pumped weed killer into the oyster beds."

In the restaurants around the port, devotees conquer mountains of crustaceans. The less intrepid settle for a dozen oysters. In some establishments, the oysters are served with tiny, sausagelike *crépinettes aux truffes*, which have been marinated in white wine. The oysters have frilled shells like the skirts of Spanish dancers, but of a delicate green, and they arrive on a bed of seaweed, with unsalted

butter, bread, and a wedge of lemon. They are small but delicious. This, with a half-bottle of Entre-deux-Mers is, by Bordelais standards, a modest repast, for the people of the Gironde eat two hearty meals a day—at noon and at seven in the evening —washed down, they confess, with at least a liter of wine.

At noon, as everyone knows, France shuts down as tightly and as securely as the vaults in the Crédit Lyonnais, while people busy themselves with the serious business of eating lunch. In Bordeaux the *quais* have an air of quiet complacency that truly represents the neat and precise, kindly and generous,

251

In a view from the vineyards of the famous Château Lafite Rothschild, above, the functional buildings of the estate appear. The small red building is one of the chais, *where grapes are pressed and the wine is aged. In the long, two-story buildings (left) the wine is bottled and crated for shipping. A veteran vineyard worker in Preignac, left, hoes the soil early in the season. Opposite (clockwise from top left): a smaller château and its vineyards; in the Jardin Public of Bordeaux, a romantic reminder of the source of wealth of the Bordelais; the cellars of Château Lafite, with some of the great wines of France; and* un cépage de Bordeaux, *a vine plant.*

emphatically bourgeois and infinitely shrewd populace, whose tastes have been refined by centuries of the wine trade and by their local produce. The restaurants in the city are packed. Wine lists are studied, menus waved at waiters, bottles uncorked, bread broken, plates cleaned, coffee served. If you feel in the mood for a liqueur or a brandy, it might as well be Armagnac, for the finest Armagnac comes from the Landes, and your choice will be met with a nod of approval, for you are among people who know a good thing when they taste it.

HUÎTRES ET SAUCISSES AU VIN BLANC   *Oysters and Sausages with White Wine*

1 dozen oysters
2 grilled pork sausages (these can be any fresh sausages, although ideally they should be special handmade sausages containing truffles)
2 slices bread, buttered generously
Generous quantities of dry white wine, such as Graves or Entre-Deux-Mers

The Bordelais often eat *charcuterie* with their oysters, e.g., *pâté de campagne, grattons de Lormont* (small pieces of pork potted in its own fat), or small peppery sausages often studded with truffles.

In this recipe they are served with hot, grilled *crépinettes*, a small coarse type of pork sausage wrapped in pig's caul. You swallow an oyster whole, eat a piece of bread and butter and a mouthful of hot sausage, and drink a draught of white wine. The purpose of the hot sausage, so they say, is to cleanse the palate. It removes the taste of the oyster so that the slightly different flavor of the next oyster can be appreciated to the fullest.

Purists never serve lemon juice or shallot vinegar with their oysters, and they eat them cooled, but not iced.

for 1 person / photograph on page 241

ANGUILLES GRILLÉES   *Grilled Eels*

12 small, live silver eels, about 2 pounds (1 kg)
A little flour
Oil (for frying)
3 cloves garlic, crushed
1 tablespoon chopped parsley
1 shallot, finely chopped
Salt, freshly ground pepper
1 tablespoon fine dried breadcrumbs
Juice of ½ lemon

Have the eels freshly killed, skinned, and cleaned (and

head and tail removed). Cover them with salt for 15 minutes before cooking. Rinse the eels and pat dry. Roll them in flour and fry them in a shallow layer of hot oil until golden brown on each side, 8 to 10 minutes. Add the garlic, parsley, and shallot. Season with salt and pepper and cook for a couple of minutes longer, then sprinkle with the breadcrumbs and the lemon juice. Serve very hot, and drink a dry white Graves or a fresh Bordeaux rosé.

for 4 people / photograph on page 249

ESCARGOTS À LA CAUDERAN   *Snails Stewed in White Wine*

4 dozen live snails, or 2 7½-ounce cans of imported snails, drained, and 48 snail shells
Handful of coarse salt
¾ cup vinegar (200 ml)
⅓ pound prosciutto (150 g)
1 tablespoon lard
10 shallots, finely chopped
2 cloves garlic, finely chopped
1 slice white bread (not too fresh), crumbled
1½ cups white Bordeaux (375 ml)
1½ cups chicken stock (375 ml)
Salt, freshly ground pepper
1 bouquet garni—see Appendix

If using live snails for this recipe, feed them nothing but a few tablespoons of flour for a week; this will purge them of any poisonous plants they may have been eating. When ready to cook them, wash several times and then soak in salted water acidulated with the vinegar for 2 hours. Wash them in plenty of cold water and blanch in boiling water for 5 to 6 minutes.

Chop the ham into small squares and fry it in the lard with the shallots and garlic. Add the crumbled bread, wine, and stock. Season the mixture with salt and pepper, add the snails and bouquet garni, and simmer for 1 hour.

for 4 people

CÈPES À LA BORDELAISE   *Cèpes with Garlic and Parsley*

Contrary to the practice of many cooks, *cèpes* need long, slow cooking to become tender and appetizing.

2 pounds fresh *cèpes* (1 kg)
½ cup olive oil (125 ml)
2 cloves garlic, chopped
1 bunch parsley, chopped
Salt, freshly ground pepper

If the *cèpes* are small and firm they should need no

washing or peeling. Cut off the stems almost level with the caps and keep the mushrooms in a damp dish towel.

Brown the *cèpes* in the hot oil for a few minutes, then lower the heat and let them cook gently, for at least 45 minutes, until tender. Add the garlic and parsley 5 minutes before serving. Season with salt and pepper and eat at once—they can't be *too* hot.

for 4 people / photograph on page 244

ALOSE À L'OSEILLE *Shad with Sorrel*

The arrival of shad in spring, when they swim upriver to spawn, is a moment for celebration. Ask your fish-monger to clean and scale the fish and to include the shad roe (for the stuffing). This recipe can also be used for sea bass or salmon trout.

1 shad, weighing about 3 pounds (1½ kg)
4 tablespoons butter (50 g)
1 pound sorrel (500 g)
Heavy cream (optional)

FOR THE MARINADE
¾ cup olive oil (200 ml)
¾ cup dry white Bordeaux (200 ml)
2 bay leaves
2 sprigs of parsley
1 onion, chopped
Salt, freshly ground pepper

FOR THE STUFFING
1 pound sorrel (500 g)
4 tablespoons butter (50 g)
Reserved shad roe
Salt, freshly ground pepper
1 egg yolk

Prepare the marinade: combine the oil and wine with the herbs, onion, salt, and pepper. Marinate the fish for about 1 hour, turning occasionally.

Prepare the stuffing: sauté the sorrel in butter for about 10 minutes, or until most of the liquid has evaporated. Add the roe, cook for 10 minutes, season with salt and pepper, and add the egg yolk to bind the mixture. (The sorrel actually softens and eventually dissolves fish bones, and is therefore useful in the cooking of any bony fish.) Make 2 or 3 diagonal cuts in each side of the fish to help it cook more evenly. Fill the fish cavity with the stuffing and sew up the opening. Preheat the oven to 350°F.

Drain the fish, reserving the marinade. Bake the fish for 45 minutes—the longer the cooking time, the more effectively the sorrel will soften the bones. Turn the fish frequently as it cooks and baste generously with the marinade.

Meanwhile, melt 4 tablespoons of butter and cook the remaining sorrel over a gentle heat, until it softens to a purée, seasoning it lightly with salt and pepper. Taste, and if you find it too acid, add heavy cream for a milder flavor. Serve the fish on top of the green sorrel purée.

for 4 people / photographs on page 247 and above

255

CARBONNADE GASCONNE *Braised Veal*

This is a traditional dish from Aquitaine, although its origins may be Flemish.

2¾ pounds veal rump in 1 piece (1¼ kg), 1½ inches thick (3 to 4 cm)
1 pound sausage meat (500 g)
4 shallots, chopped
3 cloves garlic, chopped
1 bunch parsley, chopped
Salt, freshly ground pepper
2 tablespoons olive oil
Breadcrumbs
1 lemon, halved

Preheat the oven to 425°F. Oil the bottom of a large

casserole, and put in the piece of veal. Mix the sausage with the shallots, garlic, parsley, and a little salt and pepper and spread it in a layer on top of the meat, pressing it down well with your hands. Sprinkle with the remaining oil and roast for 50 minutes. Cover loosely with foil if the sausage meat becomes too brown. In a small bowl, combine some breadcrumbs with the juice of half a lemon. Cover the meat with this mixture and baste with cooking juices.

To serve the veal, mix the cooking juices with the freshly squeezed juice of the other lemon half. Young vegetables or sautéed potatoes are delicious with the dish, as are *cèpes à la bordelaise*.

for 8 people

MACARONS DE SAINT-ÉMILION

1⅓ cups ground almonds (200 g)
1½ cups powdered sugar (200 g)
Pinch of vanilla sugar
6 tablespoons sweet white wine (90 ml)
3 egg whites
1 tablespoon butter (15 g)
About 1 tablespoon powdered sugar or granulated sugar

Preheat the oven to 350°F. Mix the almonds with the powdered sugar, vanilla sugar, and white wine. Beat the egg whites until stiff and whisk into the almond mixture. Transfer to a saucepan and whisk over the lowest heat to dry out the mixture a little, then allow to cool. When it is cold, put small blobs of the mixture onto a well-buttered baking sheet, sprinkle with powdered sugar or granulated sugar, and bake until crisp, about 15 minutes; do not allow to brown.

BARON D'AGNEAU DE PAUILLAC
Roast Lamb with Potatoes and Truffles

1 baron of milk-fed lamb (the saddle and two legs)
½ cup olive oil (125 ml)
Salt, freshly ground pepper
6 tablespoons fine fresh breadcrumbs
8 tablespoons butter (100 g)
4 pounds potatoes (2 kg)
1 truffle, thinly sliced
½ cup lamb or beef stock or water (optional) (125 ml)
6 cloves garlic
6 sprigs of parsley

Preheat the oven to 425°F. Oil a large roasting pan and put in the lamb. Rub the meat with the olive oil, salt, and pepper, and coat with the breadcrumbs. Dot with butter and sear for 15 minutes in the hot oven.

Meanwhile, peel the potatoes and slice into thin rounds. Remove the meat from the roasting pan and add the potatoes. Season with salt and pepper and sprinkle with slices of truffle. Put the lamb on top and roast for 45 minutes. If the lamb is particularly lean, add the stock to prevent the potatoes from drying out.

Chop the garlic and the parsley and sauté in a little oil until the garlic is golden. Sprinkle this mixture over the meat and potatoes and baste the lamb with its juices. Roast for 15 minutes and serve very hot.

for 8 people / photograph at left

PÉRIGORD

PÉRIGORD

PÉRIGORD lies in southwestern France, about a hundred miles inland from Bordeaux, between vast Limoges, famous for its porcelain, and dusty Cahors, which can be considered the beginning of the south. The history of Périgord starts with the earliest settlements of prehistoric humans, who found it a hospitable place, with springs and rivers full of fish, and plenty of game; you can still see fascinating traces of the Cro-Magnons' life and development in many sites around Les Eyzies-de-Tarnac. There are artifacts, drawings, and carvings to see in the museum and nearby caves and rock shelters (although the Lascaux caves are, sadly, closed), and there's a very good restaurant called the Cro-Magnon, where you can sit under the lime trees and remind yourself with slices of *foie gras en gêlée* that you, at any rate, are still alive.

Périgord once formed part of the huge inheritance of Eleanor of Aquitaine. In 1137, at the age of fifteen, Eleanor was married to Louis VII of France, but they were divorced fifteen years later. Once again the wealthiest heiress in Europe, and a rich prize for fortune-hunting barons, she quickly remarried, this time to Henry of Anjou, who shortly

In Périgord, many buildings are made with a distinctive local sandstone, which is a warm red-purple in color. One sees it in the tiny village near Turenne, preceding overleaf, and in Saint-Leon-sur-Vézère, top, a fifteenth-century town nestled in a bend of the Vézère river. Equally distinctive are the ingredients of the périgourdine cuisine. Some regional specialties, opposite, include: cou d'oie farci *(foreground), goose neck stuffed with* pâté, pork, *and chunks of truffles and usually eaten cold; a plate of* confit d'oie, *or preserved goose, with wild mushrooms; green salad dressed with vinegar and locally pressed walnut oil; and two crusty breads,* pain de froment *and* pain de seigle.

A hard-working farmer in Noaille takes a moment from his morning's chores to show off an addition to his flock.

farmyard? A ham? All farmers keep pigs. In Périgord, country feasts are frequently masterpieces of good taste."

If you go to Périgord now, not only are the people exceptionally hospitable and down-to-earth, but also the food of that earth still has a savor that is unusual in the modern world, and the countryside, full of contrasts, is superb. On the rather bare and *causse*-like heights around the vigorous farms of Saint-Julien-de-Bourdeilles in *Périgord blanc*, men still quarry huge slabs of what looks like fresh goat cheese from the limestone that lies not six inches from the surface and frequently crops out into a stony whitish desert, which gives the area its name. Further south lies *Périgord noir*, where the hills, clad with dense scrub oaks, their trunks shaggy with black moss, conceal caves and caverns, some containing subterranean lakes and unusual rock formations. In the summer these upper parts of southwestern France shimmer in parching heat, and the smell of hot juniper bushes pervades the air.

But plunge down into the river valleys and you will see a land as lush and prosperous and as beautiful as any in France. There are walnut orchards, fruit orchards, and flowery meadows bordered with poplars beside handsome rivers alive with fish. Tobacco flowers scent the air, old women in black clothes sprigged with flowers and old men in straw hats pull carts of dandelions and *blette* home for their rabbits, pots and cans and buckets full of begonias and geraniums rest on every doorstep, and the rustic architecture is some of the loveliest and most exuberant in Europe.

Everywhere you look, you see cottages and farms with extravagant stonework, sometimes chalky white, sometimes gold, sometimes pink, many with towers and steep-pitched roofs, with first-floor balconies and carved lintels, massive doorways and sagging outside staircases, beautiful pigeon towers and stone arcades. If you want to see some really extraordinary *bastides*—fortified villages—and unspoiled early farmhouses, follow the Circuit des Bastides from Issigeac to Eymet or investigate the small villages along the Dordogne river, such as Carennac. Carennac, the site of a large and lively greengage market in the summer, is where Fénélon, once tutor to the Dauphin, lived in exile from Paris and wrote *Télémache* in the tower room of his château, overlooking river and abbey.

If you visit this region, you may have occasion to taste an unusual local delicacy made with the blood of turkeys that is a flat gray-pink cake called a *régal de sang*. It looks quite sinister but becomes more appealing when you learn that it is supposed to be fried in goose fat and served with vinegar, garlic, salt, pepper, and nutmeg. You can find these cakes at the market in Périgueux, one of the main

afterward became Henry II of England. Between them they controlled the whole western side of France, more than the French king himself, and it took three hundred years for the French to get the English out of their country.

The peasants of Périgord were not well off in those times and lived chiefly on a diet of red cabbage, chestnuts, turnips, and fruit. Although the climate is usually good, they suffered droughts, frosts, deluges, and famines and were not allowed to hunt, a pleasure reserved solely for the aristocracy.

But little by little their living improved, and the Périgord art of cooking slowly developed, with outside influences helping it along. The food was always simple but savory, and as André Maurois said of Périgord: "The ingredients of *'la bonne cuisine'* are not exotic and rare here. Every cottage has them. *Foie gras*: all you have to do is force-feed a goose. Truffles? They are a miracle, a freak of nature. *Confit* or *ballotine*? Doesn't every smallholder have his markets of Périgord. The poultry there is absolutely superb, as it is throughout this region. You can buy it live or ready-plucked but with head and feet intact, as these are often eaten too—the feet, skinned, make very good soup.

Most country wives make their pocket money by rearing poultry; outside the door of the cottage throughout the summer, ducks and geese wander about under the walnut trees, gobbling up grass and weeds. But come November and the *"gavage"* and they are penned up and forcibly fed on whole corn cooked with a little fat and salt, to provide *foie gras* in time for Christmas. The best geese for *foie gras* are the *"grise de foie gras"* and the *"grise des landes,"* ponderous, broad-chested gray birds; the best ducks are pretty black-and-white crossbreds called "Mulards."

The *gavage* is exhausting for the stuffer as well as the stuffed, but ducks less so than geese, so many people now prefer to raise ducks, and *foie gras de canard* is on every menu, often sliced and briefly fried and served hot with raisins, as well as *en terrine*.

One of the great *foie gras* centers is Thiviers, where in winter the big *foie gras* markets are held. These take place every Saturday morning, but the main markets are the *Foire de Noël*, before Christmas, the *Foires des Rois* and *des Commerçants* in January, and the *Foire de Chandeleur* in February. Here the huge pink or yellow swollen livers change hands for large sums; the restaurateurs, *charcutiers*, and wholesalers have their pick, and they can buy all the rest of the geese and ducks for *confit*, stuffed

neck, and duck- or goose-breast hams.

Madame Deborde of the Hôtel des Griffons in Boudeilles on the river Dronne, cans her own *foie gras* and her own *confit*. This *confit*, made from the wings and thighs of goose or duck, spiced and seasoned and preserved in their own fat, is one of the main local dishes and makes a glorious standby. Just turn the beautifully seasoned pinkish pieces of duck, speckled with spices and bathed in yellow fat, into a heavy black frying pan, and let them cook gently until they form a golden crust on the outside. Add a .handful of sorrel if you like. Any fat and jelly left in the can is used to fry the potatoes served with the *confit*. Follow this with a salad containing dandelions and dressed with walnut oil, some goat cheese, and Reine Claude greengages, and you have a perfect meal.

Another pride of Périgord is the *cèpe*, a round-capped, fleshy mushroom with a suedelike top and spongy spores. *Rosés des près* can also be found—slender pinkish meadow mushrooms that taste delicious cooked in goose fat with sliced potatoes, garlic, and parsley. (Incidentally, the garlic of this region, which appears so frequently, is particularly mild, sweet, and harmless.) *Cèpes* are good like this too, but they should first be grilled to remove their wetness. They are also splendid served in an omelette, cooked with poultry, or made into a sauce.

Other mushrooms worth hunting are the thin black *trompettes de la mort*, which are sometimes cheatingly used in *pâté* instead of truffles, the expensive and rare *morilles*, and the beautiful *oronges*

To the weekly market in Brive-la-Gaillarde, one of the busiest in the region, local farmers and householders bring home-raised and homemade produce. The rabbits, left, were raised *by a farmer's wife; the pork sausage, center, is a thick, meaty, country-style preparation; and the speckled guinea hens, right, have been bred for the pot.*

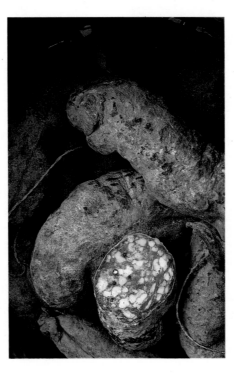

263

de *César*, which are lightly grilled for three to four minutes and then painted with butter or fresh walnut oil. Nothing more is needed but salt and pepper and perhaps a few drops of lemon juice, or better still *verjus*, the local equivalent of vinegar. This is still made by gathering bunches of still-green, but plump, grapes on a sunny day in July, and squashing them, using a mortar and pestle or a *mouli-légumes*. The juice is left to settle for an hour, then filtered and bottled. A layer of oil on top excludes air, and the bottles are corked like wine bottles and kept in the cellar (or, nowadays, in the freezer). In the cooking of Sarlat (one of Périgord's most handsome market towns), fresh *verjus* is still used with *cèpes*, while in Domme they sprinkle it on fried

Even in Périgord, where truffles and foie gras *are basic elements of the cuisine,* truffe en croûte *is an exceptionally elegant first course. It is made with black Périgord truffles, left, and a whole truffle is used for each serving. The truffle is placed on a slice of country ham, which has been spread with foie gras, below left. The whole is then wrapped in pastry dough and baked, as served at L'Hôtel Bonnet in Beynac et Cazenac, below right. Far simpler, but just as elegant, are the three essentials of French food, opposite: wine, bread, and cheese. In Périgord, the wine may be a pitcher of* vins de Cahors, *the bread a wholewheat loaf, and the cheese a farm-made cow's-milk or goat's-milk variety.*

Omelette aux boutons de scorsonères, *opposite, is flavored with the fragile flower of salsify, available fresh in the markets of Périgord for only a few days each spring. The rest of the year, the omelette must be made with preserved salsify. The finished dish, right, is prepared by M. Castannet, chef of the Restaurant Belvédère. A likely accompaniment is* salade de pissenlits, *or dandelion greens, below, sprinkled with chopped walnuts and dressed with walnut oil and vinegar.*

escalopes of fresh *foie gras*. You can squeeze the juice from unripe grapes right onto a salad with delicate results, and you can use the same juice to make a *lapin au vinaigre*.

GAME is now quite scarce in Périgord. You very occasionally see a partridge or a wild rabbit or even a pheasant that has escaped from somebody's garden—they are reared like poultry and then put out in the woods. There are, however, boar pens, and *pâté de sanglier* (wild boar) and *pâté de marcassin* (young wild

boar) are two of the many very good local *pâtés* to be found in the *charcuteries*. Here you can find *foie gras* in all its disguises (but it is available fresh only from November to February), goose fat for cooking, *confit* in jars, and walnut oil. You can also buy bottled truffles—if you do, try to obtain those preserved in cognac; they are expensive but are likely to be real Périgord truffles, black right through and the best in the world.

Truffles, which still have a wonderful mystique, are found from late November to March under certain scrub oak trees on whose fibrous roots they grow symbiotically. They are sniffed out in exciting secrecy by *"caveurs"* with trained pigs or truffle hounds (a sort of poodle-beagle cross). The owner then digs out the precious tuber and sells it at a high price, preferably with a lot of dirt stuck to its rough skin to make it heavier.

One of the largest truffle centers is Brantôme—a town worth visiting for its beautiful Renaissance riverside walk and its excellent food. It is said that in the season the streets are heavy with the aroma of truffles. A local recipe for truffle omelette produces exquisite results: You take a home-preserved truffle about the size of a potato, chop it roughly, throw it into beaten eggs, and then add some of the brandy from the jar. It must be brandy—the truffle takes heart from it. Season well and make your omelette.

In the summer, the vegetables taste wonderful. The local poultry is always superb, as are the butter and goat cheese. The lamb—from the lean, agile sheep that graze on the rocky hillsides—tastes very strong but excellent. You can also find snails on those bare hillsides; they stay in hiding until it rains, and then glide forth in great numbers. These are the huge pale-shelled Burgundian snails that look hundreds of years old. They used to live on the vines that flourished here, but most hillside vineyards in the upper Dordogne valleys have, sadly, fallen into disrepair.

The grapes of Périgord have not, in general, produced top-quality wine since the 1880s, when all the vines were destroyed by phylloxera, but there are large vineyards producing very good red wine around Bergerac. One of these is Pécharmant, a strong dark wine with a taste of the soil; this potion at three or four years old, if opened an hour before lunch, is just right with hefty winter dishes such as *civet de lièvre*, although you might want a good Bordeaux with *lièvre à la Royale*, an extraordinary, long-cooked concoction of hare in its own blood.

If you want Pécharmant, it is worth visiting Château Tiregand, just outside Bergerac, for a poignant view of the crumbling, shuttered Renaissance château, now quite charmless, one wing stacked to the ceiling with logs. The vineyards are still beautiful and in full production. Also near Bergerac, a faded old river port with a big explosives factory and a tobacco museum, is the beautiful Montbazillac area. Montbazillac is a delicious, sweet golden wine and a good substitute for Sauternes with fresh *foie gras*.

Apricots and cherries in brandy, along with regional wines and liqueurs, left. The confit de canard, *below left, duck preserved in its own fat in traditional fashion, will keep for about a year. The* tartelettes aux fruits, *below, are made with many different fruits and are usually baked in fluted molds.*

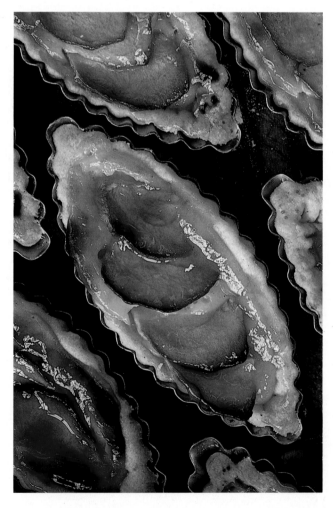

If you drive around this area in autumn, you cannot miss the fermenting grape smell that wafts around the village streets. At the pretty little Château de Planques (pronounced Plonk), the woman of the house makes and sells her own delicious *pruneaux* (sun-dried Agen plums) and you can buy a case of worthwhile 1978 Montbazillac for a few dollars a bottle.

If you visit Périgord, try to eat in a plain and everyday restaurant such as l'Auberge de Cantou in Collonges-le-Rouge; in fact, Collonges is just outside Périgord in the Corrèze, but the cooking, as is so often the case with regional cooking, has overlapped its boundaries, and here you will be able to sit by the fire and enjoy a very authentic *menu du jour* (don't take the *menu touristique*). In the friendly kitchen they make the old dishes in the usual way; the courses are brought to you (there's no choice) and will absolutely astonish you; the local wine, which is also brought without asking, may well astonish you too. Often they serve

The giant geese of Périgord, below, are raised primarily for their fat and their rosy, plump livers. The fat is used in place of butter or oil in many dishes, and the liver, of course, goes into pâté de foie gras. The pâté can also be made with duck livers, and, when studded with truffles and served with warm toast, right, is a quintessentially périgourdine dish.

mique, the famous yeast dumplings that used to be put to rise under the bedcovers, as this was the warmest place in the house, but even if they do not serve *mique* on the day you go, the meal is traditional and starts as always with *soupe*—this is essential, and housewives will ask if you have made the *soupe* rather than if you have made lunch. When you have eaten all but a spoonful or two of your soup, you pour some red wine into the bowl and drink it. This is the *chabrol* and a highly important ritual in this part of the world.

Next come some rough *rillons*, or you might be offered a tomato salad or a thick slice of raw home-made ham. *Rillons* are shreds of goose meat left over from the making of *confit* and beaten to a smooth paste with plenty of their own fat. This may be followed by half a boiled pig's head and boiled potatoes, made palatable with a scattering of parsley and some translucent pink shallots soaked in red wine vinegar.

Next comes a beefsteak (or other main dish) with fried potatoes, then cheese, then a fruit tart. Then come local liqueurs; you can choose from *eau-de-noix*, which is made from green walnuts and tastes of the nicer sort of cough syrup, or *vieille prune*, made from greengages and is perfect nectar. The greengages bottled in *eau-de-vie*, and all the many preserved fruits, cherries, plums, apricots, even walnuts, made in Sarlat and other Périgord towns, are well worth trying.

The Dordogne flows through this beautiful countryside and perch, barbel, pike, trout, and *la friture de la Dordogne*, a jumble of small, bony, but good, fried fish, are frequently on the menu. The fishermen have special black punts, which they row against the current with a single oar, although on Sundays, motorboats appear with a lot of noise and frighten off the locals. This is a dramatic river, sometimes flowing through cliffs or wooded gorges of limestone, with *châteaux* built high on the rocks, sometimes widening and running through beautiful fields, sometimes past camping sites, or past medieval towns of stunning beauty, like Souillac and Saint-Céré. The Périgord area is rich in many ways and remains very much farming and agriculture-based area where the production and selling of top-quality food are still the main occupation of most of the local people.

Mme. Valen at L'Auberge de la Porte du Prieuré in Collonges-la-Rouge, left, holds a platter of freshly made merveilles, *fritters made of a buttery dough flavored with lemon zest or orange flower water, and deep fried in oil until they are puffy and golden brown. While they are still hot, the* merveilles *are sprinkled with sugar. Two other regional desserts, opposite, along with a plate of* merveilles *(top) are* flognarde, *(foreground), a flan that can be made with sliced apples, pears, or prunes; and a stack of crisp* échaudés, *butter pastries baked until they are hollow and crackling. La Vieille Noix, a walnut liqueur, goes well with all of them.*

TRUFFE EN CROÛTE   *Truffle in a Pastry Case*

This is a regal and extremely delicious first course to serve at a celebration (even in Périgord, alas, truffles and *foie gras* are not everyday fare). This recipe comes from the Hôtel Gourmet at Beynac and Catenac, and it can hardly fail to be a success.

1 recipe *pâte brisée*—see Appendix
1 large fresh truffle
¼ pound *foie gras* (100 g)
2 thin slices smoked, streaky bacon
1 egg, beaten (for glazing)

Preheat the oven to 425°F. Roll the *pâte brisée* out into an even circle about ⅛ inch thick. Scrub and peel the truffle and cut the *foie gras* into large dice. Spread the bacon thickly with the diced *foie gras* and lay it in the middle of the pastry.

Put the truffle on top, wrap the bacon around it, and then brush the edges with water and fold the pastry over in half like a turnover. Fold the edges over to make them secure, and decorate the turnover, crimping the edges with a large fork. Brush with a glaze of beaten egg and place carefully on a buttered baking sheet. Bake for 20 to 25 minutes, covering the top lightly with foil if it is in danger of getting too brown.

for 6 people / photograph on page 264

MIQUE   *Dumpling with Salt Pork*

1 cake fresh yeast (14 g) or 1 package dry yeast (7 g)
3½ cups flour (500 g)
3 eggs
1 large tablespoon butter or pork drippings, melted
Pinch of salt
2 pounds salt pork, preferably loin (1 kg)
1 large *andouille* or boiling sausage
1 pound carrots, celery, leeks, and turnips (500 g)
1 green cabbage

Dissolve the yeast in a little warm water and leave for 15 minutes in a warm place. Put the flour in a bowl and add the eggs, butter, dissolved yeast, and salt. Work the ingredients together into a dough, adding more water as necessary, and knead thoroughly. Let rise in a warm place, covered with plastic wrap until it doubles in volume—it will take 3 hours to do so.

Meanwhile, put the salt pork into a large pot, cover generously with water, and simmer for 2 hours. Clean and trim the vegetables and cut the cabbage into 6 pieces. Add the *andouille* and the vegetables to the pot.

Remove the dough from the bowl, form it into a ball, and roll it lightly in flour. Drop it into the simmering liquid with the meat and vegetables and let it cook on one side for 30 minutes; then turn it over and cook gently for a further 30 minutes.

This huge dumpling is sliced and served hot and accompanies the meat and vegetables instead of bread.

A Sarladaise *mique* is rather different; it is made from ½ pound stale bread cut into little cubes and mixed with 2 eggs, salt, and a large tablespoon of pork drippings or a bit of pork fat, chopped extremely fine. The mixture is worked into a dough and then shaped into a ball, dusted with flour, and lowered into the simmering stock as before. This kind of *mique* takes only 30 minutes to cook.

for 6 people / photographs at left and opposite

POULE AU POT À LA FARCE NOIRE   *Chicken with a Rustic Stuffing*

1 large, 2½- to 3-pound, boiling fowl or chicken with
   giblets and its blood (1½ kg)—see Note
1 cup fresh breadcrumbs (100 g)
1 clove garlic, chopped
1 large onion, chopped
4 egg yolks
Salt, freshly ground pepper
2 tablespoons pork drippings or goose fat
5 quarts boiling, salted water (5 liters)

FOR THE POT-AU-FEU
1 pound carrots (500 g)
1 pound leeks (500 g)
1 pound Swiss chard (500 g)
1 pound turnips (500 g)
1 bouquet garni—see Appendix
1 onion, stuck with a couple of cloves

Finely chop the liver, heart, and gizzard. Soak the
   breadcrumbs in the blood, and add the liver, heart,
   gizzard, garlic, and onion. Bind the mixture with

the egg yolks. Season with salt and pepper and stuff
   the chicken with this mixture. Truss the chicken.
To prepare the *pot-au-feu*: heat pork drippings or goose
   fat in a large stockpot and brown the chicken on all
   sides. Cover with the boiling, salted water and
   simmer gently until the chicken is tender. The cooking
   time depends on the age of the chicken—a boiling
   fowl will take at least 3 hours. Clean and trim the
   vegetables. Add them to the pan, along with the
   bouquet garni and onion, 1 hour before serving.
Serve the chicken hot, well-drained, and surrounded by
   the vegetables. In Périgord it is served with *sauce verte*,
   a delicious thick green sauce, which consists of finely
   chopped shallot, parsley, chervil, chives, and the yolk
   of a hard-boiled egg, seasoned with salt and pepper
   and mixed with oil and vinegar.

Note: If chicken's blood is not available from the
   butcher, you can soak the breadcrumbs in milk and
   add ¼ pound minced prosciutto.

for 6 people

FLAN DU PÉRIGORD   *Flan, Périgord Style*

Depending on where you go in Périgord, this easy-to-
make flan is known by different names. Thicker, with
more flour and milk and flavored with rum, it becomes
the *cajassé* of Sarlat. In Limoges, with the addition of
black cherries, it is the famous *clafoutis*. Finally, mixed
with sliced fruit—apples, pears, plums, grapes, or
raisins—it is the *flognarde* of Auvergne.

4 tablespoons flour (40 g)
4 tablespoons sugar (60 g)
3 eggs
½ cup milk (125 ml)
Grated lemon peel
4 tablespoons butter (60 g)

Preheat the oven to 400°F. Stir together the flour, sugar,
   eggs, and milk. Flavor with grated lemon peel. Beat
   the batter vigorously and, still beating, pour it into a
   well-greased mold with fairly high sides. Sprinkle the
   butter, cut into pieces, over the flan, and bake until
   the flan rises and turns golden brown, about 30 minutes. The flan can be eaten hot or cold.

for 4 people / photograph on page 271

MERVEILLES   *Pastry Fritters*

These sweet pastries are found all over the southwest
—and are especially popular at Mardi Gras (Shrove
Tuesday). They have different local names according to
their shapes: round ones are *aghulets*, while the long
strip shapes are called *cambos d'oulos*.

3½ cups flour (500 g)
1 teaspoon baking powder (optional)
4 or 5 eggs
8 tablespoons butter or lard, softened (100 g)
Pinch of salt
Zest of 1 lemon or 1 tablespoon Cointreau or
   cognac
Oil (for deep frying)
Powdered sugar to taste

Sift the flour and baking powder (if you are using it, it
   will make the *merveilles* even lighter) into a bowl and
   mix in 4 of the eggs, butter, salt, and lemon zest.
   Work to a smooth dough, adding the remaining egg
   if necessary, and roll out on a floured board, to about
   ¼ inch thick. Cut into rounds or into strips about
   6 inches long by ¾ inch wide.
Heat the oil in the deep fryer, and when it bubbles,
   drop in the *merveilles*. They will puff up and brown
   very quickly. Turn them once, remove with a slotted
   spoon or skimmer, and drain on paper towels. Sprinkle
   generously with powdered sugar.
Merveilles are delicious hot, but will keep in an airtight
   container for up to 2 weeks.

for 8 people / photographs on pages 270 and 271

CIVET DE MARCASSIN   *Young Wild Boar Cooked in Red Wine*

This recipe comes from the Auberge de la Porte-du-Prieurné at Collonges-la-Rouge.

1 haunch (saddle and legs) of young wild boar
1 tablespoon lard or goose fat (15 g)
¼ pound lean, streaky bacon, cut into lardons (125 g)
6 shallots, chopped
1 tablespoon flour (10 g)
4 cups good red wine (1 liter)
Salt, freshly ground pepper
1 dozen button or pickling onions
1 pound fresh *cèpes* (or other wild mushrooms) (500 g)

FOR THE MARINADE
2 cups red wine (½ liter)
¾ cup wine vinegar (200 ml)
1 cup olive oil (250 ml)
1 onion, sliced
2 sprigs of fresh thyme
1 shallot, crushed
1 clove garlic, finely chopped
1 carrot, sliced
3 cloves
5 black peppercorns
5 juniper berries
Salt
A few fresh sage leaves

Two days ahead, combine all of the marinade ingredients in a large deep dish. Cut the boar into fairly generous pieces (as you would cut beef for a *daube*) and marinate for 48 hours, turning from time to time.

Drain and dry the meat, reserving the marinade. In a very large casserole, brown the boar meat and the bacon lardons in the lard.

When the meat is well browned on all sides, add the shallots and continue to cook, stirring, for 3 or 4 minutes. Sprinkle in the flour and let it brown. Moisten with the red wine and add the strained marinade. Season with salt and pepper, cover the pan, simmer for 1 hour, and then add the onions and cook for a further hour. Add the mushrooms and simmer for 30 minutes; serve very hot.

Accompany the *civet* with steamed potatoes and a green salad (if possible, dandelion salad) dressed with walnut oil.

for 6 to 8 people / photograph above

ACKNOWLEDGMENTS

As I mentioned in the introduction, many anonymous people made this book possible, but a few are unforgettable and deserve special thanks. I would like to express all my gratitude to the man most responsible for making this book possible, M. Marc Garai, Directeur de la Rédaction de *Marie Claire*, who first proposed doing these *reportages* for the magazine. I am also grateful to him for assigning Jacqueline Saulnier to research the regions of France and to accompany us all over France, organizing and gathering all the ingredients to make these photographs possible and the recipes publishable. When we were in Brittany this task was performed admirably by Georgette Matthews and in the Ile de France by Bob Chambers and Beth Gurney.

When *The London Sunday Times Magazine* decided to complete and republish the project in 1981, *Times* editor Susan Hodgart took on the task of translating the recipes and finding the best writers to introduce each region.

It was under the auspices of Michael Rand, Art Director of *The Sunday Times Magazine,* that I began to consider putting these fourteen regions into the form of a book. My inexperience in these matters required the impetus of my fine representatives, Peter Schub and Robert Bear. It was through their guidance that I finally met the publisher who allowed me the freedom to direct the course of this book. With the indispensable help of Art Director Nai Chang, designer Jim Wageman, and especially editor Leslie Stoker, who never ceased smiling while editing the text, translating more recipes, and abbreviating my long captions, I am happy to see my first book published.

A good deal of credit also goes to the chefs, cooks, and staff of restaurants whom I could not mention in the captions. I list them not in order of importance, but as we met them: near Lyon, Paul Bocuse, chef, photographer, *"le maître, l'empereur"* of his profession; Roger Vergé, owner and reputed chef of Au Moulin de Mougins; M. Hure, a remarkable and patient host in his first-class Hôtel de la Poste in Avallon; Patrick Lefèvre, owner of the beautiful Grange de Meslay in Tours; the brothers Haeberlin at the three-star Auberge de l'Ill in Illhausern, in Alsace; Yves and Marie Luce Mesnard, proprietors of the Restaurant de la Gironde in Bordeaux; Marc Chevillot, a great chef, a dear friend, and the owner of the lovely Hôtel de la Poste in Beaune; M. Albert Augereau and his son Michel at the Hôtel Jeanne de Laval in les Rosiers; and M. André Bonnaure from Le Maillon Restaurant in Carcassonne, who introduced us to two very good cooks, Pierre and Fauchon Vaquer in Preixan, in Languedoc. We were always received with great enthusiasm by all of these people, who devoted so much time, effort, and knowledge to our endeavor. I'm sure I have forgotten others . . . after ten years of work and so many memorable meals! Please forgive me.

Finally, it is with deep gratitude that I have dedicated this book to my wife Jeannette, who not only contributed her taste and efforts, but also her patience and navigational skills while traveling with me; and to our daughter Babette, whose mature acceptance of many long separations only brought us closer together.

R. F.

APPENDIX

About the Recipes

In this book, both standard U.S. and metric measurements have been given. As the equivalents are not exact —and the variations insignificant to the final outcome of the recipes—metric measurements have been rounded out. Conversion charts, for both liquid and solid measures, are included below.

Liquid Measures Conversion Chart

Fluid ounces	U.S. measures	Imperial measures	Milliliters
	1 tsp	1 tsp	5
¼	2 tsp	1 dessert-spoon	7
½	1 tbs	1 tbs	15
1	2 tbs	2 tbs	28
2	¼ cup	4 tbs	56
4	½ cup or ¼ pint		110
5		¼ pint or 1 gill	140
6	¾ cup		170
8	1 cup or ½ pint		225
9			250, ¼ liter
10	1¼ cups	½ pint	280
12	1½ cups or ¾ pint		340
15		¾ pint	420
16	2 cups or 1 pint		450
18	2¼ cups		500, ½ liter
20	2½ cups	1 pint	560
24	3 cups or 1½ pints		675
25		1¼ pints	700
27	3½ cups		750
30	3¾ cups	1½ pints	840
32	4 cups or 2 pints or 1 quart		900
35		1¾ pints	980
36	4½ cups		1000, 1 liter
40	5 cups or 2½ pints	2 pints or 1 quart	1120
48	6 cups or 3 pints		1350
50		2½ pints	1400
60	7½ cups	3 pints	1680
64	8 cups or 4 pints or 2 quarts		1800
72	9 cups		2000, 2 liters
80	10 cups or 5 pints	4 pints	2250
96	12 cups or 3 quarts		2700
100		5 pints	2800

Solid Measures Conversion Chart

U.S. and Imperial measures		Metric measures	
ounces	pounds	grams	kilos
1		28	
2		56	
3½		100	
4	¼	112	
5		140	
6		168	
8	½	225	
9		250	¼
12	¾	340	
16	1	450	
18		500	½
20	1¼	560	
24	1½	675	
27		750	¾
28	1¾	780	
32	2	900	
36	2¼	1000	1
40	2½	1100	
48	3	1350	
54		1500	1½
64	4	1800	
72	4½	2000	2
80	5	2250	2¼
90		2500	2½
100	6	2800	2¾

Oven Temperature Equivalents

Fahrenheit	Gas mark	Celsius	Heat of oven
225	¼	107	very cool
250	½	121	very cool
275	1	135	cool
300	2	148	cool
325	3	163	moderate
350	4	177	moderate
375	5	190	fairly hot
400	6	204	fairly hot
425	7	218	hot
450	8	232	very hot
475	9	246	very hot

Terminology Equivalents

U.S.	British
dry white beans	haricot beans
eggplants	aubergines
zucchini	courgettes
heavy cream	double cream
sugar, granulated sugar	castor sugar
powdered sugar	icing sugar
broiled	grilled
pitted	stoned
skillet	frying pan

BOUQUET GARNI   *Herb Bouquet*

Aromatic herbs or plants, tied together into a little bundle, are used for flavoring stews and sauces.

3 or 4 sprigs of parsley
⅓ to ½ bay leaf
2 sprigs of fresh thyme or ⅛ teaspoon dried thyme

Tie the herbs together with a piece of string. If dried thyme is used, wrap the herbs in a little square or bag of cheesecloth and tie it with string.

makes 1 bouquet

CRÈME FRAÎCHE

This characteristic French dairy cream, which has been fermented with a special culture until it thickens, has almost a nutty flavor. While commercially produced *crème fraîche* is available on a limited basis in this country, it doesn't compare to the French version. Heavy whipping cream, which has the same 30 percent butterfat content, can be substituted or, for a more authentic taste, try this homemade recipe.

1 cup heavy cream (250 ml)
1 teaspoon buttermilk (5 ml)

Combine the cream and buttermilk in a clean glass jar and cover it securely. Leave the jar in a warm place, such as over the pilot light or in the oven of a gas range or on a stove top of an electric range, for 6 to 8 hours, or until it thickens. It can be stored in the refrigerator (it will continue to thicken there), where it will keep for about 1 week.

makes 1 cup

CROÛTONS

Bread *croûtons* to be used as a garnish for delicate-tasting dishes can be sautéed in the butter and oil combination in this recipe or in clarified butter. If the *croûtons* are to accompany strong-flavored dishes, you may want to sauté the bread cubes in olive oil. *Croûtons* can also be toasted instead of sautéed, in which case spread the cubes on an ungreased baking sheet and toast them in a preheated 400°F oven for 2 to 3 minutes on each side.

2 slices of day-old, firm white bread, ½ inch (1 cm) thick
4 tablespoons butter (50 g)
¼ to ½ cup cooking oil (50 to 125 ml)

Remove the crusts from the bread and cut the slices into cubes (or the shape specified in the recipe). In a large skillet melt the butter and ¼ cup of the oil over medium heat. When the butter-oil mixture is hot, add the bread and turn the heat up to high. Sauté the cubes, turning them so they brown evenly on all sides, and add more oil if necessary to keep them from burning. When ready to serve, drain them on paper towels. (If you want to make them in advance, simply heat them briefly in the oven before serving.)

makes about 1 cup

BONING A BIRD

Lay the bird breast down and with a strong, sharp boning knife split the skin along the entire length of the center of the back. Starting just below the neck cavity, cut down each side of the backbone, and peel back the skin and flesh until you reach the joint of the thigh bone. Place the knife between the ball and socket of the thigh joint and twist the knife to sever the thigh bone. Cut the other joint the same way. Slide the knife in the other direction toward the neck to detach the flesh until the shoulder bone is all exposed. Do the same for the other shoulder bone. Cut through the wing joints and continue cutting, keeping the bones as free of flesh as possible, until you reach the breastbone. Left up the skeletal structure, cutting away any remaining flesh (but without puncturing the breast). Finally, sever the skeleton at the tail so that it separates completely from the flesh. Then remove the leg bones from the body, beginning from the inside of the bird. Scrape the flesh away, keeping the skin as intact as possible, by working down each bone with a knife. Remove each wing bone in the same way as the leg bones. The bird is now ready for stuffing.

VEAL STOCK

3 pounds lean, raw veal shank meat (1½ kg) and
    4 pounds cracked, raw veal bones (2 kg)
2 medium carrots, peeled
2 medium onions, peeled
2 medium celery ribs
2 teaspoons salt
¼ teaspoon dried thyme
1 bay leaf
6 sprigs of parsley
2 cloves garlic, unpeeled
2 whole cloves
2 leeks, cleaned (optional)

Place the meat and bones in a soup pot and add enough
    cold water to cover. Over moderate heat bring the
    liquid slowly to a simmer. Skim off any scum that
    rises to the surface for about 5 minutes, or until it
    almost ceases to accumulate.
Add the vegetables and salt. Tie the herbs and spices in
    a piece of cheesecloth and add them as well. Pour in
    more water if the liquid does not cover the ingredi-

ents by 1 inch. Return to a simmer, skim as necessary, and partially cover the pot. Continue to cook
the liquid at a gentle simmer for at least 5 hours.
Skim the surface occasionally. Add more water if it
evaporates below the level of the ingredients. When
the taste is strong enough to your liking, strain the
stock into a bowl. Let the stock settle for about 5
minutes and blot up the fat with a paper towel or
refrigerate until the fat hardens and scrape it off.
Taste the degreased stock and, if the flavor is weak,
boil it down to evaporate some of its water content.

Note: In the French home, a smaller quantity of veal
stock is often prepared the following way. Sauté a
piece of stewing veal, cut in pieces, in a little goose or
pork fat together with the white part of the leek,
finely sliced, a celery rib sliced, carrots cut into rounds,
and a bouquet garni. Season with salt and pepper, add
4 cups of water, and simmer for at least 1 hour.

makes 2 to 3 quarts

PÂTE BRISÉE   *Shortcrust Pastry*

2 cups flour (250 g)
½ teaspoon salt
9 tablespoons butter (125 g)
¼ to ⅓ cup water (60 to 90 ml)

Sift the flour into a bowl and add the salt. Then add the
    butter and cut it into pieces with a knife. Keep
    cutting the butter into the flour until the mixture is
    about the size of peas. Rub these pieces between
    your thumbs and fingertips. When the fat has the
    texture of cornflakes, stop rubbing. (The mixture
    shouldn't look like fine breadcrumbs, which makes
    the pastry dense rather than the flaky crust it should
    be.) Add just enough of the water to combine the
    mixture (but not too much or it will be too sticky and
    elastic) and, with your hands, mix it in until the
    dough starts to bind together. Quickly work the
    mixture into a ball and wrap it in plastic or wax

paper. Let it rest in the refrigerator several hours or
overnight. Roll out the dough into a round, about ⅛
inch thick and 2 inches larger than the pan, and trim
off the excess dough.

Note: If the recipe indicates to bake a crust blind (to
cook it partially before filling), which prevents an
undercooked and soggy crust, do the following. Line
the pan with the pastry, prick the bottom with a fork,
and cover the bottom of the pastry shell with aluminum foil, bringing up the sides as well. Then fill the
shell with dried beans or rice to weigh down the
pastry. Bake for 12 to 15 minutes in a preheated 425°F
oven or until lightly browned. Remove the beans and
foil and cook an additional few minutes so that the
bottom crust also turns a light golden.

makes an 8- to 10-inch crust

PÂTE BRISÉE SUCRÉE   *Sweet Shortcrust Pastry*

1¾ cups flour (200 g)
8 tablespoons butter, softened (100 g)
3 egg yolks
¼ cup plus 2 tablespoons sugar (75 g)
Pinch of salt
A little grated lemon rind
1 tablespoon brandy (15 ml)

Sift the flour into a bowl, make a well in the center, and
    put in the softened butter, egg yolks, sugar, salt, and
    lemon rind. Add the brandy and work everything
    together quickly and lightly with your fingertips,
    gradually drawing in the flour. When the mixture is

crumbly, mass it together into a ball, sprinkling in 1
tablespoon of water if it seems too dry. Mix well by
smearing the mixture, a couple of tablespoons at a
time, over the work top with the heel of your palm.
Gather it up with a spatula and refrigerate, wrapped
in plastic, for 30 minutes. Roll out the dough into a
round, about ⅛ inch thick and slightly larger than the
pan, and trim off the excess dough. To bake the crust
blind, see recipe for *pâte brisée*, otherwise follow
instructions for filling and baking in the individual
recipe.

makes about an 8-inch crust

INDEX

Boldface numbers indicate a recipe for a dish rather than a text description of it.

The text was set in Schneidler
by U.S. Lithograph Inc., New York, New York.

The book was printed on 115 gsm R400 gloss coated paper
by Amilcare Pizzi s.p.a.-arti grafiche, Milan, Italy.
Bound in Italy by Amilcare Pizzi.